# Lecture Notes in Computer Science    9484

Commenced Publication in 1973
Founding and Former Series Editors:
Gerhard Goos, Juris Hartmanis, and Jan van Leeuwen

More information about this series at http://www.springer.com/series/7410

Bettina Berendt · Thomas Engel
Demosthenes Ikonomou · Daniel Le Métayer
Stefan Schiffner (Eds.)

# Privacy Technologies and Policy

Third Annual Privacy Forum, APF 2015
Luxembourg, Luxembourg, October 7–8, 2015
Revised Selected Papers

 Springer

*Editors*
Bettina Berendt
Department of Computer Science
KU Leuven
Heverlee
Belgium

Thomas Engel
Université du Luxembourg
Luxembourg
Luxembourg

Demosthenes Ikonomou
ENISA
Maroussi Attiki
Greece

Daniel Le Métayer
Antenne Lyon La Doua
Inria
Villeurbanne
France

Stefan Schiffner
ENISA
Maroussi Attiki
Greece

ISSN 0302-9743                    ISSN 1611-3349    (electronic)
Lecture Notes in Computer Science
ISBN 978-3-319-31455-6          ISBN 978-3-319-31456-3    (eBook)
DOI 10.1007/978-3-319-31456-3

Library of Congress Control Number: 2016933473

LNCS Sublibrary: SL4 – Security and Cryptology

Printed on acid-free paper

This Springer imprint is published by Springer Nature
The registered company is Springer International Publishing AG Switzerland

# Preface

The European Union Agency for Network and Information Security, the European Commission Directorate General for Communications Networks, Content and Technology, and the University of Luxembourg organized APF 2015 in the framework of the presidency of the Council of the European Union. In all, 24 papers were submitted after the open call for papers; an international reviewing board selected eleven papers for presentation. After the conference, the authors submitted their revised papers for the present book, which constitutes the peer-reviewed proceedings of this event.

The contributions reflect the growing importance of networked IT services in our lives. While today the use of many of these services is optional and regarded as a mere convenience, it is to be expected that in the future many of them will become (quasi) mandatory; be it because the social environment expects a certain participation, because certain crucial services are hard to find offline, or even because – in the light of e-government – participation is legally required. Considering these developments, IT services need to be trusted by a large proportion of the population. Hence, their implications for the rights of free information and self-expression need to be studied, and thus security and privacy considerations gain importance.

The concept of privacy as a legal and social term was formed in the late 1800s. It stems from the extension of the physical integrity of the body to integrity of the mind. In their infancy, these ideas were meant to protect citizens from the ruling class. Naturally, privacy gained more importance with the rise of democracy. Together with the governmental use of technology, this development reached its preliminary peak in the development of the right to informational self-determination in the 1980s. However, since then, IT technology has been broadly adopted commercially; thus policy in this field is no longer restricted to limiting the actions of state bodies, but also needs to regulate commercial applications. The policy maker needs to set a frame in which legitimate commercial interests can co-exist with the right to privacy. Besides the legal aspect, privacy has been discussed in technical terms. In the beginning, privacy-enhancing technologies (PETs) focused on techniques for confidentiality and anonymous communication. Nowadays, PETs include technologies for controlled disclosure, fine-grained access control, destruction of data, repudiation, reputation, accountability, etc. While in the beginning many technologies were out of reach because of costs, today it is getting easier to deploy them.

However, developments in technologies, policy, and industry practices do not converge easily. APF aims to close the gap by focusing on paradigms that bridge the fields. This year, we focused on "Privacy by Design" (PbD), i.e., the attempt to combine technical and organizational measures to ensure the basic rights of the individual. It is not a method but rather a mind-set, which asks for continuous effort throughout the development life cycle. New technological trends of distributed and decentralized data management create opportunities as well as challenges for achieving privacy. Awareness of these trends further helps to bridge the gap between technology and policy.

The papers of this book were presented in three sessions.

The first session, "Measuring Privacy", contained four talks. Meiko Jensen presented a methodology for assessing the maturity of PETs as a guideline for developers and DPAs as well as policy makers to objectivize expert opinions. Vinh Thong Ta described a case study on formal accountability for biometric surveillance. Laurence Claeys showed the USEMP value model that aims at improving transparency and privacy in online social networks from a legal, economic, and technical perspective, in order to empower the users to take back control of their data. Rehab Alnemr presented a practical tool for privacy impact assessment for the cloud as an aid for cloud service customers to choose the provider that meets their needs.

The second session dealt with "Rules and Principles". Wernher Behrendt discussed open questions on consent for sensors and a codex for sensors introducing courteous sensors. Ioannis Krontiris presented a case study on Privacy-ABCs for the adoption of PETs by users and service providers. Wouter Lueks spoke on revocable privacy and presented use cases enabled by practical cryptographic protocols for real-world problems. The session was closed by Dawn Jutla, who presented PIP, a (privacy) injection pattern for inserting privacy patterns in software.

The third session covered "Legal and Economic Perspectives on Privacy". Milana Pisarić presented a case study on the surveillance of electronic communications in the Republic of Serbia, sharing with APF a view beyond EU law. Claudio Caimi described legal and technical perspectives in the definition of data-sharing agreements. Finally, Gabriela Gheorghe presented a new approach to online privacy, combining legal and technological measures and focusing on the importance of control.

Panels covered ethical aspects of data processing, privacy in the era of big data, and the economics of PETs; keynotes provided further food for thought. While Giovanni Buttarelli emphasized the EU digital single market and the importance of trust in electronic services by EU citizens, Naomi Lefkovitz gave the discussion a non-EU dimension, stressing the fact that the economy is already global. Charles Raab discussed the value of privacy for society as such and contested the idea of a trade-off between security and privacy with sceptical scrutiny. The event was closed by Bart Preneel who presented a cryptographer's view on mass surveillance, concluding with the fundamental question of why it is legal to sell unsafe technology.

A special session on "Multidisciplinary Aspects of Privacy by Design" was organized by the KU Leuven Department of Computer Science and Centre for IT and IP Law. The session was opened with a keynote by Marit Hansen; she gave insights into her practical experiences with privacy by design within a data protection authority. Dan Bogdanov, Matthias Pocs, and David Stevens then joined her for a panel chaired by Antonio Kung. The session thus brought together perspectives of data protection authorities, data protection officers, technology industry, and stakeholders involved in standardization. Lessons learned from the special session are summarized in the present book by Tsormpatzoudi, Berendt, and Coudert, the panel organizers.

In sum, APF 2015 assembled a wide range of current perspectives and state-of-the-art research on privacy, and it stimulated inspiring discussions also on the multi- and interdisciplinary challenges and solution approaches whose importance for real-world privacy is becoming increasingly clear. For the future, we aim at attracting more contributions from non-technical fields in order to broaden and deepen the insights gained. The next APF will be hosted by Goethe University Frankfurt, Germany, in September 2016. It will encourage, among other topics, discussions on privacy impact and risk assessment.

We thank everyone who made this great event possible: the sponsors, authors, reviewers, and local organizing teams of APF 2015.

February 2016

Bettina Berendt
Thomas Engel
Demosthenes Ikonomou
Daniel Le Métayer
Stefan Schiffner

# APF 2015

## Annual Privacy Forum
Luxembourg, Luxembourg, October 7–8, 2015


organized by


European Union Agency for Network and Information Security (ENISA)
European Commission Directorate for Communications Networks,
Content and Technology (DG CONNECT)
Interdisciplinary Center for Security, Reliability and Trust (SnT),
University of Luxembourg

# Organization

## Program Committee

| | |
|---|---|
| Luis Antunes | University of Porto, Portugal |
| David Basin | ETH Zürich, Switzerland |
| Rainer Böhme | University of Münster, Germany |
| Athena Bourka | ENISA, Greece |
| Claude Castelluccia | Inria Rhone-Alpes, France |
| Frédéric Cuppens | Télécom Bretagne, France |
| Nora Cuppens-Boulahia | Télécom Bretagne, France |
| Roberto Di Pietro | Bell Labs, Italy |
| Claudia Diaz | KU Leuven, Belgium |
| Mathias Fischer | International Computer Science Institute, USA |
| Simone Fischer-Hübner | Karlstad University, Sweden |
| Andra Giurgiu | University of Luxembourg, Luxembourg |
| Marit Hansen | ULD, Germany |
| Jaap-Henk Hoepman | Radboud University Nijmegen, The Netherlands |
| Kristina Irion | University of Amsterdam, The Netherlands |
| Sokratis Katsikas | University of Piraeus, Greece |
| Stefan Katzenbeisser | TU Darmstadt, Germany |
| Florian Kerschbaum | SAP, Germany |
| Klaus Kursawe | Philips Research, The Netherlands |
| Miroslaw Kutylowski | Wrocław University of Technology, Poland |
| Gwendal Le Grand | CNIL, France |
| Fabio Martinelli | IIT-CNR, Italy |
| Sjouke Mauw | University of Luxembourg, Luxembourg |
| Chris Mitchell | Royal Holloway, University of London, UK |
| Andriy Panchenko | University of Luxembourg, Luxembourg |
| Aljosa Pasic | Atos Origin, Spain |
| Siani Pearson | HP Labs, UK |
| Bart Preneel | KU Leuven, Belgium |
| Kai Rannenberg | Goethe University Frankfurt, Germany |
| Vincent Rijmen | KU Leuven, Belgium |
| Heiko Roßnagel | Fraunhofer IAO, Germany |
| P.Y.A. Ryan | University of Luxembourg, Luxembourg |
| Angela Sasse | UCL, UK |
| Jean-Louis Schiltz | SCHILTZ & SCHILTZ, Luxembourg |
| Einar Snekkenes | Gjvik University College, Norway |

| | |
|---|---|
| Radu State | University of Luxembourg, Luxembourg |
| Carmela Troncoso | Gradiant, Spain |
| Paulo Verissimo | University of Luxembourg, Luxembourg |
| Michael Waidner | Fraunhofer SIT, Germany |

## General Co-chairs

| | |
|---|---|
| Rosa Barcelo | European Commission, DG CONNECT, Belgium |
| Thomas Engel | University of Luxembourg, Luxembourg |
| Demosthenes Ikonomou | ENISA, Greece |
| Achim Klabunde | European Data Protection Supervisor, Belgium |

## Organizing Committee

| | |
|---|---|
| Athena Bourka | ENISA, Greece |
| Daria Catalui | ENISA, Greece |
| Helga Edwardsdottir | University of Luxembourg, Luxembourg |
| Thomas Engel | University of Luxembourg, Luxembourg |
| Asya Mitseva | University of Luxembourg, Luxembourg |
| Anne Ochsenbein | University of Luxembourg, Luxembourg |
| Stefanie Östlund | University of Luxembourg, Luxembourg |
| Andriy Panchenko | University of Luxembourg, Luxembourg |
| Stefan Schiffner | ENISA, Greece |

## Program Co-chairs

| | |
|---|---|
| Bettina Berendt | KU Leuven, Belgium |
| Thomas Engel | University of Luxembourg, Luxembourg |
| Daniel Le Métayer | Inria/University of Lyon, France |

## Publication Co-chairs

| | |
|---|---|
| Asya Mitseva | University of Luxembourg, Luxembourg |
| Andriy Panchenko | University of Luxembourg, Luxembourg |

## External Reviewers

| | |
|---|---|
| Reiner Kraft | Fraunhofer SIT, Germany |
| Michael Kubach | Fraunhofer IAO, Germany |
| Sebastian Luhn | Universität Münster, Germany |
| Jessica Schroers | KU Leuven, Belgium |
| Ulrich Waldmann | Fraunhofer SIT, Germany |

# Sponsors

# Contents

## Multidisciplinary Aspects of Privacy by Design

# Accountability and Quantitative Methods for Privacy

# Towards Measuring Maturity
# of Privacy-Enhancing Technologies

Marit Hansen[1]([⊠]), Jaap-Henk Hoepman[2], and Meiko Jensen[1]

[1] Unabhängiges Landeszentrum für Datenschutz, Kiel, Germany
marit.hansen@privacyresearch.eu, meiko.jensen@rub.de
[2] Radboud University, Nijmegen, The Netherlands
jhh@cs.ru.nl

**Abstract.** The assessment of the maturity of Privacy-Enhancing Technologies (PETs) is a complex and challenging task, which can only be
performed by experts in the field. However, at the same time, the need
for precise technology readiness and quality definitions for PETs emerges
rapidly. In order to overcome this gap, standardised means to assess, discuss, and compare PET maturity levels are necessary.

In this paper, we propose an approach for assessing the maturity
of PETs. We define both the scales and the methodology for measuring maturity of PETs, in a way that is independent from the domain of
application. Based on an in-depth analysis of the criteria to be met by
such a PET maturity level scheme, we propose a combined quality-and
readiness level scale to be used for this purpose.

## 1 Introduction

Since decades, the idea of incorporating privacy and data protection criteria in the design of systems has been discussed. Early work on confidentiality (e.g. based on cryptographic algorithms) or anonymity and pseudonymity
(e.g. Mix networks) showed that technology can support or even ensure privacy
and data protection features. A special category of technologies that aimed at
enhancing privacy was coined "Privacy-Enhancing Technologies (PETs)" [14].

Recent and upcoming legal norms demand "privacy by design" (the
European Data Protection Regulation [2] as well as the recently passed eIDAS
Regulation [3]). However, how to transpose this into the system design process
is either not detailed or left to secondary legislation such as delegated or implementing acts. The ENISA report on Privacy and Data Protection by Design [8]
gives an overview on today's landscape concerning privacy engineering. PETs
are recognised as an important element in the overall design task. The ENISA
report points out that the solutions, techniques, and building blocks presented
are of differing maturity levels—without providing criteria on how to assess the
individual maturity.

In this paper, we specify these criteria for the first time, and take the first
steps towards defining a full-fledged PET maturity assessment methodology,

© Springer International Publishing Switzerland 2016
B. Berendt et al. (Eds.): APF 2015, LNCS 9484, pp. 3–20, 2016.
DOI: 10.1007/978-3-319-31456-3_1

based on existing work in other fields of technology (e.g. NASA's scale of technology readiness levels (TRLs), [20]).

One crucial finding in our work is the strong belief that a mere assessment of technology readiness may yield misleading results. More precisely, a PET that is available and deployed, but shows severe shortcomings concerning its quality regarding privacy protection, should not be preferred over a better privacy technology that—perhaps because of the predominance of the worse technology—scores lower on the readiness scale. For this reason, we decided to pursue a two-fold strategy that tackles technology readiness as one dimension and privacy enhancement quality as a second dimension. The individual results then are combined into a single PET maturity score.

We aim to ensure that the assessment scheme for PET maturity we are developing is useful for a diverse set of potential stakeholders, such as Data Protection Authorities (DPAs), data controllers and data processors, developers, certification bodies, auditors, or standardisation bodies. The relevance of PET maturity for this diverse set of stakeholders demands that the information has to be easily comprehensible by experts and laypeople; potential misinterpretation of the information should be prevented as far as possible. Moreover, the methodology has to be adaptable to all kinds of PETs (e.g. protocols, algorithms, software, hardware, products, IT-based services; ideas, concepts, specifications, implementations, workable demonstrations, rolled-out versions, etc.).

The text is organised as follows: Sect. 2 introduces important terms and notions that are necessary to determine the scope of the project. In particular, the term *Privacy-Enhancing Technology (PET)* will be discussed. A survey of existing methods to measure technology readiness is given in Sect. 3. Our proposal for a PET maturity scale based on both a readiness level and a quality level is presented in Sect. 4. A first sketch of the corresponding methodology to score a given PET on the defined maturity scale is presented in Sect. 5. Finally, Sect. 6 summaries our findings and gives an outlook on our intended future work.

## 2 Setting the Stage

In this section, we introduce the basic terminology used throughout the paper, and the underlying concepts and related work we base our proposal on. We also point out some gaps and pitfalls with respect to the semantics of certain commonly used terms, and clarify how we interpret them.

For example, in this paper we distinguish levels and scales as follows. A *level* is the particular score on a metric, e.g. `pilot` as the value for the readiness level. A *scale* is the set of levels a certain metric can assume. An *indicator* is a factor that may be meaningful for determining the level; it is an input value for the assessment. *Evidence* denotes the set of indicators.

### 2.1 Privacy-Enhancing Technology

**Privacy-enhancing technologies (PETs)** have been characterised in various ways. Some authors [6] define them quite specifically as "a coherent system of

ICT measures that protects privacy by eliminating or reducing personal data or by preventing unnecessary and/or undesired processing of personal data". The OECD Report on PETs from 2002 [23] takes a broader perspective and also declares tools "that allow a user to choose if, when and under what circumstances personal information is disclosed" in scope. The European Commission [10] considers a wider range of PETs that include those that support legal compliance with data protection regulation.

For assessing PET, we aim at allowing a wide definition of PETs, encompassing all kinds of technologies that support privacy or data protection features (e.g. technologies that make use of privacy design strategies [15] or consider protection goals for privacy engineering [13]). Compared to a definition that restricts PETs to data minimisation, this approach provides greater flexibility and adaptability, albeit adds complexity when statements on the privacy enhancement properties in various categories have to be elaborated. Our approach is detailed in Sect. 5.2.

## 2.2 The Technology Lifecycle

We distinguish between seven different phases within the lifecycle of a technology, illustrated in Fig. 1, as defined by WILLIAM L. NOLTE [21]. Initially, each technology starts off with an idea, its *birth*. Then, this idea is analysed preliminarily, elaborated on, and considered useful. Thus, in the next phase, the idea is discussed on a broad scale, e.g. within research and development communities. Yet, there is no working prototype, not even a demonstrator, so the correlated phase is that of *childhood*. At some point, a proof of concept is implemented in test environments under laboratory conditions, marking a progress towards *adolescence* level. Depending on the complexity of the technology, the transition from childhood to adolescence can be rapid (e.g. if the idea gets implemented by its inventor straight away) or can take decades (e.g. if the idea cannot be implemented with current state-of-the-art technology).

The next step is that of a real-world usage of the technology under non-laboratory conditions. Typically, this step is performed with the release of a

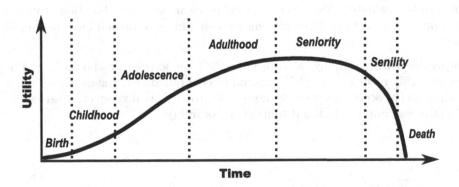

**Fig. 1.** Lifecycle of a technology (adapted from [21]).

first complete implementation, or with the advent of a pilot implementation in real-world systems. Thus, the technology matures towards a state of *adulthood*.

Subsequently, the next remarkable transition is that of a full market partici-pation of the technology, which is typically kicked off by advent of a ready-to-use product being sold (rented, consulted for, commercially supported for, etc.). This implies that the maturity of the technology has reached a point where it becomes feasible to gain profits from utilising the technology to such extent that a market emerges. The corresponding age is that of *seniority*.

Finally, the technology might become obsoleted by technological evolution. For PETs, this could mean that devastating attack techniques render the tech-nology useless in an irreparable way, or simply by the advent of a superior technology that provides the same guarantees in a more favorable way. In each of these cases, the use of the technology decreases (into what we may call the *senility* phase), until it fades out of use, and reaches its final state of *death*.

This lifecycle model has been used as the basis for our readiness metric defined in Sect. 4.1.

## 2.3   What Makes a Scale Effective?

The effectiveness of a scale depends its *comprehensibility*, its *comparability*, its *scorability*, and its *reproducibility*. We define these four criteria as follows:

**Comprehensibility.** First of all a score should be easy to understand and to apply by users looking for an appropriate PET to solve a particular problem in a certain context[1]. The meaning of a certain score should be intuitively clear.

**Comparability.** Similarly, comparing different results should be straightfor-ward. It is especially important to know for combined scores resulting from different dimensions (readiness and quality) whether — and under which condi-tions — comparability is given.

**Scorability.** Further, a particular PET should be easy to score objectively on the scale at hand by an evaluator. The score should be derived from clearly described indicators, that are easy to determine or measure for an arbitrary PET that is going to be evaluated. Moreover it should be clear how a combination of values or appreciations for the different indicators should be combined into the overall score.

**Reproducibility.** Finally, a score for a PET on some scale should be repro-ducible. This means that a PET should receive (almost) the same score, when independently scored by two or more evaluators. This further emphasises the objectiveness implicit in the definition of scorability.

---

[1] We note that in our methodology the application context of a PET is out of scope for determining its maturity, as explained further on in this report.

# 3   Related Work

Since we regard maturity of PETs as a combination of their readiness and their privacy enhancement quality, we have to consider related work from both fields.

Technology Readiness Levels (TRLs) have been used for about 40 years [22] especially by NASA [20] and in the military sector. They are based on a nine-point score (TRL 1–9) where lower TRLs express early development and readiness stages while high levels denote completely developed and thoroughly tested systems.

Similarly, the European Commission has introduced a similar nine-point scale for technology readiness for the work programme 2014–2015 (Horizon 2020) [11]—with similar advantages and disadvantages:

- TRL 1: basic principles observed
- TRL 2: technology concept formulated
- TRL 3: experimental proof of concept
- TRL 4: technology validated in lab
- TRL 5: technology validated in relevant environment (industrially relevant environment in the case of key enabling technologies)
- TRL 6: technology demonstrated in relevant environment (industrially relevant environment in the case of key enabling technologies)
- TRL 7: system prototype demonstration in operational environment
- TRL 8: system complete and qualified
- TRL 9: actual system proven in operational environment (competitive manufacturing in the case of key enabling technologies; or in space)

For being able to assess the readiness of a system, the evaluation process can be supported by a TRL Assessment Matrix and tools such as a TRL Calculator as developed for the NASA TRL scheme [5]. In the beginning, TRLs were mainly assigned to developed hardware; later, software or combined systems were taken into account, too.

Since its publication, the TRL scale has been discussed and criticised, in particular by pointing out limitations and needs for a multidimensional approach (e.g. [21]). Also for derived scales such as a Systems Readiness Level (SRL) (cf. [24]) it is being heatedly debated whether they are misleading and may be dangerous because of arbitrary assessment results, and how potential problems could be overcome (cf. [17]). Here it became evident that readiness should be understood in context and that it is usually not sufficient to assess "readiness" without regarding "quality" [25].

In the context of privacy and security this additional quality dimension is especially viable because there are many examples of widely deployed technology (that would score high on a pure "readiness" scale) that provide sub-optimal protection in practice.

In this respect, standards for software quality such as ISO/IEC 25010 on Systems and Software Quality Requirements and Evaluation (SQuaRE) [16] or, where applicable, for process quality such as ISO/IEC 15504 on Software Process Improvement and Capability Determination (SPICE) [1] have to be considered.

However, these standards are not comprehensive, but extensions are possible (e.g. shown in [12] for extending SQuaRE by green and reliability issues). Other criteria may be more or less neglected for assessment of PET maturity since they most likely won't play a role.

Moreover, measurement of privacy enhancement quality is not a trivial task. Since this is not the focus of this paper, we only mention some noteworthy contributions that may provide some input to a PET maturity debate, among others the work on comparing different degree of anonymity (e.g. concerning differential privacy [9], $k$-anonymity [27], $l$-diversity [19], or $t$-closeness [18]) or on calculations of linkability (e.g. [4,7]).

## 4    PET Maturity Metric

We are now ready to define our PET maturity metric. We will do so by defining our scale for readiness, followed by our definition of a quality scale, and continuing by describing how scores on both scales are combined to obtain the overall PET maturity level. Further, we analyse the tensions between measurable indicators and expert opinions.

### 4.1    A Scale for Readiness

We begin by defining a scale along which to express the *readiness* of a certain PET inline with the phases of the technology lifecycle described in Sect. 2.2. Readiness of a PET expresses whether a PET can be deployed in practice at a large scale, or that it can only be used within a research project to build upon to advance the state of the art in privacy protection. Readiness also says something about the amount of effort (in terms of time and money) still needed to allow the PET to be really used in practice. To ensure comprehensibility (see Sect. 2.3), we choose not to score readiness by a simple number on some linear scale. Instead we define the following readiness levels for a PET.

`idea`. Lowest level of readiness. The PET has been proposed as an idea in an informal fashion, e.g. written as a blog post, discussed at a conference, described in a white paper or technical report.

`research`. The PET is a serious object of rigorous scientific study. At least one (but preferably more) serious academic paper(s) have been published in the scientific literature, discussing the PET in detail and at least arguing its correctness and security and privacy properties.

`prototype`. The PET has successfully been implemented, and can be tested for performance and other properties in practice. "Running code" is available.

`pilot`. The PET is or has (recently) been used in some small or larger scale pilot applications with real users. The scope of application, and the user base may have been restricted (e.g. to power users, students, etc.).

`product`. The highest readiness level. The PET has been incorporated in one or more generally available products that have been or are being used in practice by a significant number of users. The user group is not a priori restricted (by the developers).

outdated. The PET is not used anymore, e.g., because the need for the PET has faded, because it is depending on another technology that is not maintained anymore, or because there are better PETs that have superseded that PET.

These readiness levels relate to the technology lifecycle; a later evolutionary level does not necessarily mean that the PET is better, because the aging process may not improve the PET's maturity or its applicability when it becomes outdated. This readiness level indicates that the PET should no longer be used. The transition from one readiness level to the next is not as sharply delineated as the previous scale suggests. In fact, different PETs that belong to the same readiness level may differ significantly. Some barely made it the level assigned to them; others are about to enter the next level. To allow people to express these differences, a readiness level may be augmented with the next higher readiness level in the scale above. So, for example, a readiness level of pilot/product may be appropriate for a PET that has been used in several pilot programmes and is currently being beta-tested as a (commercial) general purpose product.

## 4.2 A Scale for Quality

Although *quality* is somewhat dependent on readiness (a rolled out product has received so much more attention over the years than a concept still in its research stage), the quality of a PET is not only determined by its readiness. In fact several PETs at the same readiness level may have varying levels of quality. As argued in the introduction, it is important to realise that sometimes a PET with high readiness may still have a low quality. We now turn to make this notion of quality more precise.

We base our approach on the ISO/IEC system and software quality models ISO standard 25010 [16], but adjust and refine it to our needs. ISO 25010 distinguishes the following eight quality characteristics: 'functional suitability', 'reliability', 'operability', 'performance efficiency', 'security', 'compatibility', 'maintainability' and 'transferability'. Not all of these characteristics are relevant for our purposes. Some characteristics are more important than others and therefore contribute more to the overall quality score.

For example, because we want the overall maturity scale to be independent of the particular context in which a PET is applied, characteristics like functional suitability are out of scope. We believe that a PET with limited functionality has the same quality as one with a larger (or different) functionality. Which one to choose depends on the requirements to be met within a particular application context.

Similarly, 'compatibility' is deemed a less relevant characteristic.

We interpret 'operability'—which refers to the degree to which a product is easy to learn, understand, and attractive to a user—to be directed at a system developer instead of an ordinary user (because a PET is typically embedded into larger system, and not directly exposed to the user).

The 'security' characteristic is renamed to 'protection', and focuses on preventing privacy infringements. A separate characteristic 'trust assumptions' is added to capture whether and if so how much trust in certain components and agents is assumed.

Also added are two other characteristics: 'side effects' and 'scope'. This brings us to define the quality scale as comprising the following nine PET quality characteristics, listed in decreasing order of importance

**protection.** The degree of protection offered (in terms of for example unlinkability, transparency, and intervenability) to prevent privacy infringements while allowing access and normal functionality for authorised agents. Also depends on the type of threats and attacks against which the PET offers protection.

**trust assumptions.** The number of components and/or agents that need to be trusted, and the nature and extent of trust that must assumed in order to use the PET. Also depends on whether these assumptions are legal, organisational, procedural, or technical.

**side effects.** The extent in which the PET introduces (undesirable) side effects. Measured in terms of composability.

**reliability.** The degree to which a system or component performs specified functions under specified conditions for a specified period of time. Measured in terms of fault tolerance, recoverability, and compliance. Also measured in terms of the number of vulnerabilities discovered.

**performance efficiency.** The performance relative to the amount of resources used under stated conditions. Measured in terms of resource use (storage, CPU power, and bandwidth) and speed (latency and throughput).

**operability.** The degree to which the product has attributes that enable it to be understood, and easily (and in particular securely) integrated into a larger system by a qualified system developer. Measured in terms of appropriateness, recognisability, learnability, technical accessibility, and compliance.

**maintainability.** The degree of effectiveness and efficiency with which the product can be modified. Measured in terms of modularity, reusability, analysability, changeability, modification stability, and testability. Open source software typically scores high on this characteristic. Also, systems that have an active developer community, or that have official support, score high.

**transferability.** The degree to which a system or component can be effectively and efficiently transferred from one hardware, software or other operational or usage environment to another. Measured in terms of portability and adaptability.

**scope.** The number of different application domains the PET is applied in or is applicable to.

Usually, each of these characteristics is relevant for a PET, independent of its readiness level. However, the indicators that determine the score for each of the characteristics *do* depend on the readiness level. For example, the quality of a rolled out product depends on how well it is supported (by a help desk, code updates, etc.). These indicators are irrelevant for research level PETs. The quality of those is determined more by the ranking of the venues in which the research is published, for example.

For each of these nine characteristics, a PET can receive a score in the range

| $--$ (very poor) | $-$ (poor) | $0$ (satisfactory) | $+$ (good) | $++$ (very good) |
|---|---|---|---|---|

The overall quality level also utilises this five-value scale, and is comprised of the nine individual scores, according to a specific quality evaluation function, as discussed in Sect. 5.5.

### 4.3 Combining Readiness and Quality to Express Maturity

The scales for readiness and quality defined above allow us to define the real scale we are interested in: a scale for PET maturity. In fact this overall scale is simply the combination of the readiness level superscripted by the quality level.

$$\text{readiness}^{\text{quality}}$$

So for example a PET with readiness level `pilot` and quality $+$ has an overall PET maturity level of `pilot`$^+$. Thus, the total set of potential PET maturity values spans from `idea`$^{--}$ and `idea`$^{++}$ to `outdated`$^{--}$ and `outdated`$^{++}$.

### 4.4 Evidence: Measurable Indicators vs. Expert Opinions

When assessing maturity of a PET, different experts may have different opinions with respect to its readiness and quality. Hence, each assessment approach that is solely based on expert opinions is likely to be affected by the choice of experts, and thus lacks reproducibility. Having the same PET assessed by different expert groups may lead to different assessment results, due to the different viewpoints and discussion dynamics among the chosen sets of experts.

In order to mitigate this biased assessment approach, it needs to have some indisputable parameters to be taken into account. Such parameters should be assessable in a way that is unambiguous, leading to the exact same parameter value and assessment indication no matter who performs the parameter assessment. We call these types of parameters *measurable indicators*, meaning that they indicate an assessment result based on objective evidence. As such, measurable indicators are robust against change of assessors, as different assessment instances of the same measurable indicator will always result in the same indicator values, and thus in the same assessment result.

Examples for potential measurable indicators in the field of PET maturity assessment are:

- number of scientific publications referring to the PET;
- number and type of audits/certifications performed for the PET;
- number of university courses covering the PET topic;
- number of similar products in the market if the PET is a product;
- number of hits when searching for the PET in online search engines; or
- number of years since the PET was initially proposed.

As can be seen, each of these measurable indicators represents a certain characteristic with respect to the PET, and does so in an indisputable way. There can be no two different opinions on the total number of scientific publications referring to the PET, for example, at least not on a level of significance. Such a value is an objective evidence for a certain level of maturity of a PET.

However, though assessing these measurable indicators is feasible and quite robust, determining its implications with respect to the result of the assessment is more challenging. What does the number of search engine hits for the PET say about the maturity of a PET? What should be the impact of the existence of six different privacy certifications of a PET product? Each of these measurable indicators gives a small implication on the level of maturity the PET has probably reached. For instance, the existence of a substantial amount of competing products in the market of the PET to be assessed clearly implies that this PET has reached at least the `pilot` stage, more likely even the `product` stage of readiness. If there are no products in the market at all, this might indicate an earlier maturity stage, probably `research`, but it might also be the case that the PET itself is not suitable to be sold as a dedicated product. Nevertheless, it still could be utilised in many products out there, and still could be in the `product` readiness stage.

The measurable indicators are robust in assessment, but fuzzy in their implications to the result of the assessment. They need to be included in the overall assessment process, in order to mitigate the impact of assessor choices, but they are not precise enough to be used as the only, not even as the major base for a PET maturity assessment. Thus, we propose to utilise these indicators as input, but combine them with inputs from a dedicated *board of experts*.

## 5    The Assessment Process

Based on the findings described in the previous sections, we outline the process of performing a PET maturity assessment. This five-step approach is explained in the following subsections.

### 5.1    Overview

The process of assessing PET maturity along the lines defined in this document involves five steps, as illustrated in Fig. 2. The implicit initial step of an assessment consists in the determination of the assessor, as that is a very critical entity in performing the assessment. The role of the assessor is that of an expert in performing assessments. Beyond that, expertise both in terms of privacy and in the domain of interest the PET is assessed in would be beneficial. Moreover, the assessor needs to be unbiased, as far as possible, and objective in all decisions.

In the first explicit step of the assessment, it is necessary to select and precisely define the *Target of Assessment*, i.e. the concept, technology, or product that is to be assessed. Details on this step are given in Sect. 5.2.

**Fig. 2.** Overview of the PET maturity assessment process

Once the Target of Assessment is defined, the next step consists in gathering the board of experts to be asked for their opinion. Ideally, the experts should have expertise both in the domain of application the PET is evaluated for, and in the privacy engineering discipline. As with the assessor, it is necessary to gather an unbiased, objective, heterogeneous set of experts for this task (cf. Sect. 4.4), as far as this is feasible. Though there is no upper bound on the number of experts, we propose a minimum of five experts to be involved in the board.

This step also concludes the preparation phase of the assessment.

Comprising the major part of the assessment, the next two steps can be performed in parallel. On the one hand, it is necessary to gather a specific set of scores to be evaluated from public information sources. For instance, this may cover tasks such as counting the number of research publications that refer to a given PET, or similar assessment of objective indicators with respect to maturity (that is both readiness and quality) of the PET in consideration. This step would typically be performed by the assessor.

Concurrently, and somewhat independent from the previous step, the board of experts needs to be asked for their opinion with respect to the PET in consideration.

Once both concurrent steps are completed, and the total set of evidence gathered for this assessment is compiled, the final and most critical step consists in the aggregation of the assessment results. Performed by the assessor, this step involves three tasks:

1. determination of the level of technology readiness of the PET, according to the scale defined in Sect. 4.1,
2. assessment of the overall quality of the PET, according to the quality characteristics described in Sect. 4.2, and
3. aggregation of these two intermediate assessments into the final PET maturity level, as discussed in Sect. 4.3.

Finally, the documentation and logging inputs, which were collected throughout the other steps of the assessment, need to be aggregated, and comprise a PET Maturity Assessment Report accompanying the PET maturity level achieved.

Once the final PET maturity result is obtained, and the PET Maturity Assessment Report is completed, the assessment process concludes.

## 5.2   Defining the Target of Assessment

The initial step of assessing a given PET's level of maturity is the precise definition of the *Target of Assessment (ToA)*. Depending on its phase in the technology lifecycle as outlined in Sect. 2.2, a PET may consist of a few lines of demonstrator source code only, or may already have been implemented in a set of software products being sold and bought in a dedicated market of its own. Thus, the defining the correct ToA can be quite tricky.

If a PET is in one of its early stages of evolution, where it merely is made up by a concept outline or a rough set of ideas, the ToA typically consists of the major concept of the PET, as outlined by its maintainers. Being a theoretical concept without even a basic implementation, measurable quantitative maturity indicators like market share, lines of source code, etc., are not available, and thus cannot be used for maturity assessment. Available measurable maturity indicators for this stage of maturity can only be found in the research and discussion domain (such as number of research papers published that refer to this PET).

If a well-maintained implementation of a PET already exists, but no commercially available product along this implementation (such as a software product, consulting services, support desk, or the like) is found in the open markets, the ToA can be narrowed down to the scope of this implementation. Whenever a precise condition of the PET in question is required within the assessment, the concept is evaluated according to the details found in this implementation. Also, measurable maturity indicators from the source code realm (like lines of code, amount of source code documentation, etc.) can be used based on the numbers available for the existing implementation.

If a dedicated market for solutions utilising this PET already is in place, the ToA can no longer be defined as the (single) concept or implementation of the PET. Given that different products and different domains of application may result in differing privacy guarantees, the ToA in this case has to be narrowed down to one of the existing products or implementations only. This is due to the fact that different implementations of the same PET may have different characteristics, different levels of completeness, and different levels of quality. Thus, an assessment should focus on a single product or implementation only, potentially relating it to other products of the same category for comparison, but fixing the ToA on the product, not on the theoretical concept beneath. Measurable indicators for such a level of maturity may range from market share data to sales numbers, active developer community sizes, and total amount of financial capital allocated to utilisation of the PET, among others.

### 5.3    The Assessment Methodology

As shown in Fig. 3, our methodology is based on both the measurable indicators as well as the expert opinions, collected for both readiness and quality assessment. More precisely, the measurable indicators are collected and normalised according to reasonable individual scales, depending on the ToA. The expert opinions are collected by means of dedicated forms, consisting of both a scale-based assessment and a detailed opinion comment part. Then, all of these inputs are processed by the assessor to gather two separate intermediate results: a *Readiness Score* and a *Quality Assessment*. Finally, both of these are combined into the final *PET Maturity Level*.

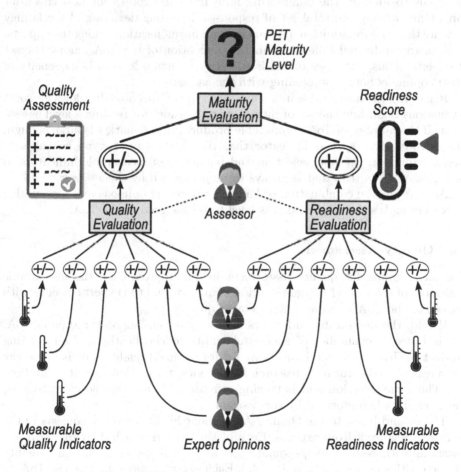

**Fig. 3.** PET maturity assessment methodology

## 5.4   Readiness Assessment

The readiness assessment of the ToA begins with the selection and harmonisation of all measurable indicators to be used, a task we propose to be performed by the assessor. The expert opinions for readiness assessment are collected by means of asking each expert on her assumed readiness level of the ToA (ranging from idea to outdated, as described in Sect. 4.1), with the option to choose two adjacent levels at once, if the expert thinks the ToA is in a transition from one level to the next.

The next step for the assessor consists in harmonising the results gathered from the initial part of our approach. Regarding the expert's feedback, the assessor needs to identify the dominating level from the votes, but also check for consistency among the total set of responses. A strong deviation of levels may indicate the need for additional discussion and harmonisation among the experts, as it clearly indicated differences in the perception of the ToA among the set of experts. Thus, the assessor needs to verify a certain level of homogeneity of expert opinions before proceeding with the assessment.

Regarding the measurable indicators, the type of ToA already allows for some estimations regarding the set of indicators to consider for readiness level assessment. If the number of ToA-comparable products in the market is large enough, this already gives a clear indicator that the level of prototype has already passed. However, the final selection and balancing of measurable indicators to be considered is a task that is always to be performed by the assessor.

As a result, the combination of harmonised expert opinions and measurable indicators makes the final readiness level to be assigned to the ToA.

## 5.5   Quality Assessment

The main inputs for quality assessment in our approach are the measurable indicators of relevance for quantification of quality, and the expert opinions with respect to the ToA's privacy enhancement quality.

Herein, the measurable indicators may vary depending on the type of ToA. For instance, the number of successful audits or certifications of an existing product as ToA has some indications for its assumed quality, but is obviously not a feasible indicator for a research-stage concept ToA that cannot be audited yet. Thus, the selection and balancing of reasonable measurable indicators for the given ToA is performed by the assessor.

The second input to the Quality Assessment in our approach consists in the dedicated feedback from experts. Each of the experts is asked to answer a few questions with respect to the quality of the ToA in terms of the nine quality characteristics as described in Sect. 4.2. Each expert is asked to rate the ToA on the quality scale ($--$ to $++$) for each of these nine criteria. Once this process is completed, the assessor evaluates these findings, elaborating the dominating quality characteristics of the ToA. Therein, the assessor may also incorporate findings from the separate comments given by the experts, e.g. in order to spot domain-specific strengths or weaknesses, or even showstopper arguments against the use of a ToA.

The result of the quality assessment part of our approach is a dedicated Quality Assessment Report, comprising of all expert opinions, including their scores for the nine quality characteristics and comments, and all measurable indicators used in the assessment. This report, which should give a quite decent estimation on the quality of the ToA, can then be used in a later stage to decide upon the final PET Maturity Level, as described in Sect. 5.6.

### 5.6   PET Maturity Assessment

The last step in performing a full PET maturity assessment of the ToA consists in combining the results from the quality assessment part with the achieved readiness level. In our approach, this task narrows down to aggregating the Quality Assessment Report's findings into a single quality indicator (on the quality scale described in Sect. 4.2), and attaching that quality indicator to the readiness level of the ToA. The combined result thus is a bipartite value anywhere in the range between $idea^{--}$ to $idea^{++}$ and $outdated^{--}$ to $outdated^{++}$.

## 6   Conclusions

### 6.1   Discussion

The PET maturity metric we propose is independent of the specific context in which the PET is applied. This is different from some technology readiness metrics that explicitly define the readiness of a technology with respect to the particular context in which it is applied (cf. e.g. [25,26]).

The advantage of our approach is that the maturity of a PET can be scored just by evaluating the PET itself. This makes it easier to assess the maturity of a PET. As a consequence, however, the maturity of a PET by itself does not say whether it is suitable to apply in a certain context. To make that decision, the requirements imposed by the context need to be matched with the functionality, properties, and guarantees as well as potential dependencies or side effects of the PET under consideration.

Our aim is to objectify the assessment of PET maturity, but at the same time we are convinced that a fully automated solution would not produce reliable results. Instead we belief that involvement of (human) experts will be necessary for a meaningful assessment, albeit supported be measurable evidence. Robustness and validity of our approach can only be achieved if an unnoticeable manipulation of the results can be sufficiently prevented. This will highly influence the choice of experts and the measurement methods, but also the transparency of the (final and probably also interim) results of the assessment so that they can be well comprehended by the various target groups, e.g. users, DPAs or funding agencies.

## 6.2   Future Work and Research Indications

Our PET maturity levels can be utilised in various different scenarios of application. For instance, they can help companies to identify PETs of relevance for their business domain, e.g. for utilisation in existing products. They can be used by funding agencies for identifying interesting PETs that are close to market, in order to provide support for entrepreneurs. DPAs can utilise the PET maturity levels for discussing the legal definition of the technological state of the art.

For all of these domains, the validity and utility of the PET maturity levels need to be thoroughly tested prior to fixation (e.g. by means of standardisation). Thus, our obvious future work consists in choosing and assessing a multitude of PETs with respect to their maturity, and thereby validate both the scale and the methodology of our approach. As this task comes with huge efforts, intense research on means to support, (semi-)automate, and optimise such broad-scale PET maturity assessments becomes necessary.

**Acknowledgements.** The work of M.H. and M.J. was partially funded by the European Commission, FP7 ICT program, under contract no. 318424 (FutureID project).

# References

1. ISO/IEC 15504-5: Information technology – Process assessment – Part5: An exemplar software life cycle process assessment model. Technical report, ISO International Organisation for Standardisation (ISO) JTC 1/SC 7 (2012)
2. European Parliament legislative resolution of 12 March 2014 on the proposal for a regulation of the European Parliament and of the Council on the protection of individuals with regard to the processing of personal data and on the free movement of such data (General Data Protection Regulation) (COM(2012)0011 C7-0025/2012 2012/0011(COD)) (2014). http://www.europarl.europa.eu/sides/getDoc.do?type=TA&language=EN&reference=P7-TA-2014-0212
3. Regulation (EU) No 910/2014 of the European Parliament and of the Council of 23 on July 2014 electronic identification and trust services for electronic transactions in the internal market and repealing Directive 1999/93/EC. OJ L 257, 28.08.2014, pp. 73–114 (2014)
4. Berthold, S.: Inter-temporal Privacy Metrics. Doctoral thesis, Karlstads Universitet (2014). http://kau.diva-portal.org/smash/get/diva2:757291/FULLTEXT01.pdf
5. Bilbro, J.W.: Systematic Assessment of the Program/Project Impacts of Technological Advancement and Insertion Revision A. Technical report (2007). https://acc.dau.mil/adl/en-US/320595/file/46759/White%20Paper%20on%20Technology%20Assessment%20Rev%20A.doc
6. Borking, J.J., Raab, C.D.: Laws, PETs and other technologies for privacy protection. J. Inf. Law Technol. (JILT) **1**(1) (2001). http://www2.warwick.ac.uk/fac/soc/law/elj/jilt/2001_1/borking
7. Clauß, S.: A framework for quantification of linkability within a privacy-enhancing identity management system. In: Müller, G. (ed.) ETRICS 2006. LNCS, vol. 3995, pp. 191–205. Springer, Heidelberg (2006). http://dx.doi.org/10.1007/11766155_14

8. Danezis, G., Domingo-Ferrer, J., Hansen, M., Hoepman, J.H., Le Métayer, D.,Tirtea, R., Schiffner, S.: Privacy and Data Protection by Design – from policy to engineering. Technical report, ENISA (2014). http://www.enisa.europa.eu/ activities/identity-and-trust/library/deliverables/privacy-and-data-protection-by-design/at_download/fullReport

9. Dwork, C.: Differential privacy. In: Bugliesi, M., Preneel, B., Sassone, V., Wegener, I. (eds.) ICALP 2006. LNCS, vol. 4052, pp. 1–12. Springer, Heidelberg (2006)

10. European Commission: Privacy Enhancing Technologies (PETs) – the existing legal framework. MEMO/07/159, May 2007. http://europa.eu/rapid/press-release_MEMO-07-159_en.htm

11. European Commission: Horizon 2020 – Work Programme 2014-2015, Annex G. Technology readiness levels (TRL). European Commission Decision C (2014)4995 of 22 July 2014. Technical report (2014). http://ec.europa.eu/research/ participants/data/ref/h2020/wp/2014_2015/annexes/h2020-wp1415-annex-g-trl_en.pdf

12. Gordieiev, O., Kharchenko, V., Fusani, M.: Evolution of software quality models: green and reliability issues. In: Proceedings of the 11th International Conference on ICT in Education, Research and Industrial Applications: Integration, Harmonization and Knowledge Transfer (ICTERI 2015), vol. 1356, pp. 432–445 (2015). http://ceur-ws.org/Vol-1356/paper_71.pdf

13. Hansen, M., Jensen, M., Rost, M.: Protection Goals for Engineering Privacy. In: 2015 International Workshop on Privacy Engineering (IWPE). IEEE eXplore (2015, to appear)

14. Hes, R., Borking, J.J.: Privacy-Enhancing Technologies: The Path to Anonymity. Technical report, Registratiekamer (1995)

15. Hoepman, J.-H.: Privacy design strategies (extended abstract). In: Cuppens-Boulahia, N., Cuppens, F., Jajodia, S., Abou El Kalam, A., Sans, T. (eds.) SEC 2014. IFIP AICT, vol. 428, pp. 446–459. Springer, Heidelberg (2014)

16. ISO/IEC 25010: Systems and software engineering – Systems and software quality requirements and evaluation (SQuaRE) – System and software quality models. Technical report, ISO JTC 1/SC 7 (2011)

17. Kujawski, E.: Analysis and critique of the system readiness level. IEEE Trans. Syst. Man Cybern. Syst. **43**(4), 979–987 (2013). http://dx.doi.org/10.1109/TSMCA.2012.2209868

18. Li, N., Li, T., Venkatasubramanian, S.: $t$-Closeness: privacy beyond $k$-anonymity and $l$-diversity. In: Chirkova, R., Dogac, A., Özsu, M.T., Sellis, T.K. (eds.) ICDE, pp. 106–115. IEEE, New York (2007)

19. Machanavajjhala, A., Kifer, D., Gehrke, J., Venkitasubramaniam, M.: $l$-Diversity: privacy beyond $k$-anonymity. ACM Trans. Knowl. Discov. Data **1**(1) (2007)

20. Mankins, J.C.: Technology readiness assessments: a retrospective. Acta Astronaut. **65**, 1216–1223 (2009)

21. Nolte, W.L.: Did I Ever Tell You About the Whale?, Or Measuring Technology Maturity. Information Age Publishing, Charlotte (2008)

22. Olechowski, A.L., Eppinger, S.D., Joglekar, N.: Technology Readiness Levels at 40: A Study of State-of-the-Art Use, Challenges, and Opportunities. MIT Sloan Research Paper No. 5127-15. Technical report, MIT (2015). http://dx.doi.org/10. 2139/ssrn.2588524

23. Organisation for Economic Co-operation and Development (OECD): Inventory of Privacy-Enhancing Technologies (PETs). Report DSTI/ICCP/REG (2001)1/FINAL, Working Party on Information Security and Privacy. Technical report (2002). https://www.oecd.org/officialdocuments/publicdisplay documentpdf/?doclanguage=en&cote=dsti/iccp/reg%282001%291/final
24. Sauser, B.J., Verma, D., Ramirez-Marquez, J.E., Gove, R.: From TRL to SRL: the concept of systems readiness levels. In: Proceedings Conference on Systems Engineering Research, Los Angeles, CA (2006)
25. Smith, J.D.: An Alternative to Technology Readiness Levels for Non-Developmental Item (NDI) Software. Technical report CMU/SEI-2004-TR-013, Software Engineering Institute, Carnegie Mellon (2004)
26. Smith, J.D.: An alternative to technology readiness levels for non-developmental item (NDI) software. In: Proceedings of the 38th Annual Hawaii International Conference on System Sciences - HICSS 2005 (2005)
27. Sweeney, L.: $k$-anonymity: a model for protecting privacy. Int. J. Uncertainty Fuzziness Knowl. Based Syst. **10**(5), 557–570 (2002)

# Formal Accountability for Biometric Surveillance: A Case Study

Vinh-Thong Ta[1](✉), Denis Butin[2], and Daniel Le Métayer[3]

[1] University of Central Lancashire, Preston, UK
vtta@uclan.ac.uk
[2] TU Darmstadt, Darmstadt, Germany
dbutin@cdc.informatik.tu-darmstadt.de
[3] Inria, Université de Lyon, Lyon, France
daniel.le-metayer@inria.fr

**Abstract.** Surveillance, especially using biometric systems, threatens the privacy of individuals. Accountability is an established approach to supporting privacy in general, but it must follow a rigorous process and involve close scrutiny of actual data handling practice to be effective. In this paper, we consider a specific, real-world biometric surveillance system, based on camcorders and bodyprint identification. We show how formalisation can be used to achieve the required level of rigour and exemplify how our formal approach to accountability — in the sense of verifiable compliance with personal data handling policies — supports the privacy of individuals monitored by the system. The formal accountability framework is general enough to be reusable in other settings.

## 1 Surveillance, Biometrics and Accountability

Surveillance systems using biometrics enjoy growing use, in particular for identification purposes [10,16,18]. A powerful feature is the possibility of identifying agents based on automatically detectable visual cues. Some features (e.g. height, hair, clothing) can be acquired without subject cooperation [9]. Even when the gathered information is insufficient to uniquely identify individuals straight away, the capture and processing of their images raises major privacy concern. As put by Campisi, *biometrics are associated with surveillance not simply for legitimate reasons (...) but also with disproportionate, imprecise and invisible use* [7]. Scope creep is therefore a worry. Advanced processing features and the possibility of communication between data controllers (DC) and third parties reinforce these concerns. Mitigating measures are required to keep potential abuse in check.

An established approach to sustain privacy is a focus on *accountability* of DC, in the sense described by the Article 29 Working Group [3]. Accountability is then defined as the duty for DC to not only put in place measures guaranteeing the privacy of data subjects (DS), but also for these measures to be verifiable. Ideally, this verification should be carried out by independent third parties or by agents acting on the behalf of DS (or, wherever practicable, by the DS themselves). This focus on transparency empowers DS and increases pressure on DC

© Springer International Publishing Switzerland 2016
B. Berendt et al. (Eds.): APF 2015, LNCS 9484, pp. 21–37, 2016.
DOI: 10.1007/978-3-319-31456-3_2

to deploy strong privacy-sustaining measures, as opposed to mere declarations of intention. Three types of accountability are distinguished by Colin Bennett [8]: accountability of policy, of procedures and of practice. The strongest variant, on which we focus here, is accountability of practice which holds that DC ought to demonstrate that their actual data handling complies with their obligations. To be effective, accountability of practice should be based on verifiable, technical information about personal data processing, for instance in the form of auditable event logs [5]. For logs to be easily mappable to privacy policies, a correspondence between low-level system events and high-level data processing can be produced [6].

Our work is inspired by the European project PARIS (PrivAcy pReserving Infrastructure for Surveillance) [1]. Privacy-preserving surveillance infrastructures require accountability models to enforce rigour, clarify process definition and avoid ambiguities. Our motivation is the specification of truly protective accountability measures. Indeed, to be more than mere smoke screens used by data controllers to avoid stronger regulations, accountability must provide concrete evidence about personal data processing and make it possible to have compliance checked by third party auditors.

**Related Work.** Most of the relevant existing work focuses on the security modelling and verification of biometric systems. Lloyd applied Unified Modeling Language (UML) and Java Modeling Language (JML) approaches to the development and security analysis of a biometric authentication system [12]. Salaiwarakul proposed a security verification method for biometric authentication protocols based on the ProVerif protocol analyser [14]. Kanak proposed a formal framework called Biometric Privacy-Security-Trust Model (BioPSTM) to describe the trade-off between privacy and security and their relationship with trust in biometric authentication systems [11].

Formal approaches for reasoning about accountability and privacy system properties are rarely investigated. Accountability has been mentioned in the context of biometrics before, but with a focus on the accountability of system users. For instance, Prabhakar considered the scenario of fingerprint-based information system access control, yielding accountability for system transactions while preserving user anonymity (no names are linked to the fingerprints) [13].

We previously introduced a formal approach to accountability for privacy, independently of the context of biometric surveillance [6]. Our focus there was the correctness of links between system events and operations on categories of personal data in a generic setting. In particular, a generic formal privacy policy language was proposed that defines, for each type of personal data, authorised purposes, deletion delays, request completion delays, admissible contexts and data forwarding policies. Trace compliance properties were defined with respect to data handling events and elements of these privacy policies. We then formalised correctness properties relating personal data handling events and system events. The genericity of this previous work contrasts with the present case study, which aims at illustrating its application (with some modifications) to a concrete surveillance scenario.

**Contributions.** We investigate the applicability of a formal approach to accountability to a biometrics surveillance system. The case study under consideration analyses a real-world system deployment by the PARIS project consortium member Visual Tools [15]. The formal approach applied here is based on [6], where the technical aspects of the framework are described in more detail. Modifications to the policy language required for this case study are proposed. To the best of our knowledge, this paper is the first work which examines this specific setting in a real-world system. In contrast to previous work [13], we examine accountability from the system owner's (DC's) perspective[1].

We aim to demonstrate the practical application of a formal framework for accountability to the example of an actual bodyprint-based surveillance system. The case study is performed in sufficient detail to provide a hands-on illustration of accountability of practice for a realistic scenario. The underlying formal framework remains general enough to be applied to different use cases.

**Outline.** The case study, the involved entities and categories of personal data are presented in Sect. 2. A privacy policy language to model accountability properties is defined next (Sect. 3). Abstract personal data handling events are then introduced to relate processing to privacy policy constraints (Sect. 4) and the compliance of a sequence of events is studied in Sect. 5. We conclude with a discussion (Sect. 6).

## 2   A Real-World Biometric Surveillance System

A PARIS consortium member has deployed a biometric system to protect equipment stored in their headquarters located in Madrid[2]. This biometric system is based on video analysis to detect unauthorised access to the office at non-working hours, when only the employees are allowed to be present. The system monitors the main transit areas of the office with camcorders, providing depth and spatial information that is analysed to detect individuals accessing the office. To this end, the camcorders are depth cameras with a video processing unit (VPU).

The biometric surveillance system is composed of two main phases: *enrolment* and *matching*. During enrolment, a group of employees are recorded and registered as authorised. Their presence in the restricted areas is permitted. Re-identification of authorised individuals as well as detection and report of unauthorised individuals takes place during matching.

The proposed biometric system uses *bodyprints* [2] for re-identification. A bodyprint is a vector of physical characteristics, such as the height and width of a person and clothing colours, which are sufficiently distinctive to make it possible to identify and differentiate individuals, even with similar clothes. Authorised individuals wear uniforms with a particular colour, which facilitates their identification.

---

[1] That is, the system owner must provide accounts to recorded individuals with respect to the handling of their personal data.

[2] Details about this use case can be found in a project deliverable [15].

**Bodyprint Extraction.** Bodyprint extraction is a two-step process. First, a person is detected by the camcorders, and his/her movement is tracked by different video frames. Second, the bodyprints of the person are created, based on the tracked frames. Bodyprints are not linked with any other personal data. Moreover, it is hard to reconstruct full images from bodyprints (Fig. 1).

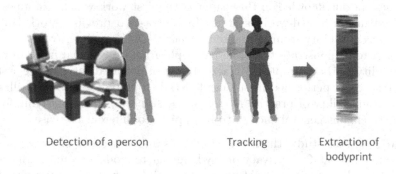

Detection of a person          Tracking          Extraction of bodyprint

**Fig. 1.** Bodyprint extraction process (taken from [15])

**Enrolment.** During enrolment, bodyprints of authorised individuals are extracted and stored in the system. The process of enrolment is performed in three steps:

1. A camcorder records a video of an authorised person, and as a result, a video sequence containing images (frames) of the person is obtained;
2. Bodyprints are extracted from the video frames, and a specific user interface facilitates the selection of the most adequate ones for matching;
3. The selected bodyprints are stored in the Authorised People Database (APDB) located in the re-identification server (RIS).

Enrolment is offline, and managed manually by the System Administrator (SA). The SA gives instruction for authorised individuals before recording them, selects adequate bodyprints and stores them in the APDB.

**Matching.** The purpose of matching is to detect and report unauthorised access to the office at non-working hours. The process is monitored by the System Operator (SO), and consists of the following steps:

1. Each camcorder continuously captures images of the scene and automatically extracts the bodyprints of the recorded individuals;
2. The camcorders periodically send new bodyprints to the RIS;
3. The RIS compares the new bodyprints with the ones stored in the APDB. The results of the comparison are copied to the alert database;
4. The SO checks the stored alerts through a specific user interface of the alert management server. In case of intrusion, the SO is responsible for reporting the incident to the local authorities.

While enrolment is managed manually by the SA, matching is fully auto-mated, involving an intervention of the SO only in the last step. Each piece of video and non-video data in the system is given a unique identifier (ID) for reference and searching purposes (Sect. 5.1.2 in [15]). In terms of personal data minimisation, no ID or basic information (civil identity, name, birthday, etc.) related to the DS is stored in the system; only the IDs of the videos and bodyprints.

In this system, the data retention period follows the Instruction 1/2006 of the Spanish Data Protection Agency [17]. On this basis, images and bodyprints can at most be stored for one month. For enrolment the videos are stored in a VPU until a corresponding set of (temporary) bodyprints has been extracted. This period in any case will not exceed one month. In the matching phase, the videos are deleted right after the bodyprints have been extracted, which is carried out automatically within a few minutes[3]. In each set of extracted bodyprints, one long-term bodyprint is selected and stored in the APDB until the system is retired. The remaining temporary bodyprints are automatically deleted within a few minutes after the long-term bodyprint has been selected. Finally, the bodyprints subject to an alarm during the matching phase are kept in the alert database until the results of the recognition are verified by the SO, with a maximum limit of one day[4]. The other bodyprints are deleted within a few minutes after they have been checked against the APDB.

Eventually, we review the roles and privileges of users in the system. The role of the SAs is to manage the whole system, hence they are granted all privileges, namely, having access to all information stored in the system. For instance, a SA can manage (add, edit, delete data) the APDB, has access to the RIS, and also access to the VPU. The SO is responsible for managing the intrusion alarms; hence, he has access to the RIS and the alert database inside it, and to the APDB as well. The SO receives alarms on a computer or mobile device, and then logs into the RIS to check the bodyprints subject to the alarm. In case of false alarms these bodyprints are deleted from the RIS alert database by the SO. We assume that accountability auditors are independent third parties such as Data Protection Authority officers. They can require access to certain information stored in the system to verify an intrusion or the compliance of the system with the regulations. To this end, they can be granted reading access to the bodyprints in the alert database, or to the bodyprints in the APDB.

## 3   Defining Privacy Policies

Based on the language introduced in [6], we propose a modified privacy policy language to model accountability properties for this case study. Due to space

---

[3] Although in Sect. 5.1.2 of [15] (alarm management part), *optionally*, the system could also directly send an image of the intruder with the alarm. We consider only the basic setting to simplify the formalism.

[4] The worst case delay authorised by Spanish law remains one month. One day is a much more realistic time frame in this case, since the verification is time-sensitive.

limitations, we only consider the videos and bodyprints of individuals during enrolment and matching. The remaining data, such as the ID of the SA and SO, can be modelled similarly. We aim to show that a formal approach to system design with accountability in mind is feasible and to illustrate the resulting benefits, such as increased clarity.

**Privacy Policies.**

**Definition 1 (Privacy Policy).** *Privacy policies are defined as tuples:*

$$\mathcal{P} = Purposes \times Time \times Time \times Context \times AccPol \times AccPol \times AccPol$$

We distinguish privacy policies for each type of personal data and phase. Specifically, $\mathcal{P}_E^{vid}$ is the policy defined for the video frames of the authorised individuals captured during enrolment. $\mathcal{P}_M^{vid}$ relates to the video frames of the DS recorded during matching. $\mathcal{P}_E^{tmp}$ is defined for the set of temporary bodyprints calculated from the video frames of a given employee recorded during enrolment. In the second step of enrolment, first a set of temporary bodyprints is extracted from the corresponding video, then the most adequate one is stored in the APDB, while the rest will be deleted. $\mathcal{P}_M^{tmp}$ is similar to $\mathcal{P}_E^{tmp}$ but deals with the temporary bodyprints during matching. $\mathcal{P}_E^{apdb}$ is the policy defined on the selected bodyprints stored in the APBD during enrolment. $\mathcal{P}_M^{alert}$ defines the policy for bodyprints stored in the alert database located in the RIS. In case of alarm, the SO will access this database to verify the bodyprint of the intruder.

Specifically, for $\pi_{ev} \in \mathcal{P}_E^{vid}$, $\pi_{mv} \in \mathcal{P}_M^{vid}$, $\pi_{et} \in \mathcal{P}_E^{tmp}$, $\pi_{mt} \in \mathcal{P}_M^{tmp}$, $\pi_{ea} \in \mathcal{P}_E^{apdb}$, $\pi_{alert} \in \mathcal{P}_M^{alert}$, let

$$\pi_* = (ap, d, gd, cx, acc^{sa}, acc^{so}, acc^{au})$$

where $* \in \{ev, mv, et, mt, ea, alert\}$.

Particularly, $ap \in Purposes$ is the set of authorised purposes for data use. The retention delay $d$ is explained in the next subsection. $gd$ is a global (worst-case) delay after which all personal data must be deleted. Unlike the retention delays specified below, global deletion delay is defined to prevent data being kept longer in the system than needed under any circumstances. $cx \in Context$ is the set of contexts in which the data can be used. *Context* is the set of constants, for instance, time or location. Finally, $acc^{sa}$, $acc^{so}$ and $acc^{au}$ specify the access policies for the SA, the SO and auditor, respectively.

Possible values for an access policy are $\downarrow_{auth}$, meaning that access to the data is allowed after a successful authentication[5], and $\uparrow$, denoting that access to the data is forbidden.

**Retention Delays.** The retention delay $d$ has a different meaning depending on the type of privacy policy under consideration:

- For $\pi_{ev}$: the delay for the DC to delete the video frames stored in a camcorder after a suitable bodyprint has been extracted and stored in the APDB.

---

[5] In case the authentication is performed by the local authorities, it may involve manual aspects.

- For $\pi_{mv}$: the delay for the DC to delete the video frames of the DS during matching after a bodyprint has been extracted from them for the matching purpose.
- For $\pi_{et}$: the delay for the DC to delete the temporary bodyprints during enrolment after the selected (adequate) bodyprint has been added to the APDB database by a SA.
- For $\pi_{mt}$: the delay after which the DC must delete the extracted bodyprint during matching, after the comparison of this bodyprint with the stored bodyprints (in the APDB) has been performed.
- For $\pi_{ea}$: the delay after which the long-term bodyprint stored in the APDB must be deleted by the DC, after the corresponding DS was disenroled or the system has been retired.
- For $\pi_{alert}$: the deletion delay for the temporary bodyprints stored in the alert database, launched after all the alerts have been examined by the SO.

**Concrete Privacy Policy Parameters.** Three examples of concrete policies for this case study can be found in Fig. 2.

---

$\pi_{ev} = (\{$"*Enrol*", "*Extract*"$\},$ 1 min, 1 month, $\{$DC Building$\}, \downarrow_{auth}, \uparrow, \downarrow_{auth})$

$\pi_{mv} = (\{$"*Match*", "*Extract*"$\},$ 1 min, 1 month, $\{$DC Building, 21:00/07:00$\}, \uparrow, \uparrow, \uparrow)$

$\pi_{et} = (\{$"*Enrol*", "*Choose*"$\},$ 1 min, 1 month, $\{$DC Building$\}, \downarrow_{auth}, \uparrow, \downarrow_{auth})$

---

**Fig. 2.** Some of the concrete privacy policies used by the system

We now discuss the parameters for $\pi_{ev}$, $\pi_{mv}$ and $\pi_{et}$ in Fig. 2. As specified in the use case description [15], the deletion delay for videos and bodyprints follows the Instruction 1/2006 of the Spanish Data Protection Agency, and should be maximum one month. Hence, we set the global deletion delay to 1 month, and for demonstration purposes, the retention delays are set to 1 min for all privacy policies. The videos are used in the DC building and the matching phase at non-working hours (the period between 9 PM and 7 AM).

In $\pi_{ev}$ the purposes of the enrolled video can be *enrolment* and *bodyprint extraction* (denoted respectively by "*Enrol*" and "*Extract*"), and the procedure takes place in the building of the data controller. Finally, only the SA and the auditor (after successful authentication) are allowed to access the enrolled videos. By contrast, the purposes of the video in $\pi_{mv}$ are *matching* and *bodyprint extraction*, which have to be done in the DC building between 9 PM and 7 AM. This video is automatically deleted within a short time, hence, no access possibility is available. Eventually, in $\pi_{et}$ the purposes of the extracted bodyprints can be either *enrolment* or the *choice* of an adequate bodyprint. The SA and the auditor have access rights to the bodyprints. In practice, the meaning of constants such as *Enrol, Extract, Match, Choose* and *DC Building* has to be defined precisely (in natural language) in documents that must be available to the auditors.

Indeed, as discussed in Sect. 6, accountability audits cannot be entirely mechanized and the application of log analysis tools should be complemented by manual verifications, in particular with respect to notions such as purpose and context which may be subject to interpretation or may require further information.

## 4  Reasoning About Personal Data Handling Events

To reason about personal data handling events with respect to privacy policies, abstract events will be defined first. Abstract states are specified later to express the combined effect of sequences of abstract events. All building blocks to define trace compliance properties (Sect. 5) will then be presented. In our context, the ultimate reason for defining trace compliance properties is to define the accountability requirements of the surveillance system.

**Abstract Events.** To reason about accountability compliance properties, we define the abstract events corresponding to the case study. Each abstract event captures a specific action, or a high-level event occurring during system execution. These events abstract away from system internals such as writing and reading from memory addresses, and are specified based on the format of privacy policies. The key requirement for the set of events is its completeness: it should include all operations that can have an impact on the compliance of the system with respect to any privacy policy. We assume that each recorded video is given a unique identifier $idv$ from the set of video identifiers $IDV$, and that each bodyprint extracted from this video is given a unique ID related to the video-ID.

Abstract events (Fig. 3) are tuples starting with an event name, followed by a timestamp capturing the time of the event, parameters of the event, and the privacy policy corresponding to the personal data created by the event (if any[6]). Note that unlike the other parameters, the policies in the events are constants. All parameters in the following list are mandatory.

Events $E_1$–$E_2$ capture the moment when the camera $cam$ (in the DC's building) records the video $video$ of type $enr\text{-}video\text{-}type$ (respectively $mat\text{-}video\text{-}type$) with a policy $\pi_{ev}$ (respectively $\pi_{mv}$) for enrolment (respectively matching). The recorded video is given a unique ID $idev$ ($idov$), where the tags $ev$ and $ov$ refer to the enrolment and matching phases, respectively. Similarly, corresponding events $E_3$–$E_4$ for bodyprint extraction during enrolment and matching exist. During enrolment and matching, the set of bodyprints $tmp\text{-}bd\text{-}set$ (respectively $tmp\text{-}bd$) of type $tmp\text{-}bd\text{-}set\text{-}type$ (respectively $tmp\text{-}bd\text{-}type$) is extracted from the video with the IDs $idev$ and $idov$, respectively.

$E_5$ expresses that during enrolment, the bodyprint $bd$ corresponding to the video identified by $idev$ is selected and stored in the APDB for matching purposes. $E_6$ occurs during matching, when the bodyprint $alert\text{-}bd$ of type $alert\text{-}bd\text{-}type$ (corresponding to the video $idov$) with the policy $\pi_{alert}$ has been subject to

---

[6] In this case study, no event leads to the creation of several pieces of personal data. However, tuples could easily be extended to include one policy per created data.

$E_1$: $(RecordEnrol, t, cam, enr\text{-}video\text{-}type, video, idev, \pi_{ev})$

$E_2$: $(RecordMatch, t, cam, mat\text{-}video\text{-}type, video, idov, \pi_{mv})$

$E_3$: $(ExtrEnrol, t, idev, tmp\text{-}bd\text{-}set\text{-}type, tmp\text{-}bd\text{-}set, \pi_{et})$

$E_4$: $(ExtrMatch, t, idov, tmp\text{-}bd\text{-}type, tmp\text{-}bd, \pi_{mt})$

$E_5$: $(ChooseEnrol, t, idev, bd\text{-}type, bd, \pi_{ea})$

$E_6$: $(AlertMatch, t, idov, alert\text{-}bd\text{-}type, alert\text{-}bd, \pi_{alert})$

$E_7$: $(CompEndMatch, t, idov, tmp\text{-}bd\text{-}type, tmp\text{-}bd)$

$E_8$: $(Use, t, idv, \theta, v, purposes, reasons)$

$E_9$: $(Delete, t, idv, \theta, v)$

$E_{10}$: $(Authenticate, t, or, idv, \theta, v)$

$E_{11}$: $(AccessReq, t, or, idv, \theta, v)$

$E_{12}$: $(Access, t, or, idv, \theta, v)$

$E_{13}$: $(SOAlertVerEnd, t, alert\text{-}bd\text{-}type, alert\text{-}bd)$

$E_{14}$: $(SysRetired, t)$

**Fig. 3.** List of abstract events

an alert, and is stored to be verified by the SO. $E_7$ captures the event when the comparison of the temporary bodyprint $tmp\text{-}bd$, extracted from the video $idov$, against the APDB has finished.

We define pairs of data types and values $(\theta, v)$, on which events are defined, in Fig. 4. From now on, let $\nabla$ be the set of these pairs. $E_8$ represents the events for the data use and $(\theta, v) \in \nabla$. This event defines the use of the data $(\theta, v)$ with the ID $idv$. In our case, $purposes$ is the set { "Enrol", "Match", "Extract", "Choose", "Store", "Verification" }, while $reasons$ is { "Alert", "AccesRequest" }.

$E_9$ is a delete event where $(\theta, v) \in \nabla$. It captures the deletion of the data of value $v$ and type $\theta$ at time $t$ during enrolment or matching. $E_{10}$ defines an authentication event performed by an originating agent $or$ at time $t$ to access the data $(\theta, v)$ with the ID $idv$.

$E_{11}$ specifies the access request received by the DC from $or$ in order to access the data $v$ of type $\theta$. In case $or$ is $SA$, $(\theta, v)$ is $(enr\text{-}video\text{-}type, video)$, $(tmp\text{-}bd\text{-}set\text{-}type, tmp\text{-}bd\text{-}set)$, or $(bd\text{-}type, bd)$, because the $SA$ has access to the VPU and the APDB. Similarly, when $or$ is $SO$, $(\theta, v)$ is the alerted bodyprints $(alert\text{-}bd\text{-}type, alert\text{-}bd)$ stored in the RIS, or the long-term bodyprints $(bd\text{-}type, bd)$ in the APDB. If $or$ is $Authority$, then $(\theta, v)$ is any data type/value pair that the $SA$ and the $SO$ can access. Note that $or$ can also be an unauthorised agent, in which case, access will be refused.

| |
|---|
| (*enr-video-type*, *video*) — videos recorded during enrolment |
| (*mat-video-type*, *video*) — videos recorded during matching |
| (*tmp-bd-set-type*, *tmp-bd-set*) — sets of temporary bodyprints extracted from the recorded videos during enrolment |
| (*tmp-bd-type*, *tmp-bd*) — bodyprints extracted from the recorded videos during matching |
| (*bd-type*, *bd*) — (long-term) bodyprints selected from the temporary sets |
| (*alert-bd-type*, *alert-bd*) — bodyprints subject to the alerts, extracted during matching |

**Fig. 4.** Data types and values

Event $E_{12}$ is the actual access by *or* to data $(\theta, v)$, where the parameters are similar to the *AccessReq* case ($E_{11}$). Finally, in $E_{13}$ the SO has terminated the verification of the alerted bodyprint *alert-bd*, while $E_{14}$ indicates that the surveillance system has retired at time $t$.

Figure 5 provides an extract of the data flow graph and the relationships between some events during enrolment and matching.

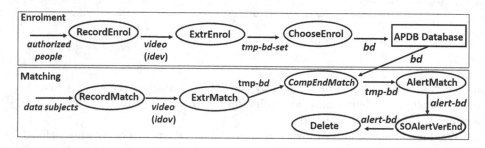

**Fig. 5.** Data flow graph extract, showing the relationships between some of the events

**Traces and Abstract States.** Sequences of abstract events are now defined. They constitute a history of personal data handling events, and will be used for compliance checking.

**Definition 2 (Trace).** *A trace $\sigma$ is a sequence of abstract events.*

We provide the notion of abstract states to define compliant traces based on the semantics of events. The main difference between our formalism and the one proposed in [6] is as follows. In this previous work, the system stores information about the DS, such as IDs. Here, only IDs about the videos and bodyprints are stored. Hence, instead of defining abstract states on the pair of data types and DS, we define them on the pair of data types and video IDs. $\mathbb{P}(S)$ denotes the power set of $S$.

**Definition 3 (Abstract State).** *The abstract state of a system associated with data types and video IDs (Type, IDV) is a function (Type, IDV) $\to$ Time $\times$ Cam $\times$ {Value} $\times$ Policy $\times$ $\mathbb{P}$(Entity, $\mathbb{N}$) $\times$ $\mathbb{P}$(Entity, $\mathbb{N}$) $\times$ $\mathbb{P}$(Entity, $\mathbb{N}$).*

We distinguish abstract states with regard to video and non-video data types such as temporary bodyprints, stored bodyprints, alerted bodyprints. A state includes the time of the current state, the camera that recorded the video with the given ID, current value of the data (video or non-video), the policy on this data, as well as the sets of SAs, SOs and Authorities who have been granted access to it. The associated value in $\mathbb{N}$ specifies the trace position where the access to this data has been granted.

For instance, in case of *enr-video-type* and *tmp-bd-set-type* we have the states:

$$(enr\text{-}video\text{-}type, idev) \to (t, cam, \{video\}, \pi_{ev}, sa, so, aud)$$

$$(tmp\text{-}bd\text{-}set\text{-}type, idev) \to (t, cam, tmp\text{-}bd\text{-}set, \pi_{et}, sa, so, aud)$$

The semantics of an abstract event at a given position in a trace is denoted:

$$\mathcal{S}_A : (Event \times \mathbb{N}) \to AbstractState \to AbstractState$$

Only an extract of the abstract state semantics is shown here for the sake of conciseness; see Fig. 6.

---

$\mathcal{S}_A((RecordEnrol, t, cam, idev, \pi_{ev}), j)\sum =$
$\sum[(enr\text{-}video\text{-}type, idev) \to (t, cam, \{video\}, \pi_{ev}, \emptyset, \emptyset, \emptyset)]$

$\mathcal{S}_A((ExtrEnrol, t, idev, tmp\text{-}bd\text{-}set\text{-}type, tmp\text{-}bd\text{-}set, \pi_{et}), j)\sum =$
$\sum[(tmp\text{-}bd\text{-}set\text{-}type, idev) \to (t, cam, tmp\text{-}bd\text{-}set, \pi_{et}, \emptyset, \emptyset, \emptyset)]$

$\mathcal{S}_A((ChooseEnrol, t, idev, bd\text{-}type, bd, \pi_{ea}), j)\sum =$
$\sum[(bd\text{-}type, idev) \to (t, cam, \{bd\}, \pi_{et}, \emptyset, \emptyset, \emptyset)]$

$\mathcal{S}_A((AlertMatch, t, idov, alert\text{-}bd\text{-}type, alert\text{-}bd, \pi_{alert}), j)\sum =$
$\sum[(alert\text{-}bd\text{-}type, idov) \to (t, cam, \{alert\text{-}bd\}, \pi_{alert}, \emptyset, \emptyset, \emptyset)]$

$\mathcal{S}_A((Access, t, or, idv, \theta, v), j)\sum =$
$\sum[(\theta, idv) \to (t, cam, \{v\}, \pi, sa \cup \{(or, j)\}, so, aud)]$, if $or = SA$, else
$\sum[(\theta, idv) \to (t, cam, \{v\}, \pi, sa, so \cup \{(or, j)\}, aud)]$, if $or = SO$, else
$\sum[(\theta, idv) \to (t, cam, \{v\}, \pi, sa, so, aud \cup \{(or, j)\})]$, if $or = Aud$,
where $(t, cam, \{v\}, \pi, sa, so, aud)] = \sum(ds, \theta)$

$\mathcal{S}_A((Delete, t, idv, \theta, v), j)\sum = \sum[(\theta, idv) \to \bot]$       where $(\theta, v) \in \nabla$

---

**Fig. 6.** Abstract states semantics (extract)

The semantics of the video recording event *RecordEnrol* is captured by an update of the state for the pair (*enr-video-type, idv*) with the tuple of the recording time, the camcorder, and (the contents of) the video itself. At this time no access is allowed to the video yet, hence, three empty sets are included. Similarly, the semantics of the bodyprints extraction event *ExtrEnrol* is defined by a tuple including the set of temporary bodyprints *tmp-bd-set* extracted from the video *idev*. At the moment of bodyprints extraction, no access right has been granted yet. The event *AlertMatch* updates the state with the time $t$, the camcorder recorded the video *idov* of the alerted bodyprint, the value and the policy of the bodyprint. The semantics of the event *Access* is based on the value of *or*, who is granted access to the data $(\theta, v)$. As a result, *or* is added to the corresponding set of SAs, SOs and Authorities, respectively. Finally, the event *Delete* captures the deletion of the data $(\theta, v)$, updating the state with the undefined state $\bot$.

Having defined abstract events and abstract state semantics, we can now define the final state of a trace. This notion captures the combined effect of all personal data handling events up to the end of a trace. The final state of a trace $\sigma = [e_1, \ldots, e_n]$ is defined as $F_A(\sigma, 1) \sum_0$ with $\forall\, \theta, \forall\, idv, \sum_0 (\theta, idv) = \bot$ and

$$F_A([\,], n) \sum = \sum$$

$$F_A([e_1, \ldots, e_m], n) \sum = F_A([e_2, \ldots, e_m], n + 1) \left( \mathcal{S}_A(e_1, n) \sum \right)$$

We set $State_A(\sigma, i) = F_A(\sigma_{|i}, 1) \sum_0$, with $\sigma_{|i} = \sigma_1 \ldots \sigma_i$ the prefix of length $i$ of $\sigma$ (i.e. the partial trace up to index $i$).

Final states will in turn be used to specify trace compliance next (Sect. 5).

## 5   Compliance of Event Traces

We now define the compliance of event traces. This notion captures the accountable operation of the biometric surveillance system. Trace compliance rules $A_1$–$A_{12}$ are stated $\forall\, i \in \mathbb{N}, \forall\, idv, \forall\, \theta$. We first describe the rules in natural language, before formalising them in Fig. 7. These rules are not an attempt at exhaustiveness with regards to privacy compliance modelling. Rather, we aim to convey the importance of clarity and precision for privacy compliance rules.

$A_1$: No data $v$ of type $\theta$ appears in an abstract state after the expiration of the global deletion delay.

$A_2$: Data $v$ of type $\theta$ is used only for purposes defined in its policy.

$A_3$: During enrolment, if the policy forbids all access to data $v$ of type $\theta$, then there is none.

$A_4$: During enrolment, every access to the personal data by the SA must be preceded by the corresponding successful authentication.

$A_5$: Every access to the personal data by the SO must be preceded by the corresponding successful authentication (matching).

$A_6$: Every access to personal data by the auditor must be preceded by the corresponding access request.

$A_7$: During enrolment, the deletion of a video must occur within the duration $\pi_{ev}.d$ after a corresponding set of (temporary) bodyprints has been extracted.

$A_1$:  $State_A(\sigma, i-1)(\theta, idv) = (t, cam, \{v\}, \pi, so, sa, aud) \implies EvTime(\sigma_i) \leq t + \pi.gd$

$A_2$:  $\sigma_i = (Use, t, idv, \theta, v, purposes, reasons) \wedge$
  $State_A(\sigma, i-1)(\theta, idv) = (t, cam, \{v\}, \pi, so, sa, aud) \implies purposes \subseteq \pi.ap$

$A_3$:  $\sigma_i = (Access, t, or, idv, \theta, v) \wedge$
  $State_A(\sigma, i-1)(\theta, idv) = (t, cam, \{v\}, \pi, so, sa, aud) \implies \pi.acc^{or} \neq \uparrow$

$A_4$:  $\sigma_i = (Access, t, SA, idev, \theta, v) \implies \exists j \mid \exists t' \mid \sigma_j = (Authenticate, t', SA, idev, \theta, v) \wedge$
  $t' < t$

$A_5$:  $\sigma_i = (Access, t, SO, idov, \theta, v) \implies \exists j \mid \exists t' \mid \sigma_j = (Authenticate, t', SO, idov, \theta, v) \wedge$
  $t' < t$

$A_6$:  $\sigma_i = (Access, t, Auditor, idev, \theta, v) \implies$
  $\exists j \mid \exists t' \mid \sigma_j = (AccessReq, t', Auditor, idev, \theta, v) \wedge t' < t$

$A_7$:  $\sigma_i = (ExtrEnrol, t', idev, tmp\text{-}bd\text{-}set\text{-}type, tmp\text{-}bd\text{-}set, \pi_{et}) \wedge$
  $State_A(\sigma, i-2)(enr\text{-}video\text{-}type, idev) = (t, cam, \{video\}, \pi_{ev}, sa, so, aud) \implies$
  $\exists j \mid \exists t'' \mid \sigma_j = (Delete, t'', idev, enr\text{-}video\text{-}type, video) \wedge (t' < t'' \leq t' + \pi_{ev}.d)$

$A_8$:  $\sigma_i = (ExtrMatch, t', idov, bd\text{-}type, bd, \pi_{mt}) \wedge$
  $State_A(\sigma, i-1)(mat\text{-}video\text{-}type, idov) = (t, cam, \{video\}, \pi_{mv}, sa, so, aud) \implies$
  $\exists j \mid \exists t'' \mid \sigma_j = (Delete, t'', idov, mat\text{-}video\text{-}type, video) \wedge (t' < t'' \leq t' + \pi_{mv}.d)$

$A_9$:  $\sigma_i = (ChooseEnrol, t', idev, bd\text{-}type, bd, \pi_{ea}) \wedge$
  $State_A(\sigma, i-1)(tmp\text{-}bd\text{-}set\text{-}type, idev) = (t, cam, \{tmp\text{-}bd\text{-}set\}, \pi_{et}, sa, so, aud) \implies$
  $\exists j \mid \exists t'' \mid \sigma_j = (Delete, t'', idev, tmp\text{-}bd\text{-}set\text{-}type, tmp\text{-}bd\text{-}set) \wedge (t' < t'' \leq t' + \pi_{et}.d)$

$A_{10}$:  $\sigma_i = (CompEndMatch, t', idov, tmp\text{-}bd\text{-}type, tmp\text{-}bd) \wedge$
  $State_A(\sigma, i-1)(tmp\text{-}bd\text{-}type, idov) = (t, cam, \{tmp\text{-}bd\}, \pi_{mt}, sa, so, aud) \implies$
  $\exists j \mid \exists t'' \mid \sigma_j = (Delete, t'', idov, tmp\text{-}bd\text{-}type, tmp\text{-}bd) \wedge (t' < t'' \leq t' + \pi_{mt}.d)$

$A_{11}$:  $\sigma_i = (SysRetired, t') \wedge$
  $State_A(\sigma, i-1)(bd\text{-}type, idev) = (t, cam, \{bd\}, \pi_{ea}, sa, so, aud) \implies$
  $\exists j \mid \exists t'' \mid \sigma_j = (Delete, t'', idev, bd\text{-}type, bd) \wedge (t' < t'' \leq t' + \pi_{ea}.d)$

$A_{12}$:  $\sigma_i = (SOAlertVerEnd, t', alert\text{-}bd\text{-}type, alert\text{-}bd) \wedge$
  $State_A(\sigma, i-1)(alert\text{-}bd\text{-}type, idov) = (t, cam, \{alert\text{-}bd\}, \pi_{alert}, sa, so, aud) \implies$
  $\exists j \mid \exists t'' \mid \sigma_j = (Delete, t'', idov, alert\text{-}bd\text{-}type, alert\text{-}bd) \wedge (t' < t'' \leq t' + \pi_{alert}.d)$

**Fig. 7.** Trace compliance rules

$A_8$: Deletion of a video must occur within the duration $\pi_{mv}.d$ after a bodyprint has been automatically extracted from it for matching.

$A_9$: Deletion of a set of temporary bodyprints must occur within the duration $\pi_{et}.d$ after an adequate bodyprint has been chosen by the SA for storage in the APDB.

$A_{10}$: Deletion of an automatically extracted bodyprint must occur within the duration $\pi_{mt}.d$ after the comparison of this bodyprint with the stored bodyprints (in the APDB) has ended.

$A_{11}$: Deletion of a long-term bodyprint in the APDB must occur within the duration $\pi_{ea}.d$ after the system has retired.

$A_{12}$: Deletion of the temporary bodyprints stored in the alert database must occur within the duration $\pi_{alert}.d$ after all alerts have been examined by the SO.

Let $EvTime$ be a function such that $EvTime(\sigma_i) = t_i$ and $\sigma_i = (X, t_i, \ldots)$, $t_i \in Time$. Trace compliance rules are formally defined in Fig. 7. $A_1$ specifies that if in the current state of $(\theta, idv)$ the time is $t$, then there cannot be any event with a timestamp later than $t + \pi.gd$ since all data must have been deleted after this time. In $A_2$ if the state of data $(\theta, idv)$ at the $(i-1)$th event includes the policy $\pi$, then its use in the next event must comply with the defined purposes. $A_3$ specifies that if $or$ accesses the data $(\theta, v)$ at the $i$th event, then this can only happen when previously the policy does not forbid access for $or$. Following this line of argument, the remaining rules can be interpreted in a similar way.

We note that accountability covers a huge number of requirements, hence, exhaustivity is beyond the scope of our paper. A sample set of compliance rules is provided to capture the most relevant aspects of accountability.

**Compliance Checking.** Trace compliance is defined with respect to the previous rules:

**Definition 4 (Trace Compliance).** *A trace $\sigma$ is compliant if it satisfies all the properties $A_1, \ldots, A_{12}$.*

The *Context* part of privacy policies did not appear in the above compliance checking rules. Generally speaking, context compliance may require manual verification by a human analyst. Even for time constraints (in our case, non-working hours), automated verification may not always be possible. Additional facts may need to be taken into account, or different context elements combined, with the final decision requiring individual appreciation. Since informal aspects can always crop up in compliance verification scenarios, manual verification must be integrated with formal verification in a single, coherent framework.

This formal definition of trace compliance can be used in practice by implementing a *log analyser*, i.e. a software tool taking as input a file containing a record of data handling events and outputting a `Compliant`/`Non-compliant` value. Data handling logs are files containing timestamped records of abstract events. They must be designed with compliance checking in mind to be usable. Such design is not trivial, and a balance must be found between semantic richness and the constraint of personal data minimisation. The issue of log design for compliance checking is explored in more detail in previous work [4].

In practice, logs generated by systems often contain events expressed at a lower level than the one relevant in conjunction with privacy policies. Events may be recorded at the system level and consist in a sequence of operations such as memory address reading, writing and deleting. However, logs at this level can also be used for compliance checking if certain conditions are met. A correspondence between different levels of abstraction is defined in [6], which makes it possible to apply the approach to low level logs.

# 6  Discussion

To the best of our knowledge, we have presented the first case-study of the application of a formal accountability framework to a biometric surveillance system. Our approach relies on the following building blocks:

1. A view of accountability as the provision, by a DC, of sufficient information to make the compliance of personal data handling verifiable to individuals or to auditors acting on their behalf.
2. The specification of distinct privacy policies for the different phases of operation of the system (enrolment and matching) and for the different categories of personal data involved.
3. The definition of abstract events, corresponding to the handling of personal data by the DC in a format compatible with the previously defined privacy policies.
4. The definition of a semantics of abstract system states for specific data types and values, and a distinction between the enrolment and matching phases.
5. Based on these abstract state semantics, the specification of data handling compliance rules for traces (sequences) of abstract events.

While formal models for accountability have been described before, this case study shows how such a framework can be tailored to a real-world setting involving biometric identification for surveillance. One specificity of this setting is that similar categories of personal data are handled in different ways depending on the stage of system processing. In this case, video frames and bodyprints are handled distinctly in different databases and at different operation stages.

Generally speaking, this example emphasises the importance of fine-grained distinction between the handling of personal data in different contexts. This need for clarity can be seen as one more argument for the importance of technical privacy policies, as opposed to privacy policies merely expressed in natural language, which are more prone to ambiguity.

Needless to say, strong measures must be taken to ensure the security (especially the confidentiality and integrity) of the log files. Their integrity must be guaranteed at two levels. At the time of their generation, log files must reflect actual system operation. It can be in the interest of DC to maliciously forge false traces to fake accountability while conducting non-compliant data handling operations. Even when this is not the case, implementation errors can break the link between system-level operations on personal data and the high-level narrative presented in the log files. Great care must therefore be taken to ensure this link is preserved. A possible technical approach is partial formal modelling of the components critically involved in log generation. In addition, the log generation process and the system itself must be documented with sufficient precision to make it possible for an auditor to check (manually) that the logs include all relevant events and form an adequate evidence for the operation of the system. Last but not least, after their generation, the integrity of log files must be preserved by preventing tampering.

To further elucidate the real-world applicability of our approach, demonstrating actual compliance checking is desirable. The feasibility of this mainly depends on the availability of exploitable logs. As discussed earlier, semantically useful log design is not obvious since both ambiguity and the presence of unnecessary personal data must be avoided. Logs must also be compatible with the chosen format of machine-readable privacy policies. Once usable logs are available, a log analyser can be implemented — a comparatively easy step in comparison if compliance semantics are well-defined. The implementation work then mainly involves a parsing module and coding compliance semantics. The task is more complicated if prior translation from system events to abstract events is required for the logs, and would need the definition of a correspondence relationship [6].

A case study fully incorporating legal and organisational aspects could be a worthwhile future work to further elucidate the concrete use of accountability.

**Acknowledgement.** This work was partially funded by the European project PARIS/FP7-SEC-2012-1, the Inria Project Lab CAPPRIS (Collaborative Action on the Protection of Privacy Rights in the Information Society) and the German Research Foundation (DFG).

# References

1. PrivAcy pReserving Infrastructure for Surveillance (PARIS) Project. http://www.paris-project.org
2. Albiol, A., Albiol, A., Oliver, J., Mossi, J.: Who is who at different cameras: people re-identification using depth cameras. IET Comput. Vis. **6**(5), 378–387 (2012)
3. Article 29 data protection working party: opinion 3/2010 on the principle of accountability (2010). http://ec.europa.eu/justice/policies/privacy/docs/wpdocs/2010/wp173_en.pdf
4. Butin, D., Chicote, M., Le Métayer, D.: Log design for accountability. In: 2013 IEEE Security and Privacy Workshop on Data Usage Management, pp. 1–7. IEEE Computer Society (2013)
5. Butin, D., Chicote, M., Le Métayer, D.: Strong accountability: beyond vague promises. In: Gutwirth, S., Leenes, R., De Hert, P. (eds.) Reloading Data Protection, pp. 343–369. Springer, Netherlands (2014)
6. Butin, D., Le Métayer, D.: Log analysis for data protection accountability. In: Jones, C., Pihlajasaari, P., Sun, J. (eds.) FM 2014. LNCS, vol. 8442, pp. 163–178. Springer, Heidelberg (2014)
7. Campisi, P.: Security and Privacy in Biometrics. Springer, London (2013)
8. Bennett, C.J.: Implementing Privacy Codes of Practice. Canadian Standards Association, Rexdale (1995)
9. Denman, S., Fookes, C., Bialkowski, A., Sridharan, S.: Soft-biometrics: unconstrained authentication in a surveillance environment. In: Digital Image Computing: Techniques and Applications (DICTA 2009), pp. 196–203. IEEE Computer Society (2009)
10. Jain, A., Ross, A., Prabhakar, S.: An introduction to biometric recognition. IEEE Trans. Circuits Syst. Video Technol. **14**(1), 4–20 (2004)

11. Kanak, A., Sogukpinar, I.: BioPSTM: a formal model for privacy, security, and trust in template-protecting biometric authentication. Secur. Commun. Netw. **7**(1), 123–138 (2014)
12. Lloyd, J., Jürjens, J.: Security analysis of a biometric authentication system using UMLsec and JML. In: Schürr, A., Selic, B. (eds.) MODELS 2009. LNCS, vol. 5795, pp. 77–91. Springer, Heidelberg (2009)
13. Prabhakar, S., Pankanti, S., Jain, A.K.: Biometric recognition: security and privacy concerns. IEEE Secur. Priv. **1**(2), 33–42 (2003)
14. Salaiwarakul, A.: Verification of Secure Biometric Authentication Protocols. Ph.D. thesis, University of Birmingham (2010). http://etheses.bham.ac.uk/1166/
15. Saornil, M., Rodríguez, F.J., Montenegro, M., Ma, Z.: PARIS project deliverable 6.1: biometrics use case description (2014). http://www.paris-project.org/images/ Paris/pdfFiles/PARIS_D6.1_Biometrics_Use_Case_Description_v1.0.pdf
16. Socolinsky, D.: Design and deployment of visible-thermal biometric surveillance systems. In: IEEE Conference on Computer Vision and Pattern Recognition (CVPR'07), pp. 1–2 (2007)
17. Spanish data protection agency: instruction 1/2006 on processing personal data for surveillance purposes through camera or video-camera systems (2006). http://ec.europa.eu/justice/policies/privacy/policy_papers/docs/ instrucciones_videovigilancia_en.pdf
18. Wheeler, F.W., Weiss, R., Tu, P.H.: Face recognition at a distance system for surveillance applications. In: Fourth IEEE International Conference on Biometrics: Theory Applications and Systems (BTAS 10), pp. 1–8 (2010)

# Increasing Transparency and Privacy for Online Social Network Users – USEMP Value Model, Scoring Framework and Legal

A. Popescu[1], M. Hildebrandt[2], J. Breuer[3], L. Claeys[3],
S. Papadopoulos[4], G. Petkos[4], T. Michalareas[6(✉)], D. Lund[5],
R. Heyman[3], S. van der Graaf[3], E. Gadeski[1], H. Le Borgne[1],
K. deVries[2], T. Kastrinogiannis[6], A. Kousaridas[6], and A. Padyab[7]

[1] CEA, Paris, France
[2] Radboud University Nijmegen, Nijmegen, The Netherlands
[3] iMinds-SMIT, Etterbeek, Belgium
[4] CERTH-ITI, Thessaloniki, Greece
[5] HW Communication Ltd, Lancaster, UK
[6] VELTI SA, Marousi, Greece
tmichalareas@velti.com
[7] Luleå Tekniska Universitet, Luleå, Sweden

**Abstract.** In this paper we present research results from the multi-disciplinary EU research project USEMP (USEMP is a project funded from EU research framework, additional information about project scope and deliverables are available at project's public website at: http://www.usemp-project.eu/). In particular, we look at the legal aspects of personal data licensing and profile transparency, the development of a personal data value model in Online Social Networks (OSNs) and the development of disclosure scoring and personal data value frameworks. In the first part of the paper we show how personal data usage licensing and profile transparency for OSN activities provides for Data Protection by Design (DPbD). We also present an overview of the existing personal data monetization ecosystem in OSNs and its possible evolutions for increasing privacy and transparency for consumers about their OSN presence. In the last part of the paper, we describe the USEMP scoring framework for personal information disclosure and data value that can assist users to better perceive how their privacy is affected by their OSN presence and what the value of their OSN activities is.

## 1 Introduction

USEMP is a multi-disciplinary research project, integrating the perspectives of lawyers, engineers, computer scientists, marketing experts and social scientists, aiming at developing a framework that will empower Online Social Network (OSN) users by enhancing their control over the data they distribute or interact with, with an eye on what can be inferred from the personal data shared in OSNs. At the core of this objective lies the idea of reducing the existing asymmetries of processing and control between OSNs organizations and citizens.

© Springer International Publishing Switzerland 2016
B. Berendt et al. (Eds.): APF 2015, LNCS 9484, pp. 38–59, 2016.
DOI: 10.1007/978-3-319-31456-3_3

For that purpose, we will briefly indicate how transparency tools operate in the legal framework of Data Protection by Design (DPbD), notably for profile transparency. Additionally, we will present how an ecosystem - as envisaged in USEMP - can evolve in the future, identifying business opportunities and challenges that could arise when the user has the means to assert more meaningful control in a sustainable manner. In addition to the proposed considerations for a personal data value model in OSNs, the USEMP research team has also developed a scoring framework that can be used to collect and compute indicators for the information disclosure and value of shared personal data, which is also described in the last part of the paper.

## 2  The Legal Angle: Data Licensing and Profile Transparency

At the global level privacy and data protection is in turmoil, creating unprecedented uncertainty over the business ethics that drive the new economy. We believe that it is pivotal that the upcoming EU GDPR stabilizes the expectations within the internal market of the EU, making sure that citizens have a legitimate expectation of the consequences of sharing data. USEMP has developed two types of legal tools to support the data-driven ecosystem of OSNs, which underpins the previous– technical and economic– account.

### 2.1   Data Licensing Agreement (DLA)

EU data protection law requires that any processing of personal data is based on one of six legal grounds. Current business models are often based on consent and on the legitimate interest of the data controller (i.e. the party that determines the purpose of processing). These are not very reliable grounds: Consent can be withdrawn at any time and the legitimate interest of the data controller needs to be balanced against the fundamental rights and interests of the data subject. In both cases the legal relationship between user and service provider remains opaque and distant, usually determined by privacy policies and terms of service that are oriented to assumptions of US law. In the context of USEMP we have opted for a Data Licensing Agreement that requires the active participation of the user, by means of mutually obligatory agreement (quid quo pro) that determines what each party commits to deliver in the context of the economic value chain. The DLA thus licenses the use– and if applicable– the re-use of personal data for explicitly defined and specified purposes by specific data controllers under the conditions set forth in the DLA. The core obligation on the side of the user is to download and install the USEMP tools on her device and to license her data for the purpose of computing a set of scores related to disclosure dimensions that can help the user understand what can be inferred based on shared data. The core obligation on the side of the provider is to provide transparency tools that deliver user-friendly visualizations of the (perceived) sensitive information that can be inferred from the user's data points. The DLA contains explicit consent for the processing of (legally) sensitive data (for the specified purpose only) and explicit consent for downloading the USEMP tools (or any other tracking mechanism).

The next version of the DLA will be modular, enabling a more granular type of licensing, comparable with the various types of Creative Commons Licenses for copyright protection. This should enable users to specify e.g. for which purposes their data may and may not be used, and/or re-used, by which parties and for what time.

## 2.2    Profile Transparency Tools

The current and the upcoming EU legislative framework of data protection requires that any automated decisions that have a significant impact on the user must comply with a number of conditions. Crucially, under the upcoming framework, three transparency requirements must be met for decisions based predominantly on automated profiling: the existence of such profiling, the logic of processing and the envisaged consequences (Hildebrandt 2012). The upcoming framework will also require the implementation of Data Protection by Design mechanisms that ensure that data controllers by default comply with their legal obligations (see [5]). This means that once state of the art mechanisms have been developed, their employment will become mandatory. USEMP is developing tools to provide profile transparency. By inferring disclosure scores based on the disclosure dimensions, USEMP is capable of indicating what kind of profiles people match, thus also indicating how they may be targeted by third parties (advertising, insurance companies, employers etc.). We hope that once USEMP-type platforms emerge as viable playgrounds for the testing of inferred user profiles, OSN providers will be forced to collaborate with them to increase the trust of their users and to improve their reputation. This may also contribute to compliance with their legal obligation to provide profile transparency. In the next section of the paper we discuss the results of research with respect to the effect of transparency in the current advertising value chain and we briefly discuss end-consumers perception of privacy.

## 3    Increasing Transparency of Use for Personal Data in OSNs

The research regarding transparency undertaken in the USEMP project has been based on conducted expert interviews with nine (9) diverse actors from the advertising ecosystem to get first hand insights; interviews covered roles from ad.networks, marketing companies, organizations related to the practices of advertising and social networks, all of which have a business interest in the utilization of users' data (the interviews method and details are described in detail in [6], we have also added a summary in Table 1).

We start with a description of the advertising and marketing ecosystem in terms of its use of personal data as it is today. The problems that users face in the value network underpinning personal data are central to the USEMP project: non-transparent re-use of personal data, often through unaccountable and untrustworthy third parties. This causes information asymmetries and power imbalances, disfavouring the user. Our research has shown that many actors on the industry side also see shortcomings in the status-quo, and we note that their interests are not per se contrary to those of users.

**Table 1.** Overview of USEMP conducted interviews with advertising/marketing industry stakeholders

| Interviewee | Role |
|---|---|
| Lien Brusselmans | L. Brusselmans Marketing Communication Manager at Engagor |
| Roland Siebelink | R. Siebelink is head of quality, productivity and best practice of Rocket Fuel |
| Theodoros Michalareas | T. Michalareas is head of product development in Velti, a provider of mobile marketing and advertising services |
| Joelle Frijters | J. Frijters is co-founder and CEO of ImproveDigital, a European provider of independent publisher monetisation technology |
| Chris Payne | C. Payne is Public Affairs Manager at World Federation of Advertisers. The federation is a global organization representing marketers and advertisers. (http://www.wfanet.org/en) |
| Niels Baarsma | N. Baarsma is co-founder and CTO of Yieldr, a demand side platform provider. |
| Kimon Zorbas & Ionel Naftanaila | K. Zorbas is Director at the Digital Business Consultancy Group (www.dbcg.eu). Before that, he was CEO and Vice President for IAB Europe. Dr. I. Naftanaila is EDAA's Programme Development Director and brings with him a wealth of industry knowledge and experience |
| Mario van Lommel | M. van Lommel is Technical Sales Engineer at Be-Mobile, a leading provider of traffic and mobility content and services for the automotive industry, mobile, media and government road operators |
| Joost Roelandts | J. Roelandts is COO at the social network Twoo |

A concrete and objective value of personal data cannot be easily defined. All actors involved in the OSNs value model depend to some degree on some kind of personal data, but each of them on different types and for different ends and purposes. Thus the value of personal data from OSN users differs for each actor. This also relates to the fact that it makes no sense to reduce 'value' to either monetary value or ethical value, as both are simultaneously at stake [11]. We propose a mechanism that can increase transparency of personal data usage in the ecosystem [1]. This would not only contribute to a business ecosystem that is more respectful to the content creators such as social network users, while enabling innovation that complies with EU Data Protection law. It would also increase the value of (personal) data for each actor and thus for the ecosystem on the whole.

The low level of trust in the industry is a main barrier in reaching such a goal (see also [2]). Trust is not only from the OSN end-user towards the industry (rightfully so in many regards), but also between commercial actors in the value network. The reason for this is among others the non-transparency of data-related operations. Linked to non-transparency, the low quality of utilized data is a major issue, impeding the industry's functioning, reducing efficiency and thus also profits. For the user, non-transparency creates not only information asymmetries, but also diminishes the user experience (for example, irrelevant advertising and longer page loading times from the effect of third party tracking).

Additionally, the USEMP team has performed a number of focus group interviews and related analysis to understand what the social requirements are for privacy enhancing tools. This social requirement analysis has highlighted the need for a personal data management platform that currently the USEMP team is building (see [16] for details of requirements and method of analysis).

### 3.1 Personal Data Business Model Evolution and Related Legal Aspects

Firstly, we will assess how the ecosystem will evolve, if the market is left to operate alone, without appropriate regulation or mechanisms as the ones suggested by USEMP.

The low quality and reliability of data is a real problem for the industry. In order to avoid being responsible and accountable for personal data issues, actors often outsource the collection and pseudo-anonymization[1] of data to data brokers or similar companies. Subsequently OSN providers purchase end-user data they need for their operations from such third parties (advertising networks, data brokers or similar companies), in some cases pseudo-anonymized. This can be seen in a similar light as rights clearance in the field of intellectual property. After buying data in this fashion, the actor may reason that it is no longer personal data, or if it is, at least lay the blame on the third party. This is– obviously– incorrect, and partly caused by the fact that some of the big players believe they can afford to base their operations on US law, even when processing personal data of EU citizens.

As the interviews with industry experts have illustrated, the functioning of the market is strongly affected by major OSNs, mostly Google, Twitter, Facebook and their related competition (for example see [8]). These actors might be able to offer a remedy regarding data quality. They have full access to personal data collected through user profiles in their respective OSNs. In addition, they have access to additional behavioural data spanning over additional data points (like web sites that include OSN tracking code).

**End-User Demand for Data Protection and the Effect to Smaller Companies.** In such an environment end-users might increasingly demand stronger data protection and prefer those actors and services that they trust and offer tools that respect their data protection rights. If the market is left alone to deal with that, the already strong position of the prominent actors today will allow them to fortify their position. In contrast to smaller companies, these actors have the necessary means at their disposal to invest and develop new tools and mechanisms. Additionally data protection and privacy tools would be

---

[1] On the legal effect of pseudo-anonymization see: Art. 29 WP Opinion 05/2014 on Anonymisation Techniques, and the upcoming General Data Protection Regulation (GDPR) that mitigates some of the obligations of data controllers if they process personal data that have been pseudo-anonymized. The legal definition of pseudo-anonymization (art. 4. 2(a) of the upcoming GDPR reads: 'pseudonjymous data' means personal data that cannot be attributed to a specific data subject without the use of additional information, as long as such additional information is kept separately and subject to technical and organizational measures to ensure non-attribution. A data controller is whoever determines the purpose of processing, i.e. the business model. The liability for compliance with EU Data Protection law rests solely with the data controller.

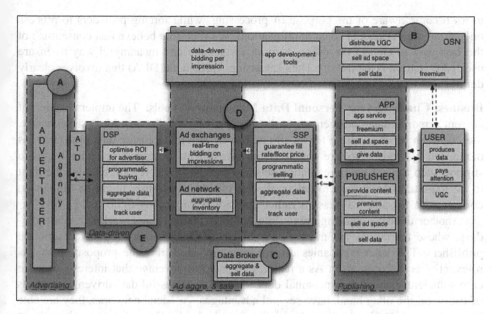

**Fig. 1.** The Value Network of Online Advertising and options to introduce transparency tools

controlled by those companies, which already misuse their access to user data today. This could be regarded in the light of feigned vendor relationship management, pretending that users have control (for examples see [3]). The advantage for OSN organizations increases even further because they can leverage user lock-in to ask for more personal data or further reaching users without losing end-users to competitors.

Our research and interviews with ecosystem actors indicates that the currently weak enforcement of data protection and privacy leads to adverse effects; it harms the European industry, weakening innovation, hurting SMEs and start-ups, while favouring big companies, especially from non-European countries that feel they can ignore the EU Data Protection legislation[2]. Moreover evidence of this harm is now documented in industry reports that show the increased use of ad-blockers plugins from end-users and the corresponding revenue losses (see for example [15]).

**Need for Personal Data Management Tools that Provide Awareness.** The concept of privacy by design, incorporating privacy from the first step of the design project, aims for a sustainable data life cycle management. Prior consent in the form of opt-in can be seen as a prime example of the failure of these types of solutions. Though consent supposedly enables the user to take all decisions over his/her data, the user basically has very little or no clue as to the consequences. One of the problems is that privacy is reduced to the ability to hide one's data, whereas the real issues reside in the inferences that may be drawn from the data. Data Protection, moreover, requires that

---

[2] Cf. expert interviews reported in [4] indicate a strong need on the side of the industry for a level playing field that will enable enterprises to act ethically sound, once they are sure that their competitors are forced to abide by the same rules.

users become aware of the purpose of processing, while forcing providers to process only those data necessary (data minimisation). We therefore believe that consent is not the best way to engage the users. A more sustainable and meaningful way to ensure user participation is the use of a Data Licensing Agreement (DLA) that involves clearly demarcated mutual obligations based on a fair exchange.

**Business Challenges for Personal Data Management Tools.** The implementation of current personal data management tools entails several challenges. Most significantly, the costs can be challenging for small companies. Efforts to ensure data protection, as demanded by legislation, are coupled with investments in respective technologies to support such tools. Cookie regulation sets an example in this regard, but also the right to be forgotten: the request to delete all data related to one user might be difficult to comply with for practical reasons rather than not being willing to do so[3].

Another decisive challenge regarding opt-in is that it cannot work as OSN providers, whose operations are mostly data-driven, are located between advertisers and publishers. The latter companies do not offer any kind of value proposition that is relevant directly to the user. As a result, they have no leverage that interests users to care sufficiently about their personal data. The most successful data-driven companies of today, on the other hand, have several advantages. As social networks, they are able to provide opt-ins simple through existing user lock-ins. The value proposition is, at least partly, that the only alternative for the user to being tracked is to stop using the service[4]. Their scale furthermore allows them to create independent data management tools, owned and controlled by them.

**Value Proposition for Personal Data Management Tools.** Thus, the value proposition of personal data management tools, i.e. the incentive to use them, is a central issue in this regard. First, it depends on the interests of the users not only in knowing what is happening with their data, but also in investing effort and time in actually controlling it. Second, even those groups in society that are concerned about their personal data do often lack the knowledge to assess their own "value". Expectation management would thus be integral to a tool in question, as an individual's data is worth much less to the industry than many would think (the value is in the connections and inferences, not in the individual data points). In addition, it needs to be clarified how much value a user already derives from using free services, as these are sponsored through the personal data market. If these two aspects are taken into account, a value proposition for a personal data management tool may become feasible.

Last but not least, such a tool could make clear that, if a user voluntarily provides certain data, for instance through tracking, a company would make money of it, while the user could benefit from free services and more personalized marketing, provided there is transparency with respect to which personal data are used and for what purpose.

---

[3] Once the legal ground or the purpose for processing has been exhausted personal data should be erased or anonymized, cf. art. 12 and 14 of the current Data Protection Directive D/95/46/EC (DPD).

[4] Note that art. 7.4 of the upcoming GDPR may prohibit this: 'the execution of a contract or the provision of a service shall not be made conditional on the consent to the processing of data that is not necessary for the execution of the contract or the provision of the service pursuant to Article 6(1), point (b)'.

This could provide re-usable data for the benefit of several actors. However, we believe that such an exchange is only sustainable if users are informed about what they inadvertently disclose when interacting with their OSN.

## 3.2   USEMP: A Centralised Tool for Transparency

In the following paragraph we present how the USEMP tool for personal data management can become effective and interesting enough for users and businesses to utilize. The research conducted in USEMP illustrates (see [6]) that direct monetization of personal data by the data subject/OSN user is unrealistic, due to the low monetary value of an individual's information. Moreover, the value that users derive from free services, such as Google, Facebook, Twitter, news etc., is already immense, yet, indirect. Instead of monetization, a tool that focuses on transparency in the first place (with the potential to be extended) seems to promise most potential, both for the user and the business. USEMP's interdisciplinary use cases and scenarios highlight the importance of transparency and awareness (see [16]). They demonstrate the need to hand over a certain amount of control to users, notably over the definition of 'privacy' and 'sensitiveness of data' (even if this will not overrule mandatory law regarding the treatment of sensitive data as defined by law). Foremost, a tool should create knowledge and awareness about the personal data market, which in itself would already be a major step forward. In privacy literature this has been coined as relating to 'institutional privacy', as opposed to 'social privacy'.

The latter concerns disclosure of personal information to one's peers, the former concerns the capturing of (inferred) personal information by public and private service providers. Whereas users have developed intricate privacy strategies with regard to social privacy, they are hardly aware of their lack of institutional privacy (see for example [9]). Not only would the actual value of personal data become more clear, not only would it clarify the actual value of personal data more clear, it would also illustrate the implications of free online services. The development of comprehensive visualisations is certainly of main importance in this regard, as it improves the user experience and comprehensibility of these complex dynamics.

From the value network perspective, which we have adopted for this work, it is a central question where such a tool:

- needs to be "inserted" in the value network, in order to be most effective,
- which actor is most directly affected by the tool, and
- how can this actor pass obligations and benefits to its partners in the value network.

Due to the strong connectedness of the ecosystem in question, the right location in the value network can affect the whole structure. Depending on where the tool is located, different advantages may also arise for different actors, and for users.

**Options for Implementing a Transparency Tool in the Ecosystem.** The broad distinction we can make regarding the value network is between 'in the middle', 'at the sides', and at the front-end (user side).

**Ad.networks and Technology Providers.** So far, much attention has gone to the actors in the middle part of the ecosystem depicted in Fig. 1. These, the publishers and app developers, are data-driven companies, and all user-related data might flow through their systems. However, they are only intermediaries, facilitators of the actions of others. Also these actors are obliged to implement consent mechanisms in their operations, due to the so-called cookie legislation (which has been twisted by the industry to force users' hand, so in point of fact such consent has little meaning [5]. This is probably the least effective spot to realize effective data protection. Although the core of their business is data, and often pseudonymous data, they have no direct contact with the user. They depend also in this regard on the sides of the value network. Focusing on the actors in the middle is unfortunate, as they create value indirectly for the user, backing the free model by increasing efficiency and relevance of advertising and other content. Without the data, they cannot work, as targeting, delivering and evaluating all depend on it.

**Publishers and Advertisers.** The actors on the sides, i.e. publishers and advertisers (A and B respectively in Fig. 1), are arguably a better location to implement a personal data management tool. Indeed, they are legally obliged to implement data protection, including transparency tools. USEMP tools will thus mitigate their liability for violations by integrating empowering tools for DPbD. This is far more effective because they have direct contact with the user or customer. They also need a good reputation to stay attractive for the user. Furthermore, almost all other actors depend on the sides. Thus, they do not only have leverage over the users, but also over the actors in the value network. Due to the strong connections and dependencies, business-to-business pressure down the value chain should be utilized as a powerful accomplice in strengthening personal data protection rights. The user can only build a trust relationship with those actors he/she has direct contact with, if these actors provide reliable insights about their operations and how these may affect the user.

**Benefits of a Centralized Tool.** The most significant outcome of all possible scenarios thus seems to be that a centralized mechanism on the side of the OSN providers promises the most desirable outcomes; this would provide a tool with overarching effects on the whole ecosystem. This is not least the case because:

- the economic value of personal data is indirect, and through centralising it in a transparent way, it becomes clearer;
- it can have benefits for both the user and the industry by increasing transparency that is missing most in the ecosystem;
- most importantly, a centralised transparency tool could also promote smaller and European companies, which might otherwise not be able to invest in appropriate tools themselves;
- centralisation that clearly complies with the legal framework of data protection, notably by providing DPbD and therefore backed by competent Data Protection Authorities, would be a good starting point for creating trust on the side of users;
- finally, a tool where all data management related operations are centralised could create legal certainty and ensure accountability through transparency.

**The Case for an Independent Platform.** We note, however, that it is not obvious that OSN providers are willing to provide the kind of transparency that is required. Below, we will explain that the emphasis is on profile transparency, which is part of mandatory data protection law. OSN providers may wish to keep their inferences behind the walls of trade-secret and IP rights, finding them to be a central part of their competitive advantage. At the same time, users may not be willing to trust OSN providers' information about what they infer. They may prefer an independent platform to secure more impartial inferring tools. The USEMP tools aim to provide precisely such an independent platform.

**Challenges for the Adoption of Centralized Platforms and USEMP Specifications.** The challenge for a centralized platform such as the one proposed by USEMP, is how this can be applied in free market conditions. There are two types of driving force that can help the adoption of such a platform: a) regulatory policies that require such tools to be implemented, and b) self-regulatory policies that can be enforced by the industry itself (see for example [17]). In addition to any regulation, the proposed solution acts also as a set of specifications that can be implemented by more than one platform by consortia of business actors that can see the benefits of introducing such solutions (for example to increase trustworthiness for the end-users).

The USEMP consortium plans to experiment in such a centralised solution where there will be contractual relationship with the user and the platform that will allow the sharing of user data on the basis of a granular license to use and/or reuse the data. This will, for instance, enable a one-time licence (or prohibition) of the processing of specific types of data, specified reuse, or particular third parties. Such granular licensing can be implemented clearly all over the value network. To render the consent that is involved in concluding a data licensing agreement (DLA) meaningful, it is important to develop indicators of personal data privacy and value to end users. In the following sections of the paper we describe the proposed USEMP framework for the collection of the necessary information and computation of such indicators.

## 4   USEMP Disclosure and Personal Value Indicators Framework

In order to develop tools that will increase the transparency of usage of personal data by advertisers and other third parties, it is important to develop personal data value and disclosure indicators that can be used to provide end-users meaningful insights. In the following paragraphs, we present a framework that has been developed as part of the USEMP project. Since these indicators are part of the personal data for each end-user of the USEMP tools (referred to also collectively as Databait), their use is also governed by the proposed DLA approach in Sect. 2.

In the early stages of the development of the USEMP disclosure scoring framework we identified a list of personal data attributes that have been qualified as sensitive or valuable by the users.[5] For users, to better perceive the different aspects of their privacy, it is useful to organize the attributes in a semantic manner. To this end we organize the identified attributes in a number of high-level categories that we refer to as disclosure dimensions[6]. This organization allows for clear and intuitive presentation and handling of the different aspects of a user's personal information.

For instance, one of the disclosure dimensions to be considered is demographics, which includes user attributes such as age, sex, etc., and another is health factors, which includes attributes such as smoking and drinking, etc. Such a grouping has multiple benefits for the end user. First, it enables him/her to form a succinct, easy to grasp mental model of the disclosed personal information and to prioritize its different parts. Second, it enables the use of different compact visualization methods that will further augment the user's awareness with respect to his/her personal information.

From a legal perspective we note that much of this data falls within the ambit of sensitive data, which has stringent legal implications. Providing these disclosure dimensions will enable users, OSN providers and other stakeholders to get a better understanding of the sensitive data that are inferred from user data and will thereby enable a clear attribution of liability for the processing of such inferred data.

On top of this disclosure dimensions framework, we develop the USEMP disclosure scoring model, by enriching it with disclosure and data value scores. Having organized the user attributes in the disclosure dimensions structure, we proceed by enriching it with disclosure and data value scores. Disclosure scores are about quantifying the potential negative impact entailed by the disclosure of different parts of the personal information of a user. The economic (though not monetary) value of a user's shared personal data in OSNs (e.g. posts) is inferred by measuring its impact on the user's social graph, i.e. audience (in terms of reactions, e.g. likes, shares, comments).

### 4.1 Disclosure Dimensions

We define eight (8) key categories of personal attributes, which we name *disclosure dimensions*. These are: (A) Demographics, (B) Psychological Traits, (C) Sexual Profile, (D) Political Attitudes, (E) Religious Beliefs, (F) Health Factors and Condition, (G) Location, and (H) Consumer Profile.

These dimensions cover a wide variety of personal information, which OSN users in many cases consider of private nature (perceived privacy), and also encompass information that is considered sensitive from a legal perspective (legally sensitive data). In addition, based on current business practices (mainly stemming from the marketing industry),

---

[5] We recognized that we need to qualify this as 'perceived' sensitivity, since when the law qualifies certain data as sensitive, based on art. 8 Data Protection Directive (DPD), this has major legal effect, which, however, does not depend on how a user 'feels' about the data.

[6] Clearly, these dimensions are not exhaustive and they do not necessarily match with the legal right to privacy as stipulated in art. 8 of the European Convention of Human Rights, or with the fundamental rights to privacy and data protection of the Charter of Fundamental Rights of the European Union. It is pivotal that perceived privacy and the right to privacy are understood on their own merits, taking note that the latter aims to provide the level playing field for users to develop their own privacy preferences.

the identified dimensions are associated with certain value levels, i.e. they carry a certain level of utility for (marketing) companies that are interested in targeting consumers. Table 2 summarizes the eight identified disclosure dimensions, along with the value levels associated with them.

This set of eight disclosure dimensions constitutes the current top-level *schema* of the USEMP privacy model, and although we do not foresee considerable changes at this level, the implementation of the overall framework is generic enough and can accommodate such changes if needed (e.g., addition of a new dimension, splitting of an existing dimension into more).

**Table 2.** Overview of USEMP disclosure dimensions

| # | Name | Description | Potential threats-Sensitivity | Value (for advertisers) |
|---|------|-------------|-------------------------------|--------------------------|
| A | Demographics | Personal data, such as Gender, Age, Nationality, Ethnic background, etc. | Discrimination in a variety of settings. The most frequently used type of information. | **High:** advertisers wish to target users of certain demographic criteria |
| B | Psychological Traits | Defined by psychologists (extraversion, openness, etc.) | Discrimination, e.g. in personnel selection | **Low:** a limited number of advertisers can connect type of personality to their product |
| C | Sexual Profile | Relationship status, preferences, habits | Discrimination, e.g. in workplace, education, housing | **High:** advertisers wish to target consumers based on their relationship status/lifestyle related to their sexual profile |
| D | Political Attitudes | Supported politicians, parties and stance | Discrimination, e.g. in workplace or personnel selection | **High:** advertisers wish to target consumers based on the political affiliations since these are related to their general profile |
| E | Religious Beliefs | Religion (if any) and beliefs | Discrimination, e.g. in the sale or rental of housing, job selection, workplace. | **Moderate:** advertisers wish to target consumers based on their religious and cultural beliefs |

*(Continued)*

**Table 2.** (*Continued*)

| # | Name | Description | Potential threats-Sensitivity | Value (for advertisers) |
|---|------|-------------|-------------------------------|-------------------------|
| F | Health Factors and Condition | Habits (e.g. smoking, drinking), medical conditions, disabilities, health factors (exercise) | Discrimination, e.g. health insurance denial or discriminatory pricing. | **High:** advertisers wish to target consumers based on their habits |
| G | Location | Characteristic locations of the individual and history of previous locations | Discrimination, e.g. house insurance, stalking | **High:** advertisers wish to target consumers based on their current location or their home location |
| H | Consumer Profile | Preferred products and brands | Ad targeting and discrimination in online price-setting | **High:** advertisers wish to target consumers based on their consumer profile attributes like the devices the use to access digital content |

The disclosure dimensions framework effectively defines a hierarchy where the top level represents the OSN personal data profile, the next level contains the eight (8) disclosure dimensions, the level below contains the set of attributes of each dimension and the lower level contains a predefined set of possible values for each attribute (please note that the word value here refers to the possible values an attribute may take and should not be confused with the concept of personal data value).

We link OSN data to this framework by considering a variety of detection and analysis mechanisms, e.g. multimedia information extraction techniques and inference techniques, and OSN presence data (typically in the form of observed user activities, e.g. likes [18], posts, user interactions, or volunteered profile information). In short, we use a user's OSN presence data (e.g. posted content, likes, set of friends), in order to predict the values of the user's attributes. This involves both utilizing explicitly provided information and also producing a number of inferences.

## 4.2   Disclosure Scoring

Initially, the USEMP research team identified the need for a scoring framework that would help the end-user understand better which OSN or web behaviour actions may disclose personal information related to the disclosure dimensions presented above. Such a mechanism is based on perceived privacy and highlights what can be disclosed about users based on inferences on their data. We make clear to the users that this disclosure is based on algorithmic decision making and need not at all be correct, but emphasize that this is how the current personal data ecosystem operates: the value chain is based on such probabilistic disclosures. Additionally, overall disclosure scores are computed at each level of the proposed hierarchy. In the next subsection we provide more details about the scoring framework.

**Structure:**  A schematic illustration of the disclosure scoring framework is shown in Fig. 2. USEMP disclosure scoring framework builds on top of the disclosure dimensions and assigns a number of scores to the elements of each level. These scores express different aspects of disclosure, e.g. the perceived sensitivity of different types of information, the confidence that some value holds for some user, an overall disclosure score and other aspects that will be described shortly Clearly, the two important characteristics of this framework are the following: (a) it is tailored to the hierarchical structure of the disclosure dimensions, (b) there are multiple scores associated with the elements of each level of the hierarchy. Hence, the framework enables the following two kinds of user awareness: (a) navigation through the levels of the hierarchy and understanding of how the scores for some particular value *affect* or *are affected by* the levels above and below it, and (b) focus on specific aspects of the factors that are related to perceived privacy; e.g., it will be possible to focus on visibility, the overall disclosure score, etc.

Here, we consider an additional level at the root of the framework, which contains any type of data that is generated as a result of a user's behaviour and interaction with the services of an OSN operator. This includes posted content (text, images), explicitly declared profile information, user network data, sets of likes, etc. We call this the *OSN presence data layer* and consider it as the primary source for populating the disclosure scores for the given user. Naturally, between the perceived privacy values level and the online presence data, there is a layer of modules that perform various mining and inference procedures. The overall framework is visualized in Fig. 2.

Computation is carried out in a bottom-up manner. That is, information that comes from the OSN and the inference mechanisms is used to fill the scores at the values level and then the computed scores at the values level are used to fill the scores at the upper levels, one level at a time. Starting from the level of values, the scores that characterize each value are the following:

(a) *Confidence.* This is a continuous value in the range from 0 to 1. It represents how confident we are that the corresponding value is true and is typically computed by the inference algorithm along with the produced inference. It needs to be noted that the confidence values under the same attribute should sum to 1 (except for the case that an attribute can take multiple values simultaneously).

(b) *Sensitivity.* This score represents how sensitive the user feels that this particular piece of information is. It also ranges from 0 to 1.

(c) *Visibility.* This score attempts to quantify the set of people to which the relevant information is accessible and consists of three sub-scores. The first is the overall visibility score and is also a continuous value in the range from 0 to 1 (lower

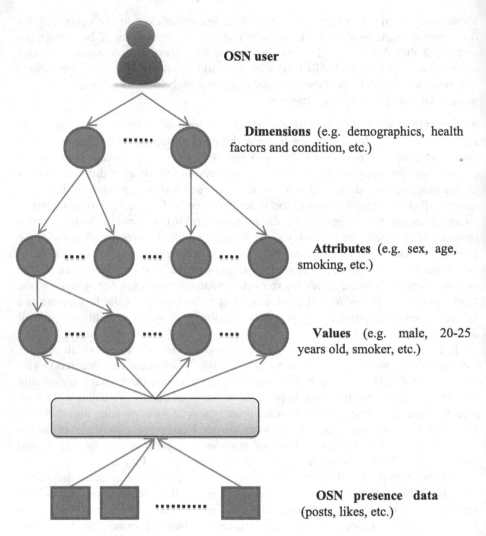

**Fig. 2.** Overview of USEMP disclosure scoring framework

values denote that the corresponding piece of information is accessible by fewer people, whereas a value of 1 denotes public information). The second visibility sub-score is a qualitative label that is related to the overall disclosure score and expresses the widest possible audience to which this information is accessible. For instance, a value whose overall visibility score is 0 has a visibility label of "Private", a value whose overall visibility score is 1 has a visibility label of "Public" and an intermediate value denotes the widest group of people that have access to the value, e.g. "Friends" or "Friends of friends", etc. This sub-score is called "visibility label". The third visibility sub-score expresses an estimate of the *actual audience* that sees this value and we refer to it as "actual visibility". It is an integer number representing the actual number of users that are aware of that value and depends on the estimates of the actual audience of the content that has been used to infer that value. It should be noted that the current implementation of the scoring framework does not compute the actual audience, however, different approaches are considered for estimating it.

(d) *Declared/Inferred.* This is a binary value that defines whether our knowledge about the particular value comes from explicitly provided information that the user has provided or has been inferred (derived). It is not an actual score but reflects information that is important for maintaining a complete view of disclosure with respect to some particular value. Additionally, in some cases a value may be both declared and inferred. In such cases, the value will be considered as declared (i.e. declared will override inferred).

(e) *Support.* This field is not really a score, but rather provides a link to the OSN presence data that support the particular value. In the case that the support for the value is associated with an inference mechanism, this field points both to the inference mechanism and the data that the inference mechanism used. This field is particularly important because it allows the user to understand the types of content that are important for his privacy.

(f) *Level of control.* This score represents the ability of a user to control the disclosure of data about him/her. It ranges from 0 to 1; low values will denote a limited ability to control the disclosure of this particular data about the user. The ability of a user to control the disclosure of data about him/her may be limited by the fact that the support of some value may involve also data posted by other users that the user him/herself cannot control. This score is set by evaluating each piece of shared information with respect to (a) ownership of the data from the end-user (or someone else), (b) the permissions framework of the social network that may allow the user to stop this information from being shared or not.

(g) *Disclosure score.* Eventually, the framework includes an overall perceived score that provides a succinct idea about the overall privacy status of an OSN user (see for example [13]). It is a function of other scores: confidence, sensitivity and visibility. Higher values of the score denote a higher exposure of personal information that is perceived to be of private nature. Note that although the disclosure score essentially summarizes the other scores, the model maintains a separate list of the individual scores (confidence, sensitivity, and visibility) in order to support richer visualization and analysis capabilities (e.g. separate visualization of visibility and sensitivity).

The three upper levels of the proposed disclosure scoring structure, namely the user, the dimensions and the attributes, are all associated with the following set of scores: (a) Visibility, (b) Disclosure score and (c) Level of control. These have the same meaning as the corresponding scores at the values level. In addition, the top level (user) is also associated with an overall personal data value score (please see the next subsection). For a full description of proposed estimators see [7, 19].

### 4.3   Personal Data Value Indicators Framework

In addition to disclosure scores, a set of personal data value indicators are required so that the end-users can be informed about the value of the data they are sharing. The proposed personal value indicators are based on the activities of the end user in the OSN environment and his/her OSN social graph. Two basic indicators are initially proposed:

(a)  a measure of influence for a specific person, referred to as Influence score and denoted with I, that is based on the history of the objects that the specific person has created in the OSN;
(b)  a measure of the importance of an object (picture/video/post), denoted with M, that is posted to the OSN. M is calculated taking into consideration the type of action on the specific object of the first- and second-hop friends of the object creator.

The *Influence score* of a specific person should be estimated based on the history of the objects that the specific person has created, while taking into consideration the

- number of connections comparing to the total number of users of the network;
- types of actions (share, like, comment) of the first and the second hop friends on the objects that the corresponding person has uploaded/created to the OSN.

For the calculation of user influence $I$, the following parameters are proposed to be collected and used:

- number of objects (i.e., picture/video/post) that a user has created
- number of first- and second-hop friends
- total number of first- and second-hop friends that had an action on each object (i.e., picture/video/post)
- type of action (i.e., share, like, comment) of user j on the object i

The parameters listed above can be collected and combined to different formulas to compute values for variables $I$ and $M$.

The proposed personal data value combines these two factors ($I$, $M$) and is calculated as follows:

$$V = I \cdot M$$

This initial set of defined value indicators (data value $V$, user influence score $I$, object importance $M$) is defined so that it can be computed from actual OSN data (like Facebook). As part of future work these parameters will be collected and computed with actual data from pilots on top of Facebook and with simulated data from theoretical models and various formulas for $I$, $M$ will be tested (for a full description of proposed estimators see [7]).

## 4.4    Experimental Tools and Visualization

In order to evaluate the ideas developed in the USEMP project, a set of pilots have been scheduled and a set of tools are developed to provide a testbed for collecting data and end-user feedback, these are referred by USEMP partners as the Databait tool. These include:

- **Databait web browser plugin:** a browser plugin that is used to collect users' browsing data during the pilot and that allows end-users to block tracking behaviour or offer users recommendations with respect to sharing data.
- **Databait webapp:** a web application that allows end-users to view indicators of their online social network sharing behaviour with respect to transparency and data value.
- **Databait backend:** a framework and set of services that collect data about user behaviour and compute a number of indicators with respect to disclosure and data value that are shared with end-users via the Databait webapp visualizations.

In the following Figs. 3, 4 and 5, we present some examples of the UI/UX of the web browser plugin and webapp visualizations for the Databait tools (this is work in progress to be validated after the completion of the USEMP pilots):

- Figure 3: presents the look and feel of the Databait web plugin that is responsible for selecting trackers and blocking (or unblocking them).
- Figure 4: presents the look and feel of the Databait web application that provides the end-user with access to a number of visualizations/tools and information from OSN shared data.
- Figure 5: presents the look and feel of two types of visualization that allow the user to understand if the shared data disclose any location (from Facebook posts analysis) or interests (derived from image analysis) and present them in an intuitive way.

**Fig. 3.** Databait web plugin – allows end users to view third-party tracking services and block them (or unblock them)

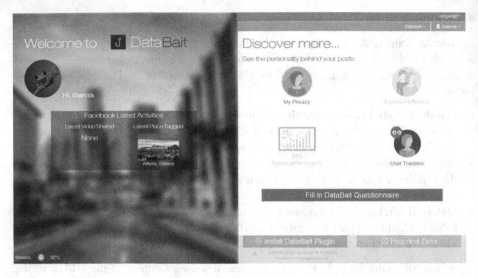

**Fig. 4.** Databait web application – access to visualizations for transparency and data value

**Fig. 5.** Databait web application – access to visualizations for transparency and data value: (a) left screen shows the concepts detected in a user's shared images, (b) right screen show the locations detected in a user's shared posts

## 4.5   Evaluation of USEMP Tools

We have performed a series of user studies within the USEMP project in order to build the Databait tools on solid grounds of user acceptance in the form three focus group sessions with end users. Hence the study acted as a formative evaluation approach by involving end users to the design and evaluation of tools while the project moves forward. Three focus group interviews were conducted in English within March 2015 together with 15 participants from Botnia Living Lab[7]. The design of the focus groups

---

[7] Botnia Living Lab is an environment in Sweden for human-centric research and the development and innovation of new ICT based solutions.

was based on gathering end user insights on main theme of transparency of personal information through USEMP tools. For this purpose we presented the participants with the mock-ups of the USEMP tools/Databait (as presented in Figs. 3, 4 and 5). Each function demonstration was then followed by questions targeted on insights for values, motivations and barriers to use. We briefly discuss the participant feedbacks here.

We first asked users about the normal social media and internet usages in order to indirectly and directly capture their awareness of the ways they disclose information. During the course of a normal social media usage there are different communicative actions which are established. Users have personal motivations and external influencing factors that force them to use social media. Therefore their usage is not totally optional and for this reason their personal information is inevitably disclosed. Among personal motivational factors that can be enumerated are the willingness to reach a wider audience in order to promote themselves for example with different political activities, keeping in touch with the families, friends, acquaintances, keeping track of their events like their friend's birthdays, to keep themselves updated about what is happening in surroundings and etc. Disclosing various types of information is evident in these types of social media usages. We asked them about the kinds of information they think they are disclosing in their everyday usage of social media to capture the level of their awareness towards privacy issues. Our analysis showed that most users think of privacy as only the basic personal information they disclose voluntarily like name, age, relationship status. The awareness towards the observed and inferred data sources is extremely low among the users.

Next, the Databait tools were presented using the mocks of the future tool and the expected results (e.g. inferences). The participants were allowed to freely discuss about the features and ask questions about the functions. Therefore we created a milieu for the lively discussion and to capture their concerns and how the tool could serve them in different scenarios. For example we could observe that most of the participants were curious about the features and at some points were shocked by the level of the tool's sophistication. One of their pivotal points was related to the unconscious disclosure of personal information that might have an impact on one's public image and how data processors could gain value of their information. The users saw the benefits in this awareness awakening through manipulation of informed disclosure. The benefits were also associated to the disclosed information at various levels determined by each and every user's beliefs, cultures, economical values gained, political outreach and etc. Databait's personality trait function showed to be beneficial in this sense since users can be sensitive to different subjects.

Photo and location leaks functionalities could draw user's attention on various levels of disclosure both those revealed intentionality and those that are unintentional. From intentional point of view users find this helpful with respect to the values of the contents to the Social Media owners. So what made them more aware of their shared content was the ability to see the profits of their contents from the social media owner's perspective; to see what could be gained from the contents and how those could be inferred. Even though they are aware of their shared contents, their perception of the contents' secondary usage was limited so that social media owner's bad intentions could hide in the user's low institutional privacy awareness. Unintentionally revealed sensitive information interpreted by Databait could help the participants learn more about the adverse effects of their actions and seek to possible solutions e.g. deleting photo/location leak or limiting audience.

To summarize, the result from evaluation of designed concepts, showed that users are curious about the revelation of values that could be drawn from personal information and generated content. We found that users are willing to be more educated through the tool about adverse effects of their sharing habits triggered by a sense of dread that could raise their awareness. Here the idea is that the users are more intrigued when they see dangers more explicitly. This has then led the users to perceive such privacy tools to be more effective. Simplicity showed to have an impact on how the users are willing to adopt a tool as well. Most of the users agreed that the tool needs to have a 'simple to use' settings with self-explanatory features. Our aim in USEMP project is to take this end user's perspective into account for the next versions of the tools.

## 5   Conclusions and Future Work

In this paper we have presented the results of the multi-disciplinary project USEMP in developing a value model for the use of personal data in advertising and OSNs that empowers the end user and offers more transparency to the use of personal data. The presented research describes:

- what are the legal aspects of users' privacy in OSNs that can be addressed by transparency tools that are based in the principle of Data Protection by Design (DPbD);
- how a DLA model is more appropriate than that of simple prior-consent to improve trust and user control on sharing personal data in OSNs;
- how a centralized tool developed as an independent platform is more appropriate for the business ecosystem to improve trust of the end-consumers to the advertising and marketing industry;
- how a disclosure scoring framework can be developed to support such a transparency tool;
- an overview of visualization methods that can be used as part of such a tool.

The ideas examined in this paper are currently implemented in the form of Databait tools and they are under evaluation from the pilot experiments organized from the USEMP project. Their impact on the end-user perception of privacy and the creation of new innovative business models that can support DPbD in OSNs and online advertising/marketing will be presented in future publications.

## References

1. Popescu, A., Hildebrandt, M., Papadopoulos, S., Claeys, L., Lund, D., Michalareas, T., Kastrinogiannis, T., Pierson, J., Padyab, A.M.: User Empowerment for Enhanced Online Presence Management– Use Cases and Tools, APC15, 2015 (forthcoming)

2. van der Graaf, S., Vanobberghen, W., Kanakakis, M., Kalogiros, C.: Usable trust: Grasping trust dynamics for online security as a service. In: Tryfonas, T., Askoxylakis, I. (eds.) HAS 2015. LNCS, vol. 9190, pp. 271–283. Springer, Heidelberg (2015). The valorization of surveillance: Towards a political economy of Facebook. Democratic Communiqué, 22(1), 5–22
3. Searls, D.: The Intention Economy (book) 2012
4. London Economics, Study on the economic benefits of privacy-enhancing technologies (2010). http://londoneconomics.co.uk/blog/publication/study-on-the-economic-benefits-of-privacy-enhancing-technologies-pets/
5. Hildebrandt, M., Tielemans, L.: Data protection by design and technology neutral law. Comput. Law Secur. Rev. **29**(5), 509–521 (2013)
6. USEMP Deliverable D3.5, Socio-economic value of personal information, 2015-04-01, this report presents a socio-economic perspective on the tool for user-centred personal data, management as envisioned by the USEMP project. http://www.usemp-project.eu/documents/deliverables
7. USEMP Deliverable D6.1 (under review), USEMP privacy scoring framework, 2015-0-15, the current deliverable is a technical report accompanying the first version of the USEMP privacy scoring framework, a tool that aims at raising the awareness of users about the disclosure and value of their personal information. http://www.usemp-project.eu/documents/deliverables/
8. Constine, J.: Facebook, Google, and Twitter's war for app install ads (2014, November 30). Retrieved January 27, 2015. http://techcrunch.com/2014/11/30/like-advertising-a-needle-in-a-haystack/
9. Young, A.L., Quan-Haase, A.: Privacy protection strategies on Facebook: The Internet privacy paradox revisited. Inf. Commun. Soc. **16**(4), 479–500 (2013)
10. Van Dijck, J.: The culture of connectivity: a critical history of social media. Oxford University Press, Oxford; New York (2013)
11. Hildebrandt, M., O'Hara, K., Waidner, M. (eds.): The Value of Personal Data. Digital Enlightenment Yearbook 2013. IOS Press, Amsterdam (2013)
12. Hildebrandt, M.: "The Dawn of a Critical Transparency Right for the Profiling Era", in Digital Enlightenment Yearbook 2012, pp. 41–56. IOS Press, Amsterdam (2012)
13. Liu, K., Terzi, E.: A framework for computing the privacy scores of users in online social networks. ACM Trans. Knowl. Discov. Data, **5**(1), Article 6 (2010)
14. Moody, D.L., Walsh, P.A.: Measuring the value of information: An asset valuation approach. In: Morgan, B., Nolan, C. (eds.) Guidelines for Implementing Data Resource Management (4th Edition). DAMA International Press, Seattle, USA (2002)
15. Pagefair 2015 ad-block Report. http://blog.pagefair.com/2015/ad-blocking-report/
16. USEMP Deliverable D4.1, Social Requirement Analysis, 2014-08-18, this document presents the methodology used and the results of the first user research including focus groups that highlight the requirements for a privacy enhancing tool. http://www.usemp-project.eu/documents/deliverables/
17. NAA ad-choices initiative for consumers opt-out for behavioural targeting. http://www.networkadvertising.org/choices/
18. Theodoridis, T., Papadopoulos, S., Kompatsiaris, Y.: Assessing the reliability of facebook user profiling. WWW (Companion Volume) **2015**, 129–130 (2015)
19. Petkos, G., Papadopoulos, S., Kompatsiaris, Y.: PScore: Enhancing privacy awareness in online social networks. In: International Workshop on Multimedia Forensics and Security (MFSec) (2015)

# A Data Protection Impact Assessment Methodology for Cloud

Rehab Alnemr[1], Erdal Cayirci[2], Lorenzo Dalla Corte[3],
Alexandr Garaga[4], Ronald Leenes[3], Rodney Mhungu[3],
Siani Pearson[1], Chris Reed[5], Anderson Santana de Oliveira[4(✉)],
Dimitra Stefanatou[3], Katerina Tetrimida[3], and Asma Vranaki[5]

[1] HP Labs, Bristol, UK
[2] Stavanger University, Stavanger, Norway
[3] Tilburg University, Tilburg, The Netherlands
[4] SAP Labs, Mougins, France
anderson.santana.de.oliveira@sap.com
[5] Queen Mary University of London, London, UK

**Abstract.** We propose a data protection impact assessment (DPIA) method based on successive questionnaires for an initial screening and for a full screening for a given project. These were tailored to satisfy the needs of Small and Medium Enterprises (SMEs) that intend to process personal data in the cloud. The approach is based on legal and socio-economic analysis of privacy issues for cloud deployments and takes into consideration the new requirements for DPIAs within the European Union (EU) as put forward by the proposed General Data Protection Regulation (GDPR). The resultant features have been implemented within a tool.

**Keywords:** Data protection impact assessment · EU GDPR · Cloud · Privacy

## 1 Introduction

A Data Protection Impact Assessment (DPIA) method aims to identify the main risks of a project with respect to the rights of data subjects concerning their personal data. It is a systematic process to elicit threats to the privacy of individuals, identify the procedures and practices in place to mitigate these threats, and document how the risks were addressed in order to minimise harm to data subjects [12, 22]. DPIAs have been recognised as a key topic for data protection governance in Europe, as they will become mandatory according to the ongoing data protection legal framework reform, in the form of the proposed General Data Protection Regulation (GDPR) [13]. The version of the European Parliament's first reading also incorporates the concept of risk into the DPIA process (cf. Article 32a), in the scope of the DPIA mechanism by mandating data controllers to carry out a DPIA in those cases likely to present specific risks to the rights and freedoms of data subjects. Hence, the concept of risk is embedded in the DPIA process as a pre-assessment stage and a risk analysis would be able to function as an awareness methodology in order for a DPIA to be carried out. Note that in the context of the present analysis the terms DPIA and Privacy Impact Assessment (PIA) are being used interchangeably [15].

© Springer International Publishing Switzerland 2016
B. Berendt et al. (Eds.): APF 2015, LNCS 9484, pp. 60–92, 2016.
DOI: 10.1007/978-3-319-31456-3_4

A DPIA seems to perform a dual function. On the one hand, it can serve as an accountability mechanism, especially where data breaches or losses occur – in the sense that it allows organisations acting as data controllers or data processors to demonstrate their awareness about the risks concerning privacy and data protection and their commitment in ensuring an effective level of protection of personal data [45]. On the other hand, it can foster the safeguard of privacy and data protection rights [35] in the case of potentially privacy intrusive projects and services, because it requires the controller to systematically consider the intended data processing, the associated privacy risks and the measures to be taken to mitigate these risks from the very outset of its activities [45]. Accountable organisations should embrace DPIAs as part of their overall risk management practices. Unfortunately, today there is a lack of tool support for organisations to perform DPIAs of cloud services.

In this paper, we present the design of a Data Protection Privacy Impact Assessment Tool (DPIAT) developed as part of the EU funded Cloud Accountability (A4Cloud) project[1]. The tool considers a number of information sources from which cloud specific risks and existing countermeasures can be collected and evaluated, in the process of supporting impact assessments for projects considering processing personal data in the cloud. We also propose updated DPIA questionnaires with respect to existing standards and recommendations, building on the expertise of experts from different disciplines from legal research to information security and risk management and to user experience design.

The remainder of the paper is organised as follows: we discuss related work in Sect. 2. We describe the rationale and approach to construct the proposed DPIA based on legal and socio-economic considerations in Sect. 3. Our approach consists of three steps: (1) conduct a pre-assessment to determine the need for a fully-fledged DPIA (see Sect. 3.2); (2) conduct the full DPIA if warranted by the previous step (see Sects. 3.3 and 3.4); and (3) perform a risk-based comparison of potential cloud service providers (CSPs) (see Sect. 4). The DPIA takes a form of a dynamic questionnaire, which aims to collect information from the user about the project under evaluation and its organisational practices. The risk evaluation of potential cloud solutions takes into account some information collected in DPIA and the implementation status of security controls by the CSP. Section 5 presents the DPIA tool design and its dynamic questionnaire to collect information about the project under evaluation and organisational practices, and its automation of steps 1–3 above. The tool produces a report containing several privacy indicators and risks based on the filled questionnaires and the selected CSP.

# 2 Related Work

Privacy impact assessments are already being rolled out as part of a process to encourage privacy by design [22]: in November 2007 the UK Data Protection Authority, the Information Commissioner's Office (ICO) launched a PIA process (incorporating privacy by design) to help organisations assess the impact of their

---

[1] Cloud Accountability Project (A4Cloud) http://www.a4cloud.eu.

operations on personal privacy. This process assesses the privacy requirements of new and existing systems; it is primarily intended for use in public sector risk management, but is increasingly seen to be of value to private sector businesses that process personal data. Similar methodologies exist and can have legal status in Australia, Canada and the US [39]. The methodology aims to combat the slow take-up to design in privacy protections from first principles at the enterprise level. Usage is increasingly being encouraged and even mandated in certain circumstances by regulators, as considered further in the following section.

The role of a risk-based approach in data protection has been considered by a number of parties, including: as an assessment of the relative values of such an approach [4]; modifying the original OECD data protection principles to take this into account [29]; analysing the relationship with accountability [18] and recent regulatory analysis [1, 7].

In terms of automation within the privacy impact assessment process, there are a few systems that have attempted this in various contexts, which we shall consider further below.

In Canada, the Treasury Board Secretariat provided in 2003 an e-learning tool for government employees interested in learning more about privacy and PIAs and how to complete them [30]. Furthermore, a new self-assessment tool, aimed at Small and Medium Enterprises (SMEs), was launched in Canada in May 2011. It was developed jointly by the Federal, Alberta and British Columbia privacy commissioners' and is a detailed online questionnaire that helps organisations gauge how well they are protecting personal information and meeting compliance standards under Canada's private-sector privacy law on both federal and provincial levels.

The US Department of Homeland Security (DHS) employs a PIA tool called the Privacy Threshold Analysis that helps users determine whether a PIA is required under the E-Government Act of 2002 and the Homeland Security Act 2002 [42]. In the UK, the PIA Guidelines provide a number of screening questions to help users decide whether a Full-Scale PIA or a Small-Scale PIA is warranted. The Guidelines also include a number of questions for a privacy law compliance check, and a Data Protection Act (1998) compliance check. Templates are also included within the Guidelines for Data Protection compliance and the Privacy and Electronic Communications Regulations (PECR) [22].

Most of these PIA tools are based upon a simple "decision-tree" approach and are mainly procedure-based with coarse-grained granularity, offered as Web applications that do not take into account the cloud or any of its characteristics. The following are PIA automated systems that are worthy of particular mention:

- A prototype decision support tool developed by the PRAIS project [20]. This tool enables personnel working with personal information to assess the privacy implications of information sharing actions dynamically and to share information and manage users' consent and other participant needs.

- HP Privacy Advisor (HP PA). It assesses risk and degree of compliance for projects that handle personal data and guides employees in their decisions on how to handle different types of data. HP PA uses a rule-based system to capture global privacy knowledge that is too complex to be easily captured via decision trees and to dynamically only present the relevant question to elicit privacy-relevant information about a project to the user [31–33].
- A privacy impact assessment tool prototype based upon ICO guidelines related to UK Data protection Act, allowing appropriate stakeholder views and input and using confidences within the knowledge representation to allow assessment of the value of the input as well as customisation of risk indicator values [38].
- Avepoint Privacy Impact Assessment System [3] and TRUSTe Assessment Manager [41] help to automate the impact assessment workflow and to track the tasks involved in the question answering process by the multiple organisational roles. However they do not focus on cloud services, which intrinsically involve third parties and data transfers.

Decision support systems for PIAs in cloud computing are a new field and there are few systems available, although there is some work targeted at the areas of clinical decision applications, and life science enterprise solutions [5]. Prior work includes tools for cloud assessment: the Microsoft "Security Assessment Tool" designed to help find weaknesses in an IT security environment, privacy impact assessment of cloud environments [40] and decision support tools for cloud service provisioning [34]. In addition, several standards propose cloud security guidance: European Network and Information Security Agency (ENISA) [16], National Institute of Standards and Technology (NIST) [27], ICO [24] and Commission Nationale de L'informatique et des Libertés (CNIL) [11], CSA Governance Risk and Compliance (GRC) stack [10].

In the next sections we explain how our DPIAT builds on the body of knowledge and recommended practices mentioned above, adjusting the DPIA process and questionnaire to make it informative, user-centric and synthetic. It differs from previous work by focusing on a profile of SMEs wishing to move to the cloud. Additionally, our approach for assessing cloud risks is founded on information disclosed voluntarily by CSPs in the CSA Security, Trust & Assurance Registry (STAR).[2]

# 3 Multidisciplinary Approach to DPIAs

The proposed GPDR provides for a series of accountability measures that aim to strengthen protection of personal data. DPIAs fall under the scope of those measures, aiming at mitigating risks resulting from certain processing operations. In practice, a DPIA screening consists of a set of questions allowing for multiple choice or free text answers, which help to assess the risks for personal data involved in the intended processing. Taking this into account, as well as the various examples of existing PIAs, this section proposes a DPIA questionnaire that is tailored to particular data protection risks associated with cloud computing services.

---

[2] https://cloudsecurityalliance.org/star/.

The DPIA tool incorporates two questionnaires. The first questionnaire (See Table 1) is a pre-screening (risk) assessment, which must be carried out to assess whether a full-scale DPIA is mandatory. The main questionnaire (See Table 2) is an extensive set of questions that comprises the full-scale DPIA [19].[3] The user of the DPIA tool will probably not be an expert in privacy and data protection. Therefore, the questions are formulated in a form and language understandable for lay users, in order to facilitate them in providing the right information [36]. We have targeted the DPIA tool to SMEs that typically lack in-house data protection experts and the resources to hire experts.[4] The tool thus should guide the user through the process as much as possible and provide meaningful feedback that helps the user to improve the privacy characteristics of their project and facilitate legal compliance with the data protection regulation.

## 3.1 Methodology

Cloud computing has several characteristics [25] that may adversely impact the privacy of personal data, including distributed nature, multitenancy, third-party hosting, potentially long supply chains. A cloud can be spread across multiple jurisdictions with different degrees of data protection and no transparency about this [16]. The multitenancy leads to risks of isolation failure and insecure data deletion which can compromise personal data. Third-party hosting can cause the cloud consumer to lose control over personal data, especially when the CSPs are not transparent about the data processing performed, the data protection measures used and the data security breaches that occurred [16]. This becomes even more apparent in the case of complex supply chains formed from different CSPs. When developing the DPIA questionnaire (see Sect. 3.3) and the cloud adoption risk assessment model (see Sect. 5) we considered these cloud characteristics and their impact on data protection.

Given that the current data protection framework within the EU is under review and that the proposed GPDR still is under extensive negotiation at the time of writing[5], we had to decide whether the questionnaires would take into account the new DPIA framework proposed within the GDPR. Following discussions within the A4Cloud consortium, all partners agreed that the DPIA tool should be as future proof[6] as possible, and therefore we took into account both the Data Protection Directive

---

[3] Note that even if the full-scale DPIA is not required, taking it nevertheless is beneficial because the questionnaire, guiding responses and assessment may help in raising the privacy bar of any project or service.

[4] A secondary user group consists of concerned individuals who consider taking their data to the cloud. The tool will help them make considered choices regarding requirements for cloud service providers. A sister tool in the A4Cloud project, the Cloud Offerings Assistance Tool (COAT) can take these requirements to filter relevant cloud offerings for the user to choose from.

[5] Both the European Parliament and the Council have agreed on their texts amending Commission's initial proposal on a GDPR. Although, there is broad agreement between the institutions on core issues, the exact wording is to be decided –probably by the end of 2015- following a series of Trilogue Meetings.

[6] For more on the concept of "future-proof" see under Sect. 3.5: Discussion.

**Table 1.** Data Protection Impact Assessment Pre-Screening Questions

| ID | Question | Explanation | Question type |
|----|----------|-------------|---------------|
| 1 | Based on the information that you process, can you identify one or more individuals about whom you are processing information? | Can the information used be associated to a particular customer or employee, either directly (e.g. by using names) or indirectly (e.g. by using license plates, social security number, addresses, telephone numbers or other information that you hold)? | Y/N |
| 2 | Does the information that you process reveal certain characteristics of individuals? | Can you, or will you, use the information you process to qualify your customer or employee, for instance on the basis of (online) behavior, attendance, marital or social status, salary level, work performance, or zip code? If you build 'profiles' of individuals, answer yes to this question. | Y/N |
| 3 | Do you deal with any kind of the following categories of information? | The following categories of information are of a particularly sensitive nature, and need to be dealt with. | [Checkbox]<br>• race or ethnic origin;<br>• political opinions;<br>• religion or philosophical beliefs;<br>• sexual orientation or gender identity;<br>• trade-union membership and activities;<br>• genetic or biometric data or data concerning health or sex life;<br>• administrative sanctions,<br>• judgments, criminal or suspected offences;<br>• data on children; |

*(Continued)*

**Table 1.** (*Continued*)

| ID | Question | Explanation | Question type |
|---|---|---|---|
| | | | • data on employees;<br>• location data;<br>• data that can be used for identity theft, such as social security number, credit card information, passport or driving license data. |
| 4 | What is the scale of your processing operations? | The scale includes, for instance, the number of persons to whom the information you deal with relates to, the amount and granularity of information per person or the number of people who have access to the information that you process. | • Large<br>• Medium<br>• Small<br>• I don't know<br>• Not applicable |
| 5 | Is the nature, scope and/or purpose of your business, profession or activity based on a regular and systematic monitoring either of any natural person(s) or of publicly accessible areas? | Think, for instance, of virtual public areas, such as social networks or public fora. | Y/N |
| 6 | How likely is that incidents will raise concerns amongst individuals and/or legal entities? | Think of, for instance, data breaches, inaccurate, incomplete or outdated data related to the information that you process, use of data for purposes other than the ones for which they were collected. | • Large<br>• Medium<br>• Small<br>• I don't know<br>• Not applicable |
| 7 | Are there any third parties involved in the storage, processing, use, or transfer of any information that you deal with? | The interplay with third parties exponentially increases the risks deriving from processing activities. | Y/N |

**Table 2.** DPIA Screening Questionnaire

| ID | Question | Explanation | Question type |
|---|---|---|---|
| Type of project | | | |
| 1 | Is the establishment of your activities in European territory? | Whether the processing of personal information of your undertaking takes place in the European Union or not is not relevant. | Y/N |
| | | If you are not established in European Union territory, but you offer goods or services to individuals in the EU or monitor them, then you should answer Y to this question. | |
| 2 | Do you gather information that can identify other people through one or more of the following activities? | Think for instance, if you use names, identification numbers or location data. The collection of information related to individuals can be potentially intrusive to the information privacy rights of these individuals. | [Checkbox] <br> - Web Browsing <br> - Account and/or Subscription Management <br> - Authentication and Authorization <br> - Customization <br> - Responding to User |
| | | In some types of projects information provided is more sensitive than in other ones e.g. Financial data | - (Service) Delivery <br> - Software Downloads <br> - Sales of Products or Services <br> - Communications Services <br> - Banking and Financial Management <br> - Payment and Transaction Facilitation <br> - Charitable Donations <br> - Government Services <br> - Healthcare Services <br> - Education Services <br> - Advertising, Marketing, and/or Promotions <br> - News and Information <br> - Arts and Entertainment <br> - Surveys and Questionnaires <br> - Online Gambling <br> - Online Gaming <br> - Search Engines <br> - State and Session Management |
| 3 | For which of the following purposes or legitimate interests do you process the information? | To be legitimate, the processing of information should be based on legitimate interests. Some interests carry more weight than others. For instance processing for historical, scientific statistical or research purposes is likely to be less intrusive to information privacy rights than processing for | [Checkbox] <br> Purposes related to the commercial objective of your undertaking <br> *Health purposes:* <br> - for preventive or occupational medicine, medical diagnosis, the provision of care or treatment or the |

(*Continued*)

**Table 2.**  (*Continued*)

| ID | Question | Explanation | Question type |
|---|---|---|---|
| | | exercise of the right to freedom of expression or information. | management of health-care services<br>- for public interest in the area of public health, such as protecting against serious cross-border threats<br>- for other reasons of public interest in areas such as social protection<br>*Employment context:*<br>- for purposes of the recruitment and job applications within the group of undertakings<br>- for the performance of the contract of employment, including discharge of obligations, laid down by law and by collective agreements,<br>- management, planning and organisation of work, health and safety at work,<br>- for the purposes of the exercise and enjoyment of rights and benefits related to employment<br>- for the purpose of the termination of the employment relationship<br>Purposes within the social security context<br>Processing for historical, scientific statistical or research purposes<br>Enforcement of legal claims and/or compliance with law enforcement agencies<br>Exercise of the right to freedom of expression or information (including in the media and the arts)<br>Other (Please specify) |
| **Collection and use of information** | | | |
| 4 | Are you relying exclusively on consent in order to process information of individuals? | Consent means 'any freely given specific, informed and explicit indication of his or her wishes by which the individual either by a statement or by a clear affirmative action signifies agreement to information relating to them being processed.' | Y/N |

(*Continued*)

**Table 2.** (*Continued*)

| ID | Question | Explanation | Question type |
|----|----------|-------------|---------------|
| 5 | How have you obtained the consent of individuals? | Consent requires prior information and an explicit indication of the intent to consent. | (a) Consent is given directly by the individual by a statement (e.g. by a consent form)<br>(b) Consent is given directly by the individual by an affirmative action (e.g. by ticking a box)<br>(c) Consent has been obtained implicitly by the individual (e.g. by the mere use of the service or inactivity) |
| 6 | If individuals have given their consent, can they withdraw it with ease and whenever they want to? | Individuals should be able to withdraw their consent at any time and every step of the processing of their information without detriment. It should be as easy to withdraw consent as it is to give it. | Y/N |
| 7 | Are the consequences of withdrawal of consent significant for individuals? | For instance, will the service to the individual be terminated *tout court*, while the individual still depends on it? | Y/N |
| 8 | On what basis do you process the information? | In order for the processing to be lawful, at least one of these grounds must be satisfied. | [Checkbox]<br>(a) The individual has given his consent<br>(b) Processing is necessary for the performance of a contract between you and the individual whose information you process<br>(c) Processing is necessary for compliance with a legal obligation you have<br>(d) Processing is necessary in order to protect vital interests of the individuals whose information you process<br>(e) None of the above |
| 9 | Do you provide clear information about: | | [Y/N Radio button]<br>- the purposes for which you process personal information<br>- the different types of information that you process<br>- your identity |
| 10 | Are all the information and its subsets you handle necessary to fulfil the purposes of your project? | The information you collect/process/handle should be adequate, relevant, and limited to the minimum necessary in relation to the | Y/N |

(*Continued*)

**Table 2.**  (*Continued*)

| ID | Question | Explanation | Question type |
|----|----------|-------------|---------------|
|    |          | purposes for which they are processed. This means that you have to use the minimum information necessary for your purposes, but you are not prohibited to have multiple purposes. |   |
| 11 | Is it possible for the individual to restrict the purposes for which you process the information? | For instance, are individuals given the possibility to opt-out of receiving email offers from you? | Y/N |
| 12 | Is the nature of your operations such that you need to comply with rules regarding data processing in more than one set of regulations? | Think for instance specific (data protection) regulation pertaining to you, such as for financial or health services. | Y/N |
| 13 | Are decisions being made on the basis of the information you process? | For instance, information can be collected for historical purposes without being used as part of a decision process. | Y/N |
| 14 | Do the outcomes of these decisions have a direct effect on the individuals whose information is processed? | For instance, are offers based on the characteristics of individuals being collected by your system? | Y/N |
| 15 | Does the information you process about individuals produce a full and correct image of these individuals? | The chances of taking wrong decisions increase if the information is incomplete, outdated or wrong. In such cases, the risk of setting individuals' rights at stake is higher. | Y/N/IDK |
| 16 | Does the information you process about the individual come from different sources? | Think, for instance, whether you obtain databases from other parties | Y/N |
| 17 | Are the individuals whose information you process aware of the fact that the information comes from different sources? | Consider whether you have informed the individuals about the information you process and which might come from other sources. | Y/N |
| 18 | Does your project involve the use of existing personal information for new purposes? | For instance, you may decide that you want to use the contact details you obtained for signaling the user that their order has been fulfilled for marketing purposes later on. | Y/N |
| 19 | Do your additional processing operations relate closely to the | For instance, using a customer's home address for frequent delivery of packages after the | Y/N |

(*Continued*)

**Table 2.** (*Continued*)

| ID | Question | Explanation | Question type |
|---|---|---|---|
| | original purposes for which you first collected the information? | first delivery is compatible use, whereas providing a patient list to one spouse, who runs a travel agency; so that he can offer special holiday deals to patients needing recuperation is not. | |
| 20 | Is the use of existing personal information for new purposes clearly communicated to the individual in a timely manner? | Consider whether you have informed the individuals about the specific (new) purposes for which you process the information. | Y/N |
| 21 | Is the use of existing personal information for new purposes clearly communicated to your organization's data protection officer? | Consider whether you have informed the data protection officer about the specific (new) purposes for which you process the information. | Y/N |
| 22 | Do you appropriately notify your national DPA before performing data processing operations subject to prior checking? | In some cases your processing activities are subject to prior checking by your national DPA. | Y/N |
| 23 | Do you process information which could potentially be perceived as discriminatory? | Think for instance, whether you process information solely on the basis of race or ethnic origin, political opinion, religion or beliefs, trade union membership, sexual orientation or gender identity etc. | Y/N |
| Storage and security | | | |
| 24 | Are procedures in place to provide individuals access to information about themselves? | Consider, for instance, whether individuals can request an overview of the information about them that you have | Y/N |
| 25 | Can the information you process be corrected by the individuals, or can individuals ask for correction of the information? | An increased level of involvement by the individual decreases the likelihood of unwarranted events (e.g. incorrect information) | Y/N |
| 26 | Do you check the accuracy and completeness of information on entry? | Consider, for instance, whether you apply specific procedures (e.g. use of journalistic archives to double-check the content) in order to ensure the validity and authenticity of the information you process. | Y/N |

(*Continued*)

**Table 2.** (*Continued*)

| ID | Question | Explanation | Question type |
|---|---|---|---|
| 27 | How often is the personal information you process updated? | Outdated information has a negative impact on the accuracy of information you process. | [Checkbox]<br>- Frequently<br>- When requested by the individual<br>- Whenever necessary to comply with technological developments<br>- Rarely<br>- Never |
| 28 | How severe would you deem the consequences, in case you process outdated information for the individuals it refers to? | For instance, having outdated information about individuals (e.g. wrong date of birth) may hold you liable. | - High<br>- Medium<br>- Low<br>- None |
| 29 | Would the fact that the information you process is not up to date lead to sanctions provided in relevant regulations? | Think, for instance, whether the nature of your activities requires you to comply with specific sets of regulations, which provide sanctions in order to keep the information updated. | Y/N/IDK |
| 30 | Do you have a Data Security Policy? | Think of aspects such as: is it clear who is responsible for security, do you adopt security standards, is the (sensitive) nature of the information you process taken into account | Y/N |
| 31 | Do you implement any technical and organizational security measure from the outset of your activities? | Think, for instance, whether you are using signatures, hashing, encryption etc. or whether you implement Privacy by Design and/or Privacy by Default mechanisms from the very design phase of your projects. | Y/N |
| 32 | Do you differentiate your security measures according to the type of information that you process? | For instance information related to race or ethnic origin, political or sexual orientation, religion or gender identity of the individuals requires specific security measures. | Y/N |
| 33 | Is the personnel in your undertaking trained on how to process the information you deal with according to the organisational policies you implemented? | Consider if you apply specific procedures or timetables to train your employees with regard to the manner in which they should process the information. | Y/N |
| 34 | How often are your Security and Privacy Policies updated? | | [Radio button]<br>- Frequently<br>- Whenever necessary to comply with technological developments |

(*Continued*)

**Table 2.** (*Continued*)

| ID | Question | Explanation | Question type |
|----|----------|-------------|---------------|
|    |          |             | - Rarely<br>- Never |
| 35 | Do you adopt one or more of the following measures and/or procedures as a safeguard or security measure to ensure the protection of personal information? | The application of one or more of the following measures may prevent potential misuse of the information you handle. | [Checklist]<br>- Personal information is kept confidential<br>- Access control is enforced<br>- Segregation of duty is used<br>- Special authorization for personnel who access the information<br>- Compliance with further regulations is ensured<br>- Use of personal information are properly documented<br>- Procedures to maintain personal information use up-to-date regularly<br>- Subcontractors follow the same guidelines on documenting the use of information<br>- Procedures to notify individuals, when necessary, are in place<br>- Procedures to take into account the impact of the information lifecycle<br>- Procedures to record individuals' requests for correction of information<br>- Specific procedures to respond to Law Enforcement access or court orders<br>- Modalities to express, withhold, or withdraw informed consent to the processing<br>- Anonymization<br>- Pseudonymisation<br>- Encryption<br>- Aggregation<br>- Separation<br>- Limitation of usage<br>- Data segregation<br>- Sticky Policies<br>- All of the above<br>- None of the above |
| 36 | If you use encryption methods, are you responsible for encrypting and decrypting the | If you are the only one responsible for encrypting and decrypting the information you process, you are subsequently the only one who has control | Y/N |

**Table 2.** (*Continued*)

| ID | Question | Explanation | Question type |
|----|----------|-------------|---------------|
|    | information that you process? | over this information. Instead, if you have given such a competence to a cloud service provider you do not have the same level of control over the information. | |
| 37 | Do the protection measures you have in place, in case of unwarranted incidents, specifically target the particular type of incident that might happen? | For instance, in case of unauthorized access/disclosure/modification, intentional or reckless destruction of or damage to your equipment, loss or theft of your assets etc. Such incidents threaten the protection of personal information | Y/N |
| 38 | Do you take action in order to notify individuals in case of (security) incidents? | E.g. by sending emails. | Y/N |
| 39 | What do you do to minimize the damages of physical, technical and/or security incidents? | | [Checklist] - Segregation of data bases - Limitation of use/transfer functionalities on system layer - Separation on system layer - Multi-tenancy limitations - Physical separation of infrastructure - None of the above - Others (please indicate) |
| 40 | Does the project(s) include the possibility by individuals to set retention periods on their own? | Setting retention periods allows you to ensure that the information that you process about individuals is kept for no longer than is necessary for your operations. | Y/N |
| 41 | For how long do you store the information you are dealing with? | | [Checklist] (a) Only for the completion of the project's purposes (b) Information is retained for a certain time after the project has been completed (c) Information is retained for the possibility of future uses or new purposes (d) Until individual requests for erasure |
| Transfer of information |  |  |  |
| 42 | Do you normally transfer the information you deal with to third parties | Do you, for instance, outsource the processing of the information you deal with to third parties? | Y/N |

*(Continued)*

**Table 2.**  (*Continued*)

| ID | Question | Explanation | Question type |
|----|----------|-------------|---------------|
| | during your normal processing operations? | | |
| 43 | Is the third parties' use compatible with the one you set for your undertaking? | If you transfer information to third parties, do they use the information in a manner consistent with your original purpose(s) and their mandate? | Y/N |
| 44 | Do you sell, rent or by any means disseminate information to third parties? | | Y/N |
| 45 | Are you transferring and/or simply disclosing personal information exclusively to countries or territories outside the EEA? | The EEA consists of the following countries: Austria, Belgium, Bulgaria, Croatia, Cyprus, Czech Republic, Denmark, Estonia, Finland, France, Germany, Greece, Hungary, Iceland, Ireland, Italy, Latvia, Liechtenstein, Lithuania, Luxemburg, Malta, Netherlands, Norway, Poland, Portugal, Romania, Slovakia, Slovenia, Spain, Sweden, United Kingdom. | Y/N |
| 46 | Are you transferring personal information exclusively to one or more of the following non-EEA countries? | Each of these countries are deemed to have adequate privacy protection in terms of the EU data protection regulations | [Checklist]<br>- Andorra<br>- Argentina<br>- Australia<br>- Canada<br>- Switzerland<br>- Faeroe Islands<br>- Guernsey<br>- Israel<br>- Isle of Man<br>- Jersey<br>- New Zealand<br>- Uruguay<br>- U.S. |
| 47 | Are measures in place to ensure an adequate level of security when the information is transferred outside of the EEA? | Not all countries have the same level of protection as regards to the processing of personal information. Transferring personal information towards countries without an adequate level of protection is a breach of EU data protection laws. | Y/N/IDK |
| Cloud specific questions | | | |
| 48 | The cloud infrastructure I use is: | The potential threats to privacy and protection of personal information are influenced by the deployment model of the | (a) owned by or operated for only me (private cloud) |

**Table 2.** (*Continued*)

| ID | Question | Explanation | Question type |
|---|---|---|---|
| | | CSP. This means that the risk is higher if the number of the subjects who operate in the system is also high. | (b) is owned by or operated for a specific group of users with common interests in a shared manner (community cloud) <br> (c) is shared amongst multiple users (public cloud) |
| 49 | Does the service provider that you use provide you just with raw computing resources, such as processing capacity or storage, for the information that you process? | Think for instance of Amazon AWS or Microsoft Azure | Y/N |
| 50 | Does the service provider you use provide you with an environment or platform in which you can develop and deploy software? | Think for instance of Google App Encine or Force.com | Y/N |
| 51 | Does the service that you use consist of the provision of end user applications run by the cloud service provider? | Think for instance of SalesForce CRM or Wuala. | Y/N |
| 52 | Are specific arrangements in place with regards to your information in case you want to terminate or transfer the cloud service? | The application of such rules/procedures gives you the ability to have control over the information you process. For instance, you can transfer the information you process to another provider if necessary (e.g. in case of bankruptcy, force majeure etc). | Y/N/IDK |
| 53 | Does the CSP apply specific procedures in order to secure the information you handle and/or process in case your business is discontinued? | Think, for instance, if the information that you process are preserved in case of merger, acquisition, bankruptcy, etc. | Y/N/IDK |
| 54 | Does the CSP have an insurance policy against the possible loss or compromise of the information you process in a cloud environment? | Think for instance if the provider is able to redress you in case of unwarranted incidents concerning the information that relates to them through an insurance scheme or similar ones. | Y/N/IDK |

(*Continued*)

**Table 2.**  (*Continued*)

| ID | Question | Explanation | Question type |
|---|---|---|---|
| 55 | Does the CSP use resource isolation mechanisms in order to secure the information you entrust it? | Think, for instance, about how the CSP ensures the isolation of your information from the information of other customers potentially located in the same physical machine, albeit of course in a different virtual one. | Y/N/IDK |
| 56 | Are the CSP's activities certified by any kind of supervisory organisation or body? | Think for instance, if the CSP has obtained a certification by a supervisory body or organization, which can guarantee the quality of his services and his compliance with the law. | Y/N/IDK |

(DPD) [14], as it is still the main legal instrument within the EU, and the drafts of the upcoming GDPR[7], rather than focusing exclusively on the legislation currently in force. The aim we set was to develop a tool that could be used effectively under both regimes.

The DPD provided us with the basic concepts and principles defining the current general data protection framework, while the GDPR provided additional concepts and concrete procedural guidelines for a practical DPIA questionnaire. In particular, the principles relating to processing of personal data, such as purpose limitation and data minimisation, derived from the DPD. Articles 6 and 7 of the current DPD, which deal with the legitimacy of data processing, gave grounds for an extensive set of questions aimed at mapping the user's intention to the legal terms incorporated in the DPD[8]. Furthermore, ICO's "Code of Practice: [23], in conjunction with the PIA Guide of the Office of the Australian Information Commissioner (OAIC) [2] also proved to be useful tools in phrasing particular questions[9]. The ICO's PIA Handbook [22] constituted the key inspirational instrument in drafting the questions related to the grounds of processing.

The GDPR (in the form of the European Parliament's first reading), was used as the starting point for both questionnaires. Articles 32a and 33 provide the conditions under which a DPIA would be mandatory.

---

[7] Which will arguably embody the current state of the art in data protection legislation, as well as the result of the doctrinal elaboration the concept had in the last two decades.

[8] For instance, Question 10 in Table 2 ("Are all the information and its subsets you handle necessary to fulfill the purposes of your project?") or Question 17 ("Does your project involve the use of existing personal information for new purposes?") were drafted by taking into consideration the already existing legal requirements.

[9] For instance, Question 11 in Table 2 ("Is it possible for the individual to restrict the purposes for which you process the information?").

The analysis of the DPD, GDPR, and various DPIA and PIA [8, 43–45] models are reflected in the construction of the questionnaire's framework[10]: the legal norms and the PIA/DPIA models utilised[11] allowed us to develop the "Question" field (for the related "Explanation" one see Tables 1 and 2), while the sources for risks in cloud environments [9, 10, 16] were used to give a logical structure to the questionnaire and to weigh the answers provided by users. The "Answer" fields were developed to steer the user throughout the questionnaire according to a logic order that was formulated mainly through the examination of the DPD and the GDPR, while assessing the impact and the likelihood of an unwarranted event happening.

Many PIAs work on the assumption that the user is aware of certain basic data protection notions, such as 'personal data' and directly ask the user whether they process personal data and for which purposes and on what ground and so forth. Our DPIA starts from the premise that the user does not know these concepts and it therefore tries to, within limits, do a legal qualification of the user's responses to simple terms. Based on the kind of information the user intends to process, the tool will 'decide' that it constitutes personal data, rather than having the user specify so in advance. The tool does provide feedback incorporating proper legal terminology where applicable.

The risk assessment, which provides the basis for probing the user about mitigation measures, is based on a series of documents (see Sect. 3.5 below) regarding the most commonly occurring incidents in cloud ecosystems; from a data protection viewpoint, these incidents provided valuable insights on the cloud's potential threats to informational self-determination, on their likelihood and on their foreseeable impact. We conceived risk as the by-product of the interplay between the likelihood of an event and of the impact that event would have. We based the construction of the questionnaire on that conception, which is to say we used literature and reports to investigate, on the one hand, the most harmful privacy-related incidents, and on the other the most likely ones, all in order to develop a better understanding of what to ask when assessing the impact of an undertaking's activities on data subjects' privacy and data protection rights. Since the questionnaire aims to assess, *grosso modo*, how and how much a cloud user's undertaking deviates or could deviate from the physiology dictated by data protection norms (as embodied currently in the DPD and for the future in the GDPR), and the impact of its activities on data subjects, it seemed proper to consider, amongst other prominent factors, the most likely and/or the most harmful incidents in cloud environments. Based on these considerations, we formulated questions embracing the notions of risk and likelihood in an intelligible manner for the tool user; for instance, the incorporation of the question: "How severe do you deem the consequences, in case you process outdated information for the individuals it refers to?" forms a clear

---

[10] The table we developed is composed by the following categories: question, explanation of the question, question type (which frames the possible answers to be given by the users, e.g. in the form of radio buttons, checkboxes, or yes/no binary answers), responses to be given to the users in order to educate them while they go through the questionnaire, actions to be performed by the tool as a consequence of the users' answers (e.g. go to the next question). A weighing of the users' activities' impact on data subjects' privacy and data protection was originally embedded in the table as well.

[11] See *supra* note 4.

example on tool's underlying perception on the notion of impact, while a question such as "For how long do you store the information you are dealing with?" captures the related perception on the notion of likelihood[12]. The situations that are most likely to threaten individuals in the cloud or that, if they occur, would harm individuals the most, provided a useful list of the risks to be incorporated in the tool. Determining their impact and likelihood turned out not to be straightforward, though. Due to the lack of available and sufficiently targeted metrics, the likelihood parameter was inferred through the review of several documents issued by public bodies tasked with the safeguard of the rights to privacy and data protection or dealing with information security, for instance [11, 12, 17, 26] among others. The impact parameter, on the other hand, is historically hard to define when correlated to the notions of privacy and, albeit to a minor extent, to the one of data protection: as it has been noted by prominent doctrinal sources, they appear "*to be about everything, and therefore [...] to be nothing*" [37]. Moreover, harms deriving from privacy and data protection violations are hardly quantifiable in that they are inherently linked to other rights, whose infringement causes the starkest impact on data subjects [37] – "*a cluster of related activities that impinge upon people in related ways*"[13]. Hence, an ontological definition of the impact deriving from a data privacy violation appears to be hardly feasible in the tool's context[14], aside, of course, from what can be directly inferred from the relevant regulations. We have therefore made reasoned assumptions about potential impacts.

It is important to stress here that this process could not capture the whole of the relevant law, which is far too complex, lengthy and granular to be represented in the tool. Qualitative decisions had to be made about which legal norms should be included, and at what level of detail. In addition, framing the questions and devising explanations of their meaning lost even more detail and richness of meaning. The version of the legal norms embodied in the tool is thus only a partial summary of the law's requirements in this area, shaped to the needs of the tool. This means that the tool cannot be relied on to identify all potentially applicable legal obligations, and that its risk assessment outputs are by definition not fully comprehensive.[15]

Despite the existence of several PIA/DPIA models which deal with traditional cases of processing, there is hardly a sufficient number of cloud-tailored DPIA models, especially when considering the growing importance and pervasiveness of the cloud

---

[12] Based on the intuition that the longer data is stored, the higher the likelihood that something happens to the data. Of course this is not necessarily, or always, the case, but as a heuristic it may suffice to make the user think about data retention.

[13] A gross negligence in an anonymization process giving ability to unduly infer a data subject's identity, for instance, which is usually a data protection violation per se, can lead to a diverse array of consequences (such as identity theft, physical harm – e.g. domestic violence victims tracked down by their assailants) depending on the concrete circumstances of the case.

[14] Our consideration of the impact deriving from privacy and data protection violations, however, was largely shaped according to Solove's classification (*Ibid.*), which taxonomizes privacy violations according to four macro-categories (Information collection, information processing, information dissemination, intrusion), each of which can be subdivided into more specific subcategories.

[15] The user may notice while going through the tool that their situation is not satisfactory covered by the questions. This may be a clear indicator to seek professional help to supplement the tool's assessment.

computing model in the market and the differences that run between traditional IT environments and the cloud. ENISA's recommendations [16] constituted, though, a helpful methodological tool in identifying and evaluating risks on the data protection rights. Also, ENISA's framework for Cloud Security Incident Reporting [17] formed the key element for the development of the evaluation scheme we propose. Several other scholarly publications [26] have been consulted for targeted guidance on particular topics in order to articulate cloud-relevant questions[16].

## 3.2 The Pre-assessment Stage

The pre-assessment stage includes a set of seven questions, fully presented in Table 1. It aims to identify whether the processing operations to be undertaken can be perceived as potentially risky to the protection of personal data of the individuals and as such trigger the full-scale DPIA when this is the case. It initially assesses whether the information s/he deals with constitutes personal data or not, and then evaluates the kind of information processed, its sensitivity, the purposes of the processing, the actors involved and the extent to which the information is likely to be diffused. Our purpose was mainly to provide the user with a very short and incisive quick-scan to assess the presence or the absence of some general factors that indicate the use of personal information, e.g. the very qualification as personal data of the information dealt with by the tool's user, or the presence of sensitive data amongst it.

## 3.3 The Assessment Stage

The (conditionally) following full-scale DPIA includes 50 questions (see Table 2 for an excerpt and [19] for the full version including explanation of implication of each answer option). The questions are grouped into to five (5) topical areas (the key inspirational document which enabled the taxonomy of these topical areas was [28]), which refer to: (1) the type of project, (2) the collection and use of data, (3) the project's storage and security policies, (4) data transfers, and (5) cloud specific issues. The aim of this set of questions is to assess how the interactions between the subjects that perform the DPIA and CSPs affects data subjects' rights to privacy and data protection.

Each question has several possible suggested answers (single selection or multi-choice), avoiding open questions, which are hard to process automatically. While answering some questions the user can get guidance from the DPIAT (see Sect. 5) on how to address the privacy issues related to the specific answers. In particular, questions 35 and 39 cover respectively a set of privacy and security controls supporting data protection; this helps the user document existing controls and to understand which others could be implemented.

---

[16] Questions 48-50 in Table 2 refer to the service models in a cloud environment.

## 3.4    Evaluation of the Results

Each question has a formula for computing the privacy impact score based on its answer and a weight prioritising the importance relative to other questions. For example, the Question 4 in Table 2 "*Are you relying exclusively on consent in order to process information of individuals?*" has the following possible answers:

(a)  *Consent is given directly by the individual by a statement (e.g. by a consent form)*
(b)  *Consent is given directly by the individual by an affirmative action (e.g. by ticking a box)*
(c)  *Consent has been obtained implicitly by the individual (e.g. by merely use of the service or inactivity)*

We assign the value for the *privacy impact score* for the answer to this question using the following formula: *If option 'a' then the score is 0, Else if option 'b' then the score is 1/4, Else if option 'c' then the score is ¾.*

Intuitively, the option 'c' would have a bigger impact on privacy than option 'b' and 'a' so the score is chosen to be proportional to the perceived impact. We compute the *final privacy impact score* (FI) taking into account the answers to all the questions:

$$FI = \frac{\sum_i^N s_i \alpha_i}{\sum_i^N \alpha_i} \tag{1}$$

Here $N$ is the number of questions in the DPIA questionnaire, $s_i$ is the score for the answer to the question $i$; and $\alpha_i = 1$ if the question $i$ is answered and $\alpha_i = 0$ otherwise.

In addition, we associate the questions with several *privacy indicators*, capturing different privacy aspects: *data sensitivity, compliance, trans-border data flow, transparency, data control, security*, and *data sharing*. For example, the answer to the question above influences the *data control* and *transparency* indicators. Some of the indicators can enhance privacy (*compliance, transparency, data c aurity*), while the others diminish it (*data sensitivity, trans-border data flow and data sharing*). Therefore, the privacy indicator scores will be either proportional to the privacy impact scores of individual answers or inverse. So in the example above a higher score for the answer (option 'c') implies less data control and transparency.

We compute the *final privacy indicator score* for the indicator $j$ ($FI_j$):

$$FI_j = \frac{\sum_i s'_{ij} \alpha_i \beta_{ij}}{\sum_i \alpha_i \beta_{ij}} \tag{2}$$

Here $s'_{ij} = s_i$ if the indicator j negatively affects privacy and $s'_{ij} = 1 - s_i$ otherwise; $\beta_{ij} = 1$ if the answer to question i impacts indicator j and $\beta_{ij} = 0$ otherwise. The ratio $\sum_i^N \alpha_i / N$ represents the coverage of the questionnaire and indicates the reliability of the indicators.

Finally, we define the overall *privacy impact level* and *privacy indicator levels* for the assessment by translating correspondingly $FI$ and $FI_j$ to a uniform qualitative scale:

*Low* < *Medium* < *High* and use color-coding to facilitate the presentation: *Low* →
Green, *Medium* → Yellow and *High* → Red.

In order to provide users with actionable guidelines, the DPIAT final report contains an additional section that delivers textual guidance generated according to the user's answers. Far from being considerable as legal advice – as the tool specifically disclaims – the section is still able to make the tool's user focus on specific privacy and data protection-related issues s/he might have overlooked. For instance, when a user indicates that data protection is not considered from the outset of the assessed project's development, the section highlights the importance of the concepts of Data Protection by Design and Data Protection by Default.

## 3.5 Discussion

Under the GDPR, as amended by the outcome of the European Parliament's first reading, there is a trend to make DPIAs compulsory when the processing operations of controllers are likely to present specific risks for rights and freedoms of data subjects (Article 32a of the Parliament's text Respect to Risk). This approach seems to confirm the importance of DPIAs to protect data subjects' rights and freedoms: this meant for us embedding in the DPIA process the concept of risk analysis introduced in the earlier stated Article 32a of the European Parliament's amended text.

As to the first area of questions relating to the type of project undertaken by the tool's user, our aim was to frame both the kind of activity performed by the CSP's client and the aim of that activity. We considered the fact that a controller could handle personal data (for instance, the controller may obtain information such as the name and e-mail address of users through online subscription forms) for a number of different reasons and aims (e.g. commercial purposes) Therefore, we decided to include two separate inquiries: one regarding the activities through which data is processed, and another regarding the purpose of the processing.

The second area of questions regards the collection of the information, the usage that processors make of that information and the means with which personal data is handled. This section draws heavily from the basic principles of both the DPD and the GDPR. For instance, it attempts to discover whether there appear to be solid, legitimate grounds for processing, identify the main risks of non-compliance with the data protection principles and assess the tool user's plans for compliance with the rights of the data subject sanctioned by law.

Storage and Security (deletion included[17]), moreover, is considered a third area, which deserves specific consideration, especially in relation to the traits of Cloud Computing.

---

[17] Note that deletion assumes particular importance in the cloud: the remoteness of the physical machines and the lack of control cloud users have over them, considered in relation to the fact that several different layers of deletion exist (from a mere drag-and-drop in the OS' virtual rubbish bin to the physical destruction of the hardware in which the virtual machine of the user lies), make deletion a focal point when assessing the risks a data subject is prone to.

The investigation we propose was developed according to an "individual-centric approach", which tried to deepen the level of protection accorded to data subjects, irrespective of who (either CSPs or their customers) exerts concrete control over the particular aspect considered: that is to say, we considered it more useful to ask SME users (and individuals using the tool) questions pertaining to the CSPs' areas of control[18], accepting the chance they might not know the answer to our inquiry, in which case the user simply refrains from answering. Leaving questions open provides a less 'accurate' assessment, but still provides guidance. Users can also return to the questionnaire after obtaining answers to questions they cannot answer from others to provide a more complete picture. The tool thus is not a one-way street, but can be used iteratively.

A major concern we had related to the "updatedness" of the information dealt with by the tool user. The questionnaire includes two questions regarding the foreseen negative consequences of the outdated information processed by the tool user's undertaking; specifically the questionnaire addresses the consequences of outdated information about individuals[19] and how such outdated information can lead to regulatory liability[20]. Whether or not outdated information may result in civil or criminal liability, however, is outside the scope of the DPIA. An individual-centric approach has also been adopted for the fourth set of questions, which relates to the transfer of information. This is because transferring information is controlled by the law to attempt to limit the risks that the data subjects are subject to by prescribing conditions for data transfer. Furthermore, due to the target of the DPIA tool, this class of inquiries caters for the possibility that the tool's user does not possess an adequate level of knowledge to answer all questions. Much like with the third set of questions, we considered the possibility of a lack of answer appropriate.

The final set of questions refers exclusively to cloud computing services. Given the complexities of cloud computing technology, it was a challenge to formulate those questions in an understandable language for an ordinary user. Each deployment model has various ramifications which are not necessarily known in the first place to the user of the DPIA tool who is to decide whether to opt for a particular cloud computing service or not.

It is important for the users of a cloud service to know how to secure the information they process within the cloud environment. Taking that into account, the cloud relevant questions aim at ascertaining the level of exposure to risk that the user may have by virtue of using a specific type of cloud service. Two major aspects are important to establish in this regard. Firstly, it is important to know whether the cloud service used by the user of the DPIA tool is public, and thus shared with third parties, or private, and thus solely used by the user. Secondly, it is important to establish what the user utilises the cloud service for.[21]

---

[18] E.g. Question 47 in Table 2.

[19] See question 28 in Table 2.

[20] See question 29 in Table 2.

[21] See Questions 48-50 in Table 2.

The inclusion of a specific part of the questionnaire targeted only to the cloud environment serves as an enabler for the applicability of the DPIA tool to a non-cloud setting as well, in an attempt to ensure that the DPIA Questionnaire remains future proof so far as technological change is concerned. This technology neutral approach enables the application of the tool to future Internet services. If the cloud-relevant questions are removed, the questionnaire can potentially be used to assist in achieving compliance with the legal framework irrespective of whether the assessed undertaking operates in the cloud or not.

Future proofing the tool in terms of its legal content is more problematic. Even once the GDPR has been agreed and becomes law, the content of the law will not be static because laws are regularly amended. More challenging is that the *meaning* of legal provisions develops and changes over time, in response to court decisions about specific sets of facts and policy decisions and guidance issued by regulators. For this reason a mechanism will need to be developed to review and update the legal content of the tool at appropriate intervals to ensure that it does not become dangerously inaccurate.

## 4 Cloud Adoption Risk Assessment Model

We employ the Cloud Adoption Risk Assessment Model (CARAM) to evaluate the risks resulting from adoption of cloud services (see [6] for full details). CARAM is designed to assist (potential) cloud customers assess all kinds of risks—not only privacy-related—that they face by selecting a specific CSP. The results of CARAM risk assessment constitute a part of the DPIA report (see Sect. 5).

CARAM is a qualitative deductive risk assessment model based on ENISA's cloud risk assessment model [16] and the Cloud Security Alliance's (CSA) Cloud Assessment Initiative Questionnaire (CAIQ).[22] Like in [16] we conceived risk as the by-product of the interplay between the likelihood of an event and of the impact that event would have. CARAM complements ENISA's approach to take into account cloud customers' assets (modelled based on the list of assets from the ENISA report) and the implementation status of security controls in CSA STAR public registry to perform a relative risk assessment of (potential) cloud solutions. This can help cloud consumers to determine which CSPs have acceptable risk profiles for security, privacy, and quality of service.

Most of the entries in STAR use a template that provides 148 questions grouped into several control areas covering the state of implementation of various security controls. We have categorised the answers of more than 50% of the CSPs from the STAR—including several big players—into the following categories:

- *Implemented*: the control is in place
- *Conditionally Implemented*: the control can be implemented under some conditions
- *Not Implemented*: the control is not in place
- *Not Applicable*: the control is not applicable to the provided service

---

[22] https://cloudsecurityalliance.org/research/cai/.

Since the answers were given in a verbose free text form instead of simple Yes/No and the number of answers was big (circa 9000) we used supervised machine learning algorithms provided by the WEKA tool [21] to automate this classification.

We used these answers together with other information from the ENISA report to calculate the vulnerability index for different risk scenarios (see Table 3 for the list of risk scenarios). The vulnerability index is defined to be proportional to the number of implemented security controls that mitigate vulnerabilities involved in the risk scenario. It is later used to adjust the probability of the risk scenario using the values provided by the experts from the ENISA report as a baseline. Eventually, the risks are grouped into three categories: risks for security, privacy and service: to provide a high level risk profile which is easier to interpret. Based on these results the customers can compare different cloud solutions and select those satisfying their risk tolerance.

Figure 1 displays the level of exposure (vulnerability index) for privacy risks among the analysed CSPs (similarly, the vulnerability index can be computed for security and service risks). According to these results, the lowest vulnerability index for a cloud solution is 0.011 while the vulnerability index for the highest risk cloud solution is 0.491. Although the later index is more than 44 times higher than the former, it is still less than 0.5. This means that the likelihood value for even the highest risk cloud solution in STAR will be reduced significantly, and become "LOW" according to the risk matrix from [6]. This is expected since all analysed CSPs report that they have implemented at least 70% of the controls from CAIQ.

In this approach, we rely on the self-assessment provided by the CSPs since it is not possible to verify independently the status of each control: only three of the analysed CSPs had a third party certification from CSA when we performed the data collection. Certification report details are not available to the public.

## 5 DPIA Tool and Report

DPIAT's web interface enables an easy and user friendly experience of a questionnaire about a perceived complex issue. Screenshots are shown in Figs. 2 and 3. The landing page asks the user whether they would like to start with pre-screening questions to determine if they need to answer the full-scale questionnaire (screening questions). The full-scale assessment questionnaire (see Sect. 3.3) contains a set of a bit more than 50 questions displayed in five stages categorising them. The stages are Type of Project, Collection and use of information, Storage and security, Transfer of information, and Cloud specific questions. During the completion of the questionnaire, the user is provided feedback on the answers and choices they make. This includes, for instance, pointing out that the chosen option increases the privacy risk, thus subtly suggesting the user to reconsider their choice. The tool does not judge, but is rather aimed at stimulating the user to think about their project from the perspective of privacy and data protection.

The output is a report including the data protection risk profile, assistance in deciding whether to proceed or not, and suggested mitigations. The report contains three sections. The first, *"Risk Related to Your Proposed Application"*, is based on the answers to the questionnaire and contains the overall data protection impact score and

**Table 3.** ENISA's list of risk scenarios and their categories

| Risk Category | Risk name |
|---|---|
| Policy & Organisational | P1.Lock-in |
| | P2.Loss of governance |
| | P3.Compliance challenges |
| | P4.Loss of business reputation due to co-tenant activities |
| | P5.Cloud service termination or failure |
| | P6.Cloud provider acquisition |
| | P7.Supply chain failure |
| Technical | T1.Resource exhaustion (under or over provisioning) |
| | T2.Isolation failure |
| | T3.Cloud provider malicious insider - abuse of high privilege roles |
| | T4.Management interface compromise (manipulation, availability of infrastructure) |
| | T5.Intercepting data in transit |
| | T6.Data leakage on up/download, intra-cloud |
| | T7.Insecure or ineffective deletion of data |
| | T8.Distributed denial of service (DDoS) |
| | T9.Economic denial of service (EDOS) |
| | T10.Loss of encryption keys |
| | T11.Undertaking malicious probes or scans |
| | T12.Compromise service engine |
| | T13.Conflicts between customer hardening procedures and cloud environment |
| Legal | L1.Subpoena and e-discovery |
| | L2.Risk from changes of jurisdiction |
| | L3.Data protection risks |
| | L4.Licensing risks |
| Not Specific to the Cloud | N1.Network breaks |
| | N2.Network management (i.e., network congestion/mis-connection/non-optimal use) |
| | N3.Modifying network traffic |
| | N4.Privilege escalation |
| | N5.Social engineering attacks (i.e., impersonation) |
| | N6.Loss or compromise of operational logs |
| | N7.Loss or compromise of security logs (manipulation of forensic investigation) |
| | N8.Backups lost, stolen |
| | N9.Unauthorised access to premises (including physical access to machines and other facilities) |
| | N10.Theft of computer equipment |
| | N11.Natural disasters |

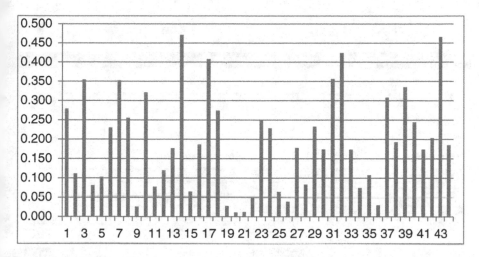

**Fig. 1.** Privacy vulnerability index for 44 CSPs in STAR (The actual CSP names were omitted for confidentiality reasons)

several privacy indicator scores (see Sect. 3.4) namely, risks related to Sensitivity, Compliance, Trans-border Data Flow, Transparency, Data Control, Security, and Data Sharing (see Fig. 4). The second part, *"Risk Related to the selected Cloud Provider"*, displays the risks based on the security controls used by the CSP (see Sect. 4). It contains the 35 ENISA [16] risk scenarios with their associated scores. The last section contains additional information related to the GDPR article 33. It also explains to the user that DPIA is meant to be an ongoing process and guides the user on the general phases of the assessment. The final decision of whether to proceed with the desired transaction (which triggered the DPIA in the first place) is up to the user or his manager (i.e. an approver in case the result of the DPIA is *high risks*).

The implementation of the *server-side* application and web-service (Questionnaire Provider) is written in Java. This application provides access to the Questionnaire data and also provides a rules-engine that helps determine the flow of the questionnaire for the client as well as providing further details and information based on the user's responses to the questions offered. The *rules engine* is based on the Drools[23] library. The *client-side* application is implemented using HTML5 and JavaScript and utilises a number of open-source libraries to simplify the underlying business logic layer. We use RESTful[24] API as a transport layer and JSON[25] as the data-interchange format.

During the development of the tool, testing on how the user experience should look like was conducted. The tool was presented to several users including partners in HP Privacy Office and the feedback received was incorporated in the final implementation of the tool. Positive feedback was given on the amount of guidance provided for the

---

[23] Drools Business Rules Management System Solution: http://www.drools.org/.

[24] RESTful is a standard for web APIs and transport protocol.

[25] JSON Data Interchange Format: http://www.json.org/.

**Fig. 2.** DPIAT initial screen

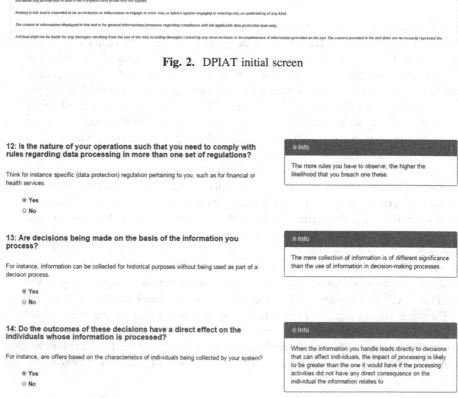

**Fig. 3.** DPIAT tooltip displaying information about the selected options

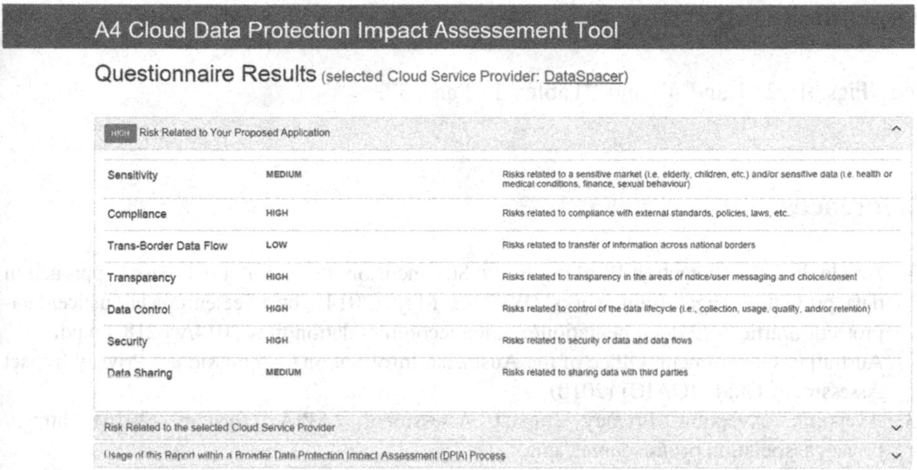

**Fig. 4.** DPIAT output report - details of first section

user in terms of information text for both the questions and the answers. Also, dividing the 50 questions into five stages was considered a good impact on the tool's usability. Additional testing was carried out with privacy researchers from a variety of inter-disciplinary backgrounds, and further changes are planned to the tool in respect of this feedback. In particular, there was a strong perceived need for more explanation about both how the tool derives its recommendations and about how these recommendations should be interpreted and acted upon.

# 6 Conclusions

We have presented a contemporary Data Protection Impact Assessment methodology focusing on the use of cloud services, supported by a tool that aims at helping users to understand privacy risks of their intended project and help them consider means to mitigate these concerns. The DPIAT is based on existing PIAs, legal sources and specific cloud risk scenarios. It is aimed specifically at SME users that typically have limited knowledge about privacy and data protection and have restricted resources to consult experts in the field, yet will have a legal obligation (once the GDPR comes into effect) to conduct a DPIA. Although the tool does not incorporate advanced intelligence to help the user, we believe that the way we have structured the issues, framed the questions and provide situation specific feedback and a crude likelihood/impact score, actually will help the target audience understand the importance of privacy and data protection in their context and help improve legal compliance.

**Acknowledgement.** This work is part of the EU-funded FP7 project grant number 317550 titled as "Accountability for Cloud and Other Future Internet Services" (A4Cloud - http://www.a4cloud.eu/).

# Appendix

See "Figs. 1, 2, 3 and 4" and "Tables 1, 2 and 3".

# References

1. Article 29 Data Protection Working Party: Statement on the role of a risk-based approach in data protection legal frameworks (WP218), May (2014). http://ec.europa.eu/justice/data-protection/article-29/documentation/opinion-recommendation/files/2014/wp218_en.pdf
2. Australian Government, Office of the Australian Information Commissioner: Privacy Impact Assessment Guide (OAIC) (2010)
3. Avepoint: Avepoint Privacy Impact Assessment (APIA) System (2015). https://privacyassociation.org/resources/apia
4. Bennett, C.J., Raab, C.D.: The Governance of Privacy: Policy Instruments in Global Perspective. MIT Press, Cambridge (2006)
5. CambridgeSoft: ChemBioOffice Cloud–An Integrated Decision Support System for CHDI (2010). http://chembionews.cambridgesoft.com/WhitePapers/Default.aspx?whitePaperID=43
6. Cayirci, E., Garaga, A., Santana de Oliveira, A., Roudier, Y.: A cloud adoption risk assessment model. utility and cloud computing (UCC). In: 2014 IEEE/ACM 7th International Conference, pp. 908–913 (2014)
7. Centre for Information Policy Leadership (CIPL): A Risk-based Approach to Privacy: Improving Effectiveness in Practice (2014). http://www.hunton.com/files/upload/Post-Paris_Risk_Paper_June_2014.pdf
8. Clarke, R.: Privacy impact assessment: its origins and development. Comput. Law Secur. Rev. **25**(2), 123–135 (2009)
9. Cloud Security Alliance (CSA): Security guidance for critical areas of focus in cloud computing, v3.0 (2011). http://www.cloudsecurityalliance.org/guidance/
10. Cloud Security Alliance (CSA): The notorious nine: Cloud computing top threats in 2013, v.1.0 (2013). http://cloudsecurityalliance.org/research/top-threats/
11. Commission Nationale de L'informatique et des Libertés (CNIL): Recommendations for Companies Planning to Use Cloud Computing Services (2012). http://www.cnil.fr/fileadmin/documents/en/Recommendations_for_companies_planning_to_use_Cloud_computing_services.pdf
12. Commission Nationale de L'informatique et des Libertés (CNIL): Methodology for Privacy Risk Management (2012)
13. COM 11 final 2012/0011 (COD) European Commission: Proposal for a Regulation of the European Parliament and of the Council on the protection of individuals with regard to the processing of personal data and on the free movement of such data (General Data Protection Regulation). Brussels, 25.1.2012 p. 1. (2012)
14. Directive 95/46/EC of the European Parliament and of the Council of 24 October 1995 on the protection of individuals with regard to the processing of personal data and on the free movement of such data OJ L281/31 (DPD) (1995)
15. De Hert, P.: A human rights perspective on privacy and data protection impact assessment. In: Wright, D., De Hert, P. (eds.) Privacy Impact Assessment. Law, Governance and Technology Series, vol. 6, pp. 33–76. Springer, Netherlands (2012)

16. European Union Agency for Network and Information Security - European Network and Information Security Agency. Cloud Computing - Benefits, risks and recommendations for information security (2009)
17. European Network and Information Security Agency: Cloud Security Incident Reporting: Framework for reporting about major cloud security incidents, ENISA (2013)
18. Felici, M., Pearson, S.: Accountability, risk, and trust in cloud services: towards an accountability-based approach to risk and trust governance. In: IEEE Proceedings of SERVICES, pp. 105–112 (2014)
19. Garaga, A., Santana de Oliveira, A., Cayirci, E., Dalla Corte, L., Leenes, R., Mhungu, R., Stefanatou, D., Tetrimida, K., Alnemr, R., Felici, M., Pearson, S., Vranaki, A.: D:C-6.2 Prototype for the data protection impact assessment tool. A4Cloud Deliverable D36.2 (2014). http://www.a4cloud.eu/sites/default/files/D36.2%20Prototype%20for%20the% 20data%20protection%20impact%20assessment%20tool.pdf
20. Harbird, R., Ahmed, M., Finkelstein, A., McKinney, E., Burroughs, A.: Privacy Impact Assessment with PRAIS (2007). http://www.cs.ucl.ac.uk/staff/A.Finkelstein/papers/hotpets. pdf
21. Hall, M. et al.: The WEKA Data Mining Software: An Update; SIGKDD Explorations, vol. 11, no. (2009)
22. Information Commissioner's Office: Privacy Impact Assessment Handbook (2011). http:// ico.org.uk/pia_handbook_html_v2/files/PIAhandbookV2.pdf
23. Information Commissioner's Office: Conducting privacy impact assessments code of practice (2014). https://ico.org.uk/media/for-organisations/documents/1595/pia-code-of-practice.pdf
24. Information Commissioner's Office: Guidance for Companies on the Use of Cloud Computing, v1.1 (2012). http://ico.org.uk/for_organisations/data_protection/topic_guides/ online/cloud_computing
25. Mell, P., Grance, T.: The NIST Definition of Cloud Computing. NIST Special Publication 800, Washington (2011)
26. Millard, C.J. (ed.): Cloud Computing Law. Oxford University Press, Oxford (2013)
27. National Institute of Standards and Technology NIST: Guidelines on Security and Privacy in Public Cloud Computing, SP 800-144 (2011). http://csrc.nist.gov/publications/nistpubs/800-144/SP800-144.pdf
28. NOREA: Privacy Impact Assessment: Introductie, handreiking en vragenlijst. beroepsorganisatie van IT-auditors (2013). http://www.norea.nl/readfile.aspx?ContentID= 36650&ObjectID=343968&Type=1&File=0000040117_NOREA%20A4%20Privacy% 20Impact%20Assessment%2003%20WEB.pdf
29. Organisation for Economic Co-operation and Development OECD: Guidelines Concerning the Protection of Privacy and Transborder Flows of Personal Data (2013). http://www.oecd. org/sti/ieconomy/2013-oecd-privacy-guidelines.pdf
30. Office of the Privacy Commissioner of Canada: Securing Personal Information: A Self-Assessment Tool for Organisations (2011). http://www.priv.gc.ca/resource/tool-outil/ security-securite/english/AssessRisks.asp?x=1
31. Pearson, S: Simple Mode: Addressing Knowledge Engineering Complexity in a Privacy Expert System, HP Labs External Technical Report, HPL-2010-75, June (2010). http:// www.hpl.hp.com/techreports/2010/HPL-2010-75.html
32. Pearson, S., Sander, T.: A decision support system for privacy compliance. In: Data Mining: Concepts, Methodologies, Tools, and Applications, pp. 1496–1518. Information Science Reference, Hershey (2013). doi:10.4018/978-1-4666-2455-9.ch078

33. Pearson, S., Rao, P., Sander, T., Parry, A., Paull, A., Patruni, S., Dandamudi-Ratnakar, V., Sharma, P.: Scalable, accountable privacy management for large organizations. In: Enterprise Distributed Object Computing Conference Workshops, EDOCW 2009, vol. 13, pp. 168–175 (2009)

34. Sander, T., Pearson, S.: Decision support for selection of cloud service providers. Int. J. Comput. (JoC) GTSF 1(1), 106–113 (2010)

35. SEC 72 final, Commission Staff Working Paper: Impact Assessment Accompanying the document Regulation of the European Parliament and of the Council on the protection of individuals with regard to the processing of personal data and on the free movement of such data (General Data Protection Regulation) and Directive of the European Parliament and of the Council on the protection of individuals with regard to the processing of personal data by competent authorities for the purposes of prevention, investigation, detection or prosecution of criminal offences or the execution of criminal penalties, and the free movement of such data. Brussels, 25.1.2012, p. 81 (2012). http://ec.europa.eu/justice/data-protection/document/review2012/sec_2012_72_en.pdf

36. Svantesson, D., Clarke, R.: Privacy and consumer risks in cloud computing. Comput. Law Secur. Rev. 26(4), 392 (2010)

37. Solove, D.J.: A taxonomy of privacy. Univ. PA Law Rev. 154, 477 (2006)

38. Tancock, D., Pearson S., Charlesworth. A.: The emergence of privacy impact assessments (2010). http://www.hpl.hp.com/techreports/2010/HPL-2010-63.pdf

39. Tancock, D., Pearson, S., Charlesworth, A.: Analysis of privacy impact assessments within major jurisdictions. In: Proceedings of PST 2010, pp. 118–125. IEEE, Ottawa (2010)

40. Tancock, D., Pearson, S., Charlesworth, A.: A privacy impact assessment tool for cloud computing. In: Pearson, S., Yee, G. (eds.) Privacy and Security for Cloud Computing. Computer Communications and Networks, pp. 73–123. Springer, London (2013)

41. Truste: TRUSTe Assessment Manager. https://www.truste.com/resources?doc=516

42. United States Department of Homeland Security: Privacy Threshold Analysis (PTA) (2007). http://www.dhs.gov/xlibrary/assets/privacy/DHS_PTA_Template.pdf

43. Wright, D.: The state of the art in privacy impact assessment. Comput. Law Secur. Rev. 28 (1), 54–61 (2012)

44. Wright, D., De Hert, P.: Introduction to Privacy Impact Assessment. Springer, Netherlands (2012)

45. Wright D.: Should privacy impact assessments be mandatory? Commun. ACM, 54(8), pp. 121–131 (2012)

# Building Blocks and Fundamental
# Privacy Principles

# Courteous Sensors - Rules and Methodology

Wernher Behrendt[(✉)]

Salzburg Research, Salzburg, Austria
wernher.behrendt@salzburgresearch.at

**Abstract.** We posit that sensors of the emerging Internet of Things (IoT) should behave courteously. This means that the sensor makes itself known to a subject, that it stops sensing upon request, that it respects the subject as originator of the data and that it negotiates further use of the subject's data before activating such further use. We state and justify the four fundamental rules for sensor behaviour and outline a methodology for responsible design of sensor-based information systems.

## 1 The Internet of Sensing Things

A year 2020 scenario is that many spaces utilized by humans will be sensorized in a variety of ways. Think of a typical modern hotel: smoke detectors will not only detect smoke but may have inbuilt cameras. Walls and hallways will have pressure sensors that are able to identify the walking pattern of the guest in room 2411 and will then know where guest 2411 is moving, throughout his stay.

Our approach to the imminent, artificial sensorization of the environment is to assume that sensors are extensions of human sensory means and that each sensor has an owner who is responsible for that sensor and for the information gleaned from the sensor.

The paper presents on the one hand, a proposed methodology for designing sensor-based information systems with privacy enhancing technologies, and it is on the other hand, an opinion paper because it presupposes that privacy is closely related to human rights and that taking away privacy is an assault on human rights. Others may think that privacy is a commodity that people can buy if they so wish.

## 2 Governance of Information Disclosure

Humans tend to have a finely balanced approach to information disclosure. They are cautious about sharing very personal information and they have certain views on what is right or wrong with somebody else's dealing with information disclosure. What has changed over the past 20 years is that much of our life is copied into cyberspace and there, the governance of informaton disclosure is fundamentally different: information about human activity is actively collected, value-added and made a traded commercial good. As a result, humans need no longer worry about what their neighbours know or think, but rather, what unknown commercial companies know and what automated conclusions they draw from the data that they collected.

© Springer International Publishing Switzerland 2016
B. Berendt et al. (Eds.): APF 2015, LNCS 9484, pp. 95–103, 2016.
DOI: 10.1007/978-3-319-31456-3_5

## 2.1 Psychological Predispositions for Information Disclosure

Borcea-Pfitzmann [1] points out three psychological predispositions of humans when dealing with personal information:

1. *Nondisclosure:* human beings tend to presume that other human beings do not disclose information that is very personal.
2. *Natural process of oblivion:* human beings gradually forget or lose track of information that they did not use for some time.
3. *Conscience:* human beings are able to distinguish right from wrong and factor this into their interactions with other human beings.

## 2.2 Inverse Privacy

Gurevich et al. [2] introduced a very useful concept into the privacy discussion: they define inverse privacy as the items of information that others (organisations, in particular) have about you, but you don't know what they know about you. The authors suggest that the main problem of the current privacy discussion is the immense scale at which inverse privacy has grown in recent years. To explain their concept in more detail, they define first, the infoset P about a person. This info set is split into four buckets:

1. *Directly private* - information that only P has about himseif.
2. *Inversely private* - information that X has the information about P but P does not have that information.
3. *Partially private* - information that P has and a limited number of other parties, as well.
4. *Public* - information about P that is generally available.

Gurevich et al. rightly identify the problem of the vastly growing, inversely private information but fall short of remedies. Their proposal of institutions sharing back information - thus making it partially private - accepts that the information was taken "from the people" in the first place. Our position is that taking information first and giving some of it back, later, is not at all courteous.

## 3    The Four Rules of Courteous Sensing

Note that in principle, the notion of sensing applies to any gathering of information about others. For the purpose of this paper, we apply it just to "real" sensors that we can expect to be deployed in large numbers practically everywhere, in the near future. So what we propose for such physical sensors could also be applied to browser "cookies" that improve so much, our Web-browsing experience - as every website tells us.

## 3.1   Rule 1: Thou Shalt Signal a Sensor's Presence

According to our psychological predisposition, we are used to believing that we are not being observed when we are alone in some room and when there is no human in sight. Except for very paranoid people, we tend not to check under the bed or behind mirrors, whether somebody is there, watching us.

In the case of shared spaces where one party has not yet noticed the other party, it is most common behaviour to somehow make one's presence known to the other party. This seems to be due to a natural drive for symmetry in inter-personal relationships. You may want to play this Gedankenexperiment in a crowded restaurant: are you normally recording people's faces? Are you staring at them? Are you trying to hide in a place where you can see all others, but they cannot see you? We normally do not hide in places to observe others.

Hidden sensors do to physical spaces what "cookies" do to our web spaces: the cookies "observe" us by storing information about visited pages and making this information available to the web site owner and - very often - also to third party analytical tools. Whereas in the web space we have already lost our privacy, we still have a little time to go before the same situation will arrive in physical spaces. In the *old virtual* world, we used to have a choice of reducing our engagement with that world if we were unhappy about the level of observation. Once *physical* spaces are getting virtualised, observed and recorded by similar mechanisms as we have got used to in the web-space then there is literally no space left anymore, for disengaging.

When humans share a space then they signal their presence, mutually. Since the sensor is the extended sensory device of somebody who has an interest in that shared space, let us oblige that other party to signal its presence.

**Technical Implementation of Presence Signalling for Sensors.** Classical security cameras (CCTV) have no active signalling capacity, but usually make their presence known by readable signs and icons that a specific area is under surveillance. Future sensor systems will be much more varied, including cameras, pressure sensors, or card readers. We can distinguish two types of technology: identity recognizers and (human) presence detectors. Note that with this distinction, the classical CCTV is more a presence detector than an identity recognizer, whereas the aforementioned set of pressure sensors for walking patterns is an identity recognizer, just like cameras that are connected to a face recognition system. The simplest form of presence signalling would be to tell people in iconic language which kinds of presence detection devices and identity recognition devices are covering the space in which the person is moving right now. That same iconic language could be used by sensors to transmit their presence electronically to people's smartphones and other electronic devices.

## 3.2   Rule 2: Thou Shalt Be Able to Switch the Sensor Off

Scene 1: Two people talk in the coffee room about a private matter. A third person enters and the two people will change topic or perhaps engage the third person in a topic of mutual interest. Scene 2: Two people enter a meeting room for some negotiation and a colleague is still sitting there, finishing his notes from the previous meeting. One of the two people entering informs the person that they are having a confidential meeting and the previous occupant packs his things and leaves the room. Scene 3: Two people are entering the meeting room talking about some non-confidential matter. They do not mind a third person sitting there listening in on the conversation. The third person will most likely not be interested, either and will soon have forgotten what the conversation was about.

The important issue in these three scenes is the behaviour of the parties involved, and of the third person, in particular. In the first scene, the conversation stops and moves to a mutually acceptable new situation, triggered by the presence of the third party. In the second scene, when the third party receives a signal that the others wish to make this a private space, the third party leaves that space out of courtesy, at the latest upon a specific request. In the third scene, the three parties signal to each other that they do not mind occupying the same space for their respective conversations. The third party in these scenes can now be replaced by one or more sensors, and we would expect the same rules of courtesy to apply.

Since a sensor is the extended sensory device of a third party, this third party should be obliged to remove that device upon request, from the shared space!

**Technical Implementation of an Off-Switch for Sensors.** We expect sensors to react accordingly, to a "mute" signal which we may send out, using a technical device. Such a device may either be a smart phone or a simple "do not track" (DNT) emitter. For the state of affairs in implementing DNT, https://en. wikipedia.org/wiki/Do_Not_Track is illuminating: the proposed standard exists and there are technical implementations, but they are by and large ignored. If and when the law gets teeth for this matter, then its implementation could be technically challenging: suppose subjects A and B are in a sensor's range. subject A has enabled "DNT" whereas subject B is willing to be sensed. How many subjects will the sensor report? One or two? Under what circumstances is "one" the correct answer? What if there is a fire and only one person (B) is being reported as in danger? To summarize: it should be a human right for free citizens to switch unwanted sensory detection off. Denying a "switch off" request would then require an active denial signal from the sensor ("I am sorry, but I am owned by Metropolitan Police and my continuous detection activity is backed by law"). A common criticism against this type of requirement is that it would make sensing very expensive. The position of this author is that the sensing of unconvicted, presumed innocent citizens should indeed remain very expensive, as any form of surveillance should.

### 3.3   Rule 3: Thou Shalt Respect That My Data Is My Body

In the physical world, we all have bodies, we obey the rules of physics and we are normally aware of the causal relationships between our behaviour and that world.

Think of running into a tree. In the virtual world, there are no physical trees, but we all have "bodies" made of data. Every link we click is a walk down some avenue and our browsers and smartphone apps are the recorders of those walks. In fact, many smartphone apps record our steps in the physical world too, without ever asking whether we want that. If in the physical world, somebody wants to know who you are and why you are walking down this road, they have to ask you. And you are free to ignore the request, you even have the right to be left alone and not being asked. Only under very specific circumstances are police or the public allowed to interfere with your free movement. These strong rights go back 800 years when the gentry demanded better securities in view of the feudal system that left their well-being at the mercy of the monarchs. Now replace gentry with modern citizen and replace monarch with Apple or Google and replace body with "data about me". If the reader is willing to accept the analogy then he or she will see the relationship with the Magna Carta of 1215: Article 39 of the Magna Carta (1215) states https://en.wikipedia.org/wiki/Law_of_the_land:

*"No freeman shall be taken or imprisoned or disseised or exiled or in any way destroyed, nor will we go upon him nor will we send upon him except upon the lawful judgement of his peers or the law of the land."*

It is our contention that inverse privacy constitutes the equivalent of a "freeman being taken" in cyberspace. What else is there in cyberspace, except my data? So if that data is collected without my notice and stored somewhere in an aggregation that I do not know of, then my cyberbody has been imprisoned without reason. A sensor taking measurements of my body, locating these measurements in the real world and referencing them with some time interval is making a copy of my cyberbody and is imprisoning that copy until it gets deleted. Deletion of personal data is giving back freedom in Cyberspace, whereas keeping a copy is maintaining data body imprisonment. This may sound extreme but imagine that 20 years from now, my purchase history of good wines could be used by the Radical Anti-Alcoholics Church to convict me of crimes against the Holy Soberness and punish me to one whip for every bottle purchased as proved by the supermarket's customer data.

There are of course in 2015, many aspects that the Magna Carta did not foresee, e.g. that my data body is separated from my physical body and that my data body is a distributed set of data, with many overlaps and inconsistencies. It should also be noted that the Magna Carta itself was a pragmatic succession of document rewrites establishing minimal respect between rulers and the next level in the feudal hierarchy (see e.g. [3]). So we only want to point out that human rights have been the result of struggles between those in power and those with less power.

For those who do not wish to follow the Magna Carta analogy, we can offer the "My Life is a Piece of Art" analogy: If you concede that each individual life is a piece of art then any data my life produces is part of that piece of art and cannot be copied without infringing my copyright.

**Technical Implementation of the Virtual Magna Carta.** This requires a paradigmatic change otherwise known as a revolution. As Bruce Schneier puts it (https://www.schneier.com/news/archives/2014/04/surveillance_is_the.html): *Surveillance is the business model of the Internet.* Cloud computing, media platforms, electronic commerce platforms are the Monarchs and we, the citizens have not asked for our rights back, yet.

Technical directions for such a revolution could be *data banking* where we can choose between conservative investments (storing data long-term) or quick profits (giving very private data away for a good price). Alternatively, we could opt for the strict *life is a piece of art* approach where all data is managed by the individual and where we will have to learn how to deal with our data. This will be a new cultural skill like reading and writing. Most citizens are at present illiterate in this respect and most Monarchs want to keep it that way.

### 3.4   Rule 4: Thou Shalt Be Courteous in Requesting Data Shares

This fourth rule is a consequence of the third rule, but it is worth spelling out. Since my data is my body and since you are only allowed to make copies of myself if I have given you the right to do so, any copying of representations of my data body requires my agreement. If you request to keep some data, then explain what the data will be used for, and give the reason for keeping it, as well as the time frame. Also, do not proliferate my data body! Note that the latter is the default in most big data consumer analytics. If big data is the new crude oil, then I am the Sheik and I want money for you putting oil rigs on my land!

**Technical Implementation of Courtesy in Data Sharing.** Since this rule is not strictly independent of the third rule and thus, could perhaps be subsumed in the third, the technical directions could be similar. One first step would be to require data collectors and aggregators to answer any request of citizens as to what data is stored about them - this is Gurevich's inverse privacy argument. The cost of answering must strictly remain with the data collector. We are well aware that the use of many "free" applications is bound to license agreements that by and large state: "you pay with your data". This form of licensing needs to be outlawed until we have a better understanding of the real value of data. The abovementioned data banking approach might be a way of achieving at least a better deal for the customer/citzen.

## 4   Outline Methodology for Responsible Design of Sensor-Based Information Systems

For our outline methodology we consider three sources:

1. Cavoukian - Privacy by Design [4]
2. Jackson - Problem Frames [5]
3. Borcea-Pfitzmann - Privacy 3.0 [1]

## 4.1  Privacy by Design

In 2009, Ann Cavoukian, The former Information and Privacy Commissioner
for the Canadian province of Ontario published a summary of her work dealing
with Privacy by Design, a set of seven guidelines for IT systems that deal with
personal data [4]. The seven principles are:

1. Proactive and Preventative - catch privacy invasive events before they happen.
2. Privacy as the Default Setting - No action is required on the part of the
   individual to protect their privacy it is built into the system, by default.
3. Privacy Embedded into Design - Privacy is integral to the system, without
   diminishing functionality.
4. Positive-Sum, not Zero-Sum - accommodate all legitimate interests and objectives in a positive-sum win-win manner.
5. Full Lifecycle Protection - secure lifecycle management of information, end-
   to-end.
6. Visibility and Transparency assure all stakeholders that Information Systems
   are operating according to the stated promises and objectives, subject to
   independent verification.
7. Repect for User Privacy by Design requires architects and operators to keep
   the interests of the individual uppermost.

Principle 1 stipulates that a sensor should by default be switched off. If switching
off defeats the object then the least invasive sensor should be the first to switch
on. Principle 2 could be interpreted very strictly, saying that by default, sensors
are always off and get switched on either because I wish this, or because there is
some other legitimate interest (Principle 5) that takes precedence over my wish.
This brings us to the next issue: how can we determine the "legitimate interests
and objectives" of the stakeholders?

## 4.2  Context Diagrams

M. Jackson devised a structuring method for software development problems
called "Problem Frames" [5]. He describes the context diagram as a means of
bounding the problem space of an IT solution (pp. 24–25): *"The context diagram
locates the problem within quite an exact boundary. If you leave something out
of the context diagram, you are leaving it out of the problem - deciding that it
will play no part in your work. You will never consider it, so it won't affect
the outcome. If you include something, you are undertaking to give it serious
attention and effort. So it's important to think carefully about the diagram and
to question the decisions it expresses"*.

This means for the design of sensor based information systems that we always
need to have the observed subject ("target") in our context diagram, as well as
the third party who is responsible for the sensors that are doing the observations.

### 4.3   Contextual Integrity

Borcea-Pfitzmann et al. [1] introduce the previously mentioned human predisposition for information disclosure and then discuss three approaches to privacy: (a) the principle of data minimisation established in the 1980s which fails to account for the phenomena of social networks. (b) the notion of user control of data disclosure starting in the late 1990s but also reaching its limits in a ubiquitously connected mobile data world. They therefore propose the notion of *contextual integrity* and hope to support users in controlled data disclosure by always giving a situational frame for which that data is valid. We suggest that this approach poses too much burden on the observed subject (who is incidentally, not really a "user"). We therefore favour the perspective of "courteous sensors" to lay the burden again on those who do the observing, as the causators of any data dilemmas we may have.

## 5   Conclusions and Further Work

Our work addresses the question how future information systems can be developed with a "Privacy by Design" approach and it gives justifications put forward elsewhere in the literature, why privacy considerations are strongly linked to basic human rights. By implication, protagonists of the "you have no privacy" dictum have to answer what their interests are, in weakening human rights.

We have proposed four rules of courteous behaviour of sensors, taking the view that every sensor has some legal entity responsible for its workings and for the information that it produces. It is the responsibility of the owner to guarantee such courteous behaviour of its sensors.

In many real-life cases, there is a multitude of interests at stake and even ownership of sensors may be shared and may have inconsistent sets of interests associated. We proposed Jackson's context diagram as a mechanism for analysing stakeholder interests.

### 5.1   How Much Intelligence Does One Need for Courtesy?

One specific issue is and will be that individual sensors may not have the processing power and inference capability ("intelligence") to behave courteously. Let that be no excuse, particularly not for technologists! We envisage motes (processing nodes close to the edge of the IoT) to have sufficient reasoning capability for acting courteously, on behalf of a group of "dumb" sensors. Work needs to be invested to ensure that these processing agents embody compliance regulations set out by privacy regulators. The argument that "this cannot be done" is like arguing that running over pedestrians must be accepted because we don't know how to build brakes into our cars. If you can build a sensor that senses then you can build a switch to switch it off. If you cannot build courteous sensor systems then why should anyone agree to having them installed anywhere?

## 5.2    Symmetry, Balance and Equality

There is a huge asymmetry developing, which Gurevich rightly named as "inverse privacy". We contend that any asymmetry creates imbalance and in society, imbalance creates inequality and injustice. Therefore, asymmetry and imbalance are problematic. Inequality is definitely not desirable and injustice is not acceptable. Taking this further, the "bending" of judicial systems to perpetuate or increase asymmetry is a threat to society. Important research questions manifest themselves *beyond* the question "how can we detect feature X in the set of all data streams?". One of these questions beyond is "how do we develop an Internet of Things that keeps symmetry, that lets consumers learn as much about marketing strategies as companies learn about consumer behaviour?" Another question is "how do we ensure that the Internet of Things does not become the instrument of choice for a modern form of fascism?" Will the implanted chip increase security or just help to distinguish the "chosen ones" from the "rest of mankind"? Our proposal is to give equal instruments to the "chosen ones" and the "rest of mankind".

# References

1. Borcea-Pfitzmann, K., Pfitzmann, A., Berg, M.: Privacy 3.0 := data minimization + user control + contextual integrity. it - Inf. Technol. **53**, 34–40 (2011)
2. Gurevich, Y., Hudis, E., Wing, J.: Inverse privacy, Technical report. MSR-TR-2014-100, July 2014
3. Linebaugh, P.: The Magna Carta Manifesto : The Struggle to Reclaim Liberties and Commons for All. University of California Press, Berkeley (2008)
4. Cavoukian, A.: Privacy by design - the 7 foundational principles (2009). https://www.privacybydesign.ca/content/uploads/2009/08/7foundationalprinciples.pdf
5. Jackson, M.: Problem Frames: Analysing and Structuring Software Development Problems. Pearson Education, Harlow (2001)

# Privacy-ABCs as a Case for Studying the Adoption of PETs by Users and Service Providers

Ioannis Krontiris[3]($\boxtimes$), Zinaida Benenson[1], Anna Girard[1], Ahmad Sabouri[2], Kai Rannenberg[2], and Peter Schoo[3]

[1] Friedrich-Alexander-University Erlangen-Nuremberg, Erlangen, Germany
zinaida.benenson@cs.fau.de, anna_girard@hotmail.de
[2] Goethe University Frankfurt, Frankfurt, Germany
{ahmad.sabouri,kai.rannenberg}@m-chair.de
[3] European Research Center, Huawei Technologies, Munich, Germany
{ioannis.krontiris,peter.schoo}@huawei.com

**Abstract.** Although in the last years there has been a growing amount of research in the field of privacy-enhancing technologies (PETs), they are not yet widely adopted in practice. In this paper we discuss the socioeconomical aspects of how users and service providers make decisions about adopting PETs. The analysis is based on our experiences from the deployment of Privacy-respecting Attribute-based Credentials (Privacy-ABCs) in a real-world scenario. In particular, we consider the factors that affect the adoption of Privacy-ABCs as well as the cost and benefit trade-offs involved in their deployment and usage, as perceived by both parties.

## 1   Introduction

Safeguarding privacy is vital for building trust in the online environment and facilitating economic development. It is important to show to citizens that going online is not just convenient, but also trustworthy and that their data won't be mismanaged or misused, sold or stolen. To strengthen trustworthiness in the online environment in a practical and effective way, "privacy by design" is becoming an essential principle, meaning that data protection safeguards should be built into products and services from the earliest stage of development.

One way of realizing privacy by design is by using Privacy-Enhancing Technologies (PETs). During the last years, there is a growing amount of research in the field of PETs enabled by major advances in cryptography. They provide advanced privacy features such as anonymous protection of real-time communication, privacy-respecting identity management and methods for anonymously retrieving online content.

Yet, PETs are not widely adopted in practice so far [16]. One cannot expect a simple explanation to this, as online privacy is a complex and interdisciplinary issue. Several of the technical aspects have been addressed at a satisfactory

B. Berendt et al. (Eds.): APF 2015, LNCS 9484, pp. 104–123, 2016.
DOI: 10.1007/978-3-319-31456-3_6

degree, but there are still several socioeconomical aspects of PETs adoption that only now begin to draw attention. In this paper we discuss in particular the cost-benefit trade-offs involved in adopting such technologies, as perceived by both users and service providers.

In 2010, the European Commission sponsored a study of the economic costs and benefits of PETs [15], which shows clearly that costs and benefits are technology specific as well as dependent on the applications in which PETs are deployed. Therefore, in this paper we narrow down the discussion by focusing on a specific PET and on a particular application scenario. More specifically, during the last four years, the EU-funded research project ABC4Trust[1] concentrated on the advancement of Privacy-respecting Attribute-based Credentials (Privacy-ABCs) and its applicability in real-world scenarios. In this paper we report our experiences from working within this project and especially our analysis from one of the user trials.

In the first part of the paper we explore the adoption of Privacy-ABCs from the users' side. Which factors influence their intention to use such tools and how do they perceive the trade-off between benefits and costs connected with the usage? User acceptance of advanced PETs had rarely been studied outside the laboratory, and so we are one of the first to present such results. In the second part of the paper we discuss the factors that might affect the adoption of Privacy-ABCs by service providers. In deciding whether to invest in PETs, service providers engage in a cost-benefit trade-off involving many factors related not only to internal processes and business models but also to the external environment, such as legislation, user demand or global infrastructure readiness.

## 2   The Privacy-ABCs Case

Providing privacy in the identity management area means moving towards a claims-based architecture [9]. In this kind of architecture, the service provider publishes a *Policy* on accessing a specific resource and expects to receive claims from trusted sources that satisfy this policy. The trusted sources that issue such security tokens are the identity service providers (IdSP), sometimes also called identity providers for simplicity. An important characteristic of claims-based architecture is the separation between service providers and IdSPs, so that there is no direct exchange of information between them. Instead, the user resides in the middle, having control over the exchange of his identity information.

Claims-based architectures can use privacy-respecting credential systems (i.e., Privacy-ABCs) to provide untraceability and minimal disclosure. Examples of such credential systems are Idemix [8] and U-Prove [7]. Over the last few years, Idemix and U-Prove have been developed to offer an extended set of features, even though these features are named differently and they are realized based on different cryptographic mechanisms. In 2010, the EU research project ABC4Trust was initiated with the goal to alleviate these differences and unify

---

[1] https://abc4trust.eu/.

the abstract concepts and features of such mechanisms. Privacy-ABCs are privacy respecting credentials that are defined over these concepts and features and are independent from the specific cryptographic realization beneath.

One of the main achievements of ABC4Trust project was to test Privacy-ABCs in real-world situations within the scope of two large-scale user trials. This gave us valuable experiences regarding the interaction of users and system designers with the technology. More specifically, one of the user trials was conducted at Patras University in Greece, the results of which we present here.

The main goal of the user trial in Patras was to enable university students to login onto an online evaluation system at the end of the semester and evaluate the courses they attended, remaining anonymous to the system. At the same time, the system had to guarantee that only eligible students have access to the evaluation of a course. That is, the system had to first verify that a student (1) had registered to the course and (2) had attended most of its lectures.

To be able to prove the they satisfy the above conditions, students collected Privacy-ABCs and stored them in smartcards that they had been provided with. Specifically, they collected two credentials from the university, one for being enrolled as students at the institution and one for being registered for the specific course. During the semester, they obtained an attendance unit (implemented as increasing a counter value) per lecture by waving their smartcard in front of a contactless reader at the end of the lecture.

At the end of the semester, the students could use their smartcards to login anonymously at an online Course Evaluation System (CES) and fill the course evaluation form. During the authentication process, the students were first presented with the Policy of the CES at the user interface. Then they could select different attributes from their credentials and produce a presentation token corresponding to this policy and in that way authenticate to the CES, revealing only the minimum required information.

Privacy-ABCs are an attractive solution for the course evaluation scenario, prividing advantages for students as well as for the lecturers. On the one hand, students don't reveal their identity to the CES, but present themselves under a random pseudonym. Moreover, the CES cannot link the evaluations of two different courses back to the same student. On the other hand, privacy-ABCs assure that only students that actually attended a specified amount of lectures are able to evaluate the course. Students can evaluate each course only once and when they do so a second time, the new evaluation replaces the old one.

## 3    User Acceptance of Privacy-ABCs in a University Course Evaluation

The user trial in Patras gave us a unique opportunity to study the reactions of users while they interacted with the Privacy-ABC technology and get an empirical understanding of the factors that influence user acceptance of Privacy-ABCs. Below we present our findings and discuss lessons learned from the trial about the trade-offs between the benefits of Privacy-ABCs and the costs perceived by the users. More details on the trial organization can be found in the full report of the trial [29], whereas for the more specific details of the theoretical development and validation methodology we refer the interested reader to [4].

## 3.1 Theoretical Background and Methodology

**Theoretical User Acceptance Factors for Privacy-ABCs.** In order to investigate user acceptance factors of Privacy-ABCs, we first developed a theoretical model for possible acceptance factors, drawing from related work on general technology acceptance [10,24,34], as well as acceptance of security- and privacy-related technologies [18,28,30]. We identified possible user acceptance factors that are presented in Table 1 and will be explained below in more detail.

**Table 1.** Factors of user acceptance of Privacy-ABCs and their correlations to the intention to use Privacy-ABCs for course evaluations. $m$ denotes the mean values for the corresponding scales, $\sigma$ denotes standard deviations. For details on the measurement results, see Fig. 1. Correlation results are discussed in depth in Sect. 3.2.

| Factor (psychometric scale) | Definition in the context of the Patras Privacy-ABCs trial | $m$ | $\sigma$ | Kendall's $\tau$ |
|---|---|---|---|---|
| Perceived Usefulness for the Primary Task | The degree of agreement that Privacy-ABCs are useful for course evaluation | 4.10 | 0.66 | 0.726** |
| Perceived Usefulness for the Secondary Task | The degree of agreement that Privacy-ABCs are useful for privacy protection | 3.93 | 0.74 | 0.420** |
| Perceived Ease of Use | The degree of agreement Privacy-ABCs usage is free of effort | 3.83 | 0.65 | 0.498** |
| Perceived Risk | The degree of agreement that course evaluation using Privacy-ABCs is risky | 1.80 | 0.99 | −0.444** |
| Trust | The degree to which the Privacy-ABC System is perceived to be trustworthy | 4.13 | 0.73 | 0.326* |
| Situation Awareness | The perception of being well informed about what is going on in the system | 3.87 | 0.63 | 0.319* |
| Understanding of the Technology | The ability to correctly answer questions about the key aspects of Privacy-ABCs | 0.51 | 0.45 | 0.065 |

Significance levels: * $p < 0.05$;  ** $p < 0.01$
Correlation strength: $0.1 < \tau \le 0.3$ weak, $0.3 < \tau \le 0.5$ moderate, $\tau > 0.5$ strong

Considering the general technology acceptance, the most influential theoretical model is *Technology Acceptance Model (TAM)* [10,32,33], that has been later extended to the *Unified Theory of Acceptance and Use of Technology (UTAUT)*. Although UTAUT [34] and its recent extension UTAUT2 [35] are more successful models than TAM in predicting technology acceptance, we identified TAM as being more suitable in the context of the Privacy-ABC trial (see Appendix A for an in-depth discussion). In a nutshell, as we knew the demographic characteristics of our participants in advance, we could predict from the existing literature and from out previous experience with Privacy-ABCs [5] that testing additional UTAUT and UTAUT2 factors would not be possible and would only overload the (already very substantial) questionnaire.

TAM considers *Perceived Ease of Use* and *Perceived Usefulness* of a technology as main factors in user acceptance, while user acceptance is conceptualized as intention to use the technology in the future. However, security- and privacy-enhancing technologies rarely serve *primary* user goals, such as communication or online shopping. They are expected to work in the background, protecting the user and thus facilitating the successful execution of the primary task. Therefore, we decided to distinguish between *Perceived Usefulness for the Primary Task* (i.e., the course evaluation) and *Perceived Usefulness for the Secondary Task* (i.e., the privacy protection during the course evaluation). *Perceived Ease of Use* did not need any special adaptation.

Security- and privacy-sensitive scenarios usually involve perceived risk and trust as factors of user participation. User's assets (such as data, money or reputation) can be put at risk, and the decision to participate in such a scenario involves risk assessment and depends on the trust in other parties and in the underlying technology. Pavlou [24] integrated trust and perceived risk into the TAM in the context of online shopping. Building on his work, we consider *Trust* into the Privacy-ABC technology and *Perceived Risk* of usage of the Privacy-ABC technology as important acceptance factors.

Trust is defined as "beliefs that a specific technology has the attributes necessary to perform as expected in a given situation in which negative consequences are possible" [21, p. 7]. We note that users' expectations from the technology in the context of the trial refer not only to privacy protection during the course evaluation, but also to other properties of the course evaluation system that is implemented using Privacy-ABCs, such as reliable collection of course attendance credentials or error-free storage and processing of the course evaluation results.

Spiekermann [28] investigates situation awareness as a possible factor that drives adoption of privacy-enhancing technologies for RFID. Building on her research, we consider this factor in our investigation as well. *Situation Awareness* is defined as "personal perception to be informed about what is going on" [28, p. 134]. In connection with Privacy-ABCs, Situation Awareness includes knowing which information will be disclosed in order to get a credential, who receives the data, which data is stored on the smart card, etc.

Usually, people do not need to understand exactly how a technology works in order to be able to use it. Much more important than the exact understanding is the development of a *mental model* of the technology that enables correct usage.

Mental models are representations of reality in people's minds, their conceptions about how things work. As discovered by Wästlund et al. [36], correct mental models of Privacy-ABCs are especially difficult to convey.

Although expert technical knowledge might not play an important role in user acceptance, *misunderstanding* of some key concepts could result in poor adoption. For example, Sun et al. [30] discovered that some users think that their login credentials are given to every participating party when they use single sign-on, which lead to (wrongly) perceived additional insecurity, and thus to unwillingness to use the technology. Therefore, we investigate *Understanding of the Technology* as a possible factor of user acceptance.

**Methodology for Validation of User Acceptance Factors.** In order to assess the relative importance of the user acceptance factors, we developed a quantitative standardized questionnaire that the participants filled in shortly after the course evaluation deadline. In this way, they were able to assess all available functions of the Privacy-ABC System, such as credentials collection, backup of the smartcard data and course evaluation.

We developed Likert scales [14] for all constructs presented in Table 1, apart from *Understanding of the Technology* that was assessed by means of a knowledge quiz. Each scale consists of several statements, called items. The users rated the items from 1 = "strongly disagree" to 5 = "strongly agree". The scales are presented in Appendix B. All developed multi-item scales fulfill the following quality criteria: one-dimensionality (Kaiser-Meyer-Olkin criterion > 0.5, total variance explained > 50 %) and reliability (Cronbach's $\alpha$ > 0.7) [14]. More details on scale construction and quality criteria are presented in [4].

**Participants.** 30 out of 45 participants of the Patras trial answered our questionnaire and so all further analyses relate to the sample size of 30 subjects (23 male, 7 female, 23 years old on average).

The participants are active Internet users: 25 participate in online social networks, 23 shop online, and 17 use online banking. 26 participants expressed a high or very high level of Internet privacy concerns ($m = 4.03$, $\sigma = 0.86$)[2] on a 5-point Likert scale developed by Dinev and Hart [12]. Most participants exhibit privacy-aware behavior: more than two thirds said that they at least sometimes delete cookies, clean browser history, use their browser in private mode and provide fake information when creating a web account. However, only three participants ever used a PET before (TOR in all cases).

Participation in course evaluations was reported as being important or very important by 21 participants, and 28 participants indicated that protection of anonymity during course evaluations is important (9) or very important (19) for them, with the remaining two participants reporting a neutral attitude.

---

[2] $m$ denotes mean value, $\sigma$ denotes standard deviation.

## 3.2   Results on User Acceptance Factors

**Descriptive Statistics.** The measurements for the user acceptance factors[3] are presented in Fig. 1. Overall, the Patras users found Privacy-ABCs useful, trustworthy, and usable. The positive evaluation results are mirrored by the high level of intention to use Privacy-ABCs for course evaluation in the future: 29 out of 30 users expressed this intention. Comparing the Privacy-ABC System with the paper-based course evaluation that is usually conducted at their university, 28 participants indicated that they prefer using a Privacy-ABCs-based system over a paper-based system.

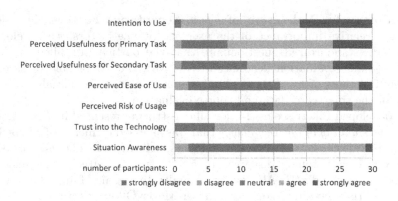

**Fig. 1.** Measurements of intention to use and acceptance factors.

Considering the results in more detail, more than two thirds of the users (22) perceived Privacy-ABCs to be useful for course evaluation (primary task), and 19 users found Privacy-ABCs to be useful for privacy protection (secondary task) as well. 14 participants found the system easy to use, with additional 14 participants expressing a neutral usability attitude. Participants expressed a low level of risk perception and a high level of trust into the system: cumulatively, 24 users (80 %) disagreed or strongly disagreed with the system usage being risky, and agreed or strongly agreed with the system being trustworthy. Finally, 12 users agreed that the Privacy-ABC system provides a good overview of what happens during the usage (Situation Awareness), with additional 16 users demonstrating a neutral attitude.

**Statistical Correlations.** In order to understand in more detail the relation between the acceptance factors and the intention to use Privacy-ABCs, we explored statistical correlations between the acceptance factors and the reported intention of the participants to use Privacy-ABCs for course evaluations in

---

[3] Understanding of the Technology factor will be discussed later in Sect. 3.3 for readability reasons.

the future. We conducted bivariate non-parametric two-tailed correlations using Kendall's correlation coefficient ($\tau$). This test does not require normal data distribution and works for ordinal data and small sample sizes. We report the results in Table 1. The correlation coefficient $\tau$ indicates the strength of the association between the variables, whereas the significance level $p < x$ means that the probability of the corresponding correlation to occur by chance is less than $x$.

Ease of Use, both kinds of Perceived Usefulness, Trust and Situation Awareness are significantly positively correlated to the intention to use Privacy-ABCs for the course evaluations, whereas Perceived Risk is significantly negatively correlated. The correlation coefficients are medium for all correlations except for Perceived Usefulness for Primary Task with the large effect size (0.726), which points at this factor as the most important one for user acceptance.

Quite surprisingly, there is no correlation between the understanding of Privacy-ABCs and the intention to use them, although we would have expected some connection. For example, people who understand the pseudonymization properties of Privacy-ABCs especially well might had felt more inclined to use them, or people who misunderstand some Privacy-ABCs' properties might had felt averse towards Privacy-ABCs usage. In the next section, we discuss the understanding of Privacy-ABCs in more details.

## 3.3 Understanding of Privacy-ABCs

The participants in the Patras trial have high technical literacy and were given an introductory lecture on the topic of Privacy-ABCs properties. Nevertheless, the understanding of fundamental properties of the system turned out to be unexpectedly low. We measured how well the participants understand the concepts behind the Privacy-ABCs by means of a knowledge index consisting of five statements that could be rated as true or false, with the "don't know" answer option also available. Due to space limitations, we discuss only the most important results here, more details are available in [4,29].

The participants expressed a low level of understanding of the pseudonymization property of Privacy-ABCs: Only 14 participants rightly stated that their matriculation number (a unique identifier) is not transmitted to the Course Evaluation System during the authentication process. Considering the weak understanding of Privacy-ABCs, the high level of perceived usefulness of Privacy-ABCs for privacy protection (Fig. 1) seems to be non-rational.

Even less participants (11) rightly indicated that the number of their class attendances (a potentially identifying and unnecessary piece of information) is not transmitted when they evaluate the course. Actually, only the fact that a student attended more than half of the course's lectures is disclosed to the system, which qualifies the student to evaluate this course.

These results indicate that users' perception to be well informed about what is happening in the system (Situation Awareness) and the overall high level of trsut into the system may be more important than the actual understanding of the system.

### 3.4  Cost-Benefit Trade-Offs in User Acceptance

From the economics point of view, user acceptance of a technology is tightly connected to a (sometimes unconscious) cost-benefit assessment of the technology [2,13]. We directly assessed the perceived cost-benefit relation by asking the users to rate their corresponding perception. 23 participants agreed or strongly agreed that the benefits outweigh the costs, additionally 6 participants showed a neutral attitude, and one participant disagreed.

The benefits of Privacy-ABCs can further be expressed in terms of their perceived usefulness. Most participants found the system useful for course evaluations as well as for privacy protection, as discussed previously.

The costs of the Privacy-ABCs in the Patras trial are mostly incurred by usability issues. According to users' ratings of the Perceived Ease of Use presented in Fig. 1, the usability costs were perceived as relatively low. Additionally, we also examined the usability costs in more detail. We asked the participants to rate statements about concrete usability characteristics of the system:

- *Mental effort:* Interaction with the Privacy-ABC system requires a lot of mental effort
- *Physical effort:* Interaction with the Privacy-ABC system takes too much time for manual operations (for example clicks, data input, handling the smart card)
- *Learnability effort:* Usage of the Privacy-ABC system is difficult to learn
- *Memorability effort:* Remembering how to interact with the Privacy-ABC system is difficult
- *Low helpfulness:* Help information provided by the the Privacy-ABC system is not effective
- *Error recovery effort:* Mistakes made during the Privacy-ABC system usage are difficult to correct
- *Worries about smartcard loss:* Users' anxiety about the possibility of losing his/her smartcard
- *Uneasiness about data on smartcard:* User feels uncomfortable knowing that his/her personal data is saved on a smartcard

As can be seen in Fig. 2, the incurred costs are mostly perceived as low, e.g., only 5 participants found that the system usage requires physical effort, and 3 participants found the system difficult to learn. The only "expensive" task was remembering how to interact with the system (5 participants found this easy to do). We hypothesize, however, that high system helpfulness (22 participants disagreed or strongly disagreed with the low helpfulness of the system) and good error recovery probably mitigated this disadvantage.

We conclude that users' perception that the PET usage does not require a lot of physical and mental effort, and the resulting positive cost-benefit assessment of the Privacy-ABC technology might play an important role in user acceptance. Moreover, some usability costs (such as low memorability) can be compensated by other, more usable features.

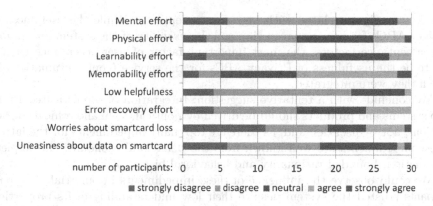

**Fig. 2.** Usability costs of Privacy-ABCs usage in the course evaluation.

We note, however, that it is impossible to draw causal conclusions from our trial. Did the high system usability influence perceived usefulness and users' high intention to use the system in the future? On the contrary, probably the high perceived usefulness of the system influenced user's positive usability perceptions. More research is needed to answer these questions.

## 3.5   Limitations of the Study Results

The results of the Patras pilot have to be further verified in other studies, as our trial had a lot of limitations that might have influenced the results. For example, users that found Privacy-ABCs inconvenient or untrustworthy could have refused to participate (so-called self-selection bias), such that we were unable to investigate their opinions and technology rejection factors.

Furthermore, the trustworthy university environment could have increased trust into the system, and thus also the perceived usefulness for privacy protection. Moreover, computer science students are more likely to be early adopters, which could imply exaggerated user acceptance results in comparison to the general population. Also good usability results may have been positively influenced by the high technical literacy of the users.

## 3.6   Promoting PETs Usage by the End Users

According to the conventional wisdom, in order to adopt PETs, people need to understand their benefits. It is also often assumed that risk perception is connected to the understanding of privacy risks. The reasoning is that if the users would perceive risk for their privacy as high, and the efficacy of PETs in reducing this risk as high, then they would adopt PETs. However, we see a different picture in our trial. Although the participants did not understand the properties of Privacy-ABCs well, they expressed a high level of trust into the system. Moreover, their perception of the overall system as useful for the primary task is strongly correlated with high user acceptance. While the usefulness of Privacy-ABCs for privacy protection and the usability of the system are important acceptance factors, the most important factor of user acceptance turned out to be the usefulness of Privacy-ABCs for the service (course evaluation) in which they were integrated.

We conclude with a tentative suggestion: Integration of sophisticated PETs into systems and products should be driven by political, legal and ethical considerations, not by user demand, as there are too many impediments for the latter. These impediments are well known from the behavioral economics: incomplete information, bounded rationality and behavioral biases [3].

We could observe the influence of these impediments in our trial: The participants trusted the system despite their low understanding of its properties, and expressed the wish to use it because they perceived the system as useful for the task that is important for them (course evaluation). Especially interesting is that these results were obtained for technically savvy and privacy-aware users.

Therefore, our results may also be valid for general Internet population. We think that the users would only adopt PETs that are integrated into useful services. In this case, we think that people may accept some usability drawbacks that arise from the PET integration, such as having to use a smart card or to consult a user manual sometimes. Although good usability and usefulness for privacy protection are important factors of user acceptance, our empirical results indicate that perceived usefulness of the primary (not privacy-related) service is much more important.

## 4    Adoption of PETs by Service Providers

For many PETs, like Privacy-ABCs, adoption from the users is not enough, but they rather require that service providers also support their use from their side. In this regard, the results of an expert survey [27] investigates the factors that may become a driver or an inhibitor for service providers' decision to adopt such kind of PETs in their processes. In this section we give an overview of the relevant factors and report our experiences from the Patras pilot, wherever appropriate.

### 4.1    Which Factors of Acceptance to Consider?

The literature in Information Systems research provides a handful list of theories explaining adoption of new innovations. From the prominent ones that have been verified by various empirical studies, four theories that focus on the organizational level of technology adoption [11, 19, 25, 31] could be combined into a single conceptual model to highlight the factors influencing adoption of technologies like PETs. Below we discuss in more details the resulted set of factors, which we have grouped into five categories.

**Technology.** Most PETs are newly introduced technologies and their characteristics may have a strong influence on the decision of the potential adopters.

*Compatibility.* It refers to the degree to which an innovation is perceived as consistent with the existing values, needs, and past experiences of the potential adopters. Therefore, higher compatibility of PETs' specification with the existing protocols and standards that are commonly used would support the adoption.

*Complexity.* It refers the degree to which an innovation is perceived as relatively difficult to understand and use. For example, Privacy-ABCs are based on difficult cryptographic concepts, which are not easy for people beyond the cryptographers to understand. In this regard, further effort to provide the policy makers and application developers with supporting materials facilitating their understanding as well as developing better user-interfaces for the end users seems to be crucial.

*Trialability.* It is defined as the degree to which an innovation may be experimented and tested on a limited basis. In other words, it concerns how easy it would be for a potential adopter to test (or partially test) the features that the new technology provides. This concern exists for example among the scientific community around Privacy-ABCs, as they have been constantly developing and publishing supporting-materials such as reference implementation and online resources to facilitate examining Privacy-ABCs.

*Observability.* It refers to the extent to which the innovation or its results are visible to the others. Unlike many other innovations that have visible results and can be well demonstrated, some PETs like Privacy-ABCs are very challenging to present. They are not like stand-alone products or services, but instead they are integrated into those. Therefore, demonstrators have difficulties showing all the added values of PETs in demos.

**Organization.** Beside the characteristics of an innovation itself, several organizational characteristics of the potential adopters have an influence on their decision to adopt or reject an innovation.

*Top Management Support.* This is in general necessary for adopting a new technology. Concerning PETs, top management's attitude towards changes caused by PETs can influence their adoption.

*Business Dependency on User Data Collection.* Dependency of the organization's business model on the collection of excessive personal data can negatively influence adoption of PETs like Privacy-ABCs, as some of these technologies are built to reduce the amount of collected personal data only to the minimum necessary.

*Technology Competence.* Our experience from the ABC4Trust pilots shows that typical developers often have difficulties to integrate Privacy-ABCs into services on their own, and constant support of technology providers would be needed. At the same time developers with scientific background and technical understanding of the technology went through the integration process smoothly. Hence, lack of technical competency can hinder PETs adoption.

**External Pressure.** Various sources of external pressure may influence the adoption of new innovations and in particular PETs.

*Regulatory Pressure.* A regulatory body may be the source of coercive pressures [26]. The regulations may directly address privacy and require the business to implement privacy enhancing mechanisms, or they may indirectly touch the topic, for instance by defining more costly requirements to protect the collected personal data.

*Social Pressure.* There have been major incidents recently, which we expect to have an influence on the adoption of PETs in general. The most well-known incidence was brought up by Edward J. Snowden, which indeed highly stimulated the public opinion on the need for a raise of privacy in online environments. So, we expect that social pressure on service providers will increase and push them towards employing mechanisms that reduce personal data collection in their processes.

*Extent of Adoption among Competitors.* Knowing a competitor has adopted an innovation and it has been a success, a firm tends to adopt the same innovation. We also consider that adoption of PETs by the competitors of a firm motivates it to follow the same approach not to lose trust.

*Standardization.* It is very typical for industries to employ procedures, processes or protocols that are standardized in order to ensure interoperability and sustainability of their products and services. In this regard, Standardization can become a source of normative isomorphism.

**Environment.** Here we refer to the external conditions that do not introduce any pressure, but they can facilitate or hinder adoption of an innovation. For instance, it is more likely to succeed in implementing the idea of a remote movie rental company in a country that has cheaper, faster and more reliable postal services around.

*Established Infrastructure Readiness.* Having the already established infrastructure ready to support PETs, the integration of these technologies into the platforms of service providers could become less costly and more attractive. Let us take eIDs as an example, which have been implemented in various countries around the world. Service providers can benefit greatly from the established infrastructure to perform authentication and access control in their online businesses. It is important that PETs, like Privacy-ABCs, can be integrated with the existing eID infrastructure without requiring any modifications to this infrastructure [6]. The EU Project FutureID[4] is studying in depth how such an integration can be done to take full advantage of Privacy-ABCs.

---

[4] http://futureid.eu.

**Perceived Benefits and Costs.** There are several factors not included in the four categories above and which encompass monetary benefits but also costs, obligations and potential lost revenue. The trades-off and the resulting monetary effects are discussed separately in Sect. 4.3.

## 4.2 Influence Level of the Factors

The aforementioned factors have been formulated into a questionnaire targeting experts from various relevant domains in order to collect their opinion on the influence level of these factors on the adoption of Privacy-ABCs [27]. The statistical results demonstrate that the experts considered *Business Model Dependency to Data Collection, Complexity for User, Observability, Top Management Support, Trialability, Cost of Integration, Complexity for Developers,* and *Regulations for Data Collection* as the top 8 most important or influential factors impacting the decision of the service providers to employ Privacy-ABCs.

## 4.3 Cost-Benefit Trade-Offs

Here costs can be seen as investments, but also potentially lost revenue from a risk analysis point of view. Likewise, benefits can be seen as reducing liabilities and costs, but also gaining reputation and new users.

**The Costs of PETs for Service Providers.** Certainly, several of the factors that affect service providers' decision to adopt a specific PET are related to the financial aspects around the collection of personal data. Currently service providers benefit from the collection of excessive personal data that allows them to personalize advertisement of goods and services and also improve new ones. For example, price discrimination or targeted advertising is based on such data, while the whole realm of big data today is based on the principle of collecting as much data as possible and find use of this data later.

This holds especially for big data categories *analysis* and *predict & project*, where it is assumed that the quality of data analysis will increase over time. Thus history information has a specific high value. For personal data this can in turn be harmful. Consent to use their personal data was given by end users not being able to identify at time of agreement those analysis, prediction, or projection methods that could be used in the future. For these big data categories suitable PETs will be extremely helpful.

In these lines, if PETs diminish the usefulness of personal data, this could be seen as a cost associated with their deployment. However, this is not always the case and PETs may make it possible to reach a new economic equilibrium where data holders can still profit from the value of data, while subjects' individual information stays protected. For example, Acquisti has argued that using PETs like Privacy-ABCs is compatible with price discrimination strategies [1].

There is also a social loss associated with the uncertainty created to users about the deployment of PETs at the service provider, as usually service providers do not reveal details about the level of protection offered. However, sometimes the quality of data protection is certified by seals that 3rd parties testified, which can help mitigate the problem.

Another kind of costs is related to the investment costs for the integration and deployment of PETs inside the service provider. The implementation of several PETs is now available as an Open Source Software (including Privacy-ABCs[5]), but their integration to a specific service or product can still require a lot of effort. This was experienced in the case of the Patras pilot, where the adaptation of the core reference implementation to the specific scenario took considerable effort, with additional complexity introduced by the use of smart cards and the enhancements regarding the revocation and inspector services. In general, there is lack of engineering techniques that would facilitate the smooth integration of PETs and only recently this area has started to attract interest[6].

Furthermore, investment can become especially troublesome in cases of international companies that operate worldwide and need to conform their services to different standards and privacy regulations. This was experiences in a smaller scale within ABC4Trust, where one partner company had the role of data processor developing part of the system and University of Patras had the role of data controller. To minimize the contact of the former with personal data kept by the latter, a step-by-step procedure with several safeguards had to be established through a legal contract, which limited the flexibility of the data processor [17].

Finally, sometimes the service provider might need to educate the users about the usage of a new PET, which can also be considered as a cost. We saw this in the Patras user trial, where the University gave to the students an introduction to Privacy-ABCs before they start using it and it distributed an extensive user manual about the system. During the user trial, the students requested additional support sending in total more than 150 emails to the support team, mostly regarding problems with the use of smart cards.

**The Benefits of PETs for Service Providers.** One of the benefits for using PETs is the limitation concerning the liabilities and costs due to lost or misused personal data. Indeed, one privacy risk that service providers face today is related to insufficient protection of personal data that are collected and stored by them. For example the insufficient deletion of personal data and the insufficient response to data breaches can have huge financial consequences to the company. There have not been reliable estimates of the potential loss from a privacy incident, but according to the upcoming EU data protection reform, data protection authorities will be able to fine companies that do not comply with EU rules with up to 2 % of their global annual turnover[7]. So from a risk management point of

---

[5] https://github.com/p2abcengine/p2abcengine.

[6] E.g., see the Internet Privacy Engineering Network initiative (https://secure.edps. europa.eu/EDPSWEB/edps/EDPS/IPEN).

[7] http://europa.eu/rapid/press-release_MEMO-14-186_de.htm last visited May 15th, 2015.

view, handling personal data can become very costly and using PETs can help address these risks.

Another aspect that promotes investments in PETs is the concerns about the harms in reputation associated with high-profile privacy incidents, which is expected to have a bigger impact as regulation is becoming stricter in mandating disclosure of privacy failures. Even though is has been suggested that firms lose billions of dollars due to privacy concerns, there are still not clear data to support this. An aspect to be considered here is how consumers' behavior is affected after privacy breach notifications, given that people's intentions with regard to privacy differ from their actual behavior [22].

An indirect but important benefit from PETs is that they can help service providers save costs by decreasing the risk of fraud or by protecting the organization's trade secrets. For example, in the identity management ecosystem it can be a competitive threat, if IdSPs learn all the users of the service providers. The use of Privacy-ABCs prevent this by placing the user between IdSPs and service providers.

## 5   Concluding Remarks

The results of the Patras trial indicate that users may not need to understand a PET in order to use it, as long as they trust the technology. The most important acceptance factor is the usefulness of the technology for the service they want to access, leaving ease of use (usability) to play a less important, but still significant role. Overall the benefits of Privacy-ABCs for the users overtook the costs.

Although the participants of the trial are not representative for the general Internet population, these results may still be generalizable, as the Patras pilot was conducted with the users that had probably the best possible chances and the best incentives for understanding Privacy-ABCs: technically savvy and privacy-aware computer science students.

For the service providers, economic forces, cryptographic technologies, and targeted regulatory guidelines would have to conspire to lead to adequate adoption. This is what Laudon called "co-regulative" solutions to privacy problems [20]. But the right balance will be decided from a societal viewpoint and may thus be different from society to society.

Looking to the future, we are still missing more and broader field trials to explore the socioeconomic factors of privacy technologies. There are some EU-wide surveys on public perception of privacy (e.g., [23]), but more focused ones on the adoption factors of PETs is still missing. Moreover, we should investigate not only adopters, but also non-adopters of PETs in order to better understand the acceptance factors. We are also especially missing controlled user acceptance experiments that would shed light on the causal relation between the user acceptance factors.

From the service providers' point of view, firms are more likely to utilize cost-benefit analysis if there is reliable data to inform the analysis. Until today however we are still missing large-scale data. For example, there have not been reliable estimates of the potential loss from a privacy incident. Also there is little data on the reputation impact of privacy breach notifications or on the revenue loss of firms due to privacy concerns.

## A    Discussion on the Applicability of UTAUT and UTAUT2

Although UTAUT [34] and UTAUT2 [35] are more successful models than TAM in predicting technology acceptance, we identified TAM as being more suitable in the context of the Privacy-ABC trial.

TAM considers two main factors that influence user adoption: Perceived Usefulness (called Performance Expectancy in UTAUT) and Perceived Ease of Use (called Effort Expectancy in UTAUT). UTAUT extends TAM with one additional factor that directly influences intention to use the technology: Social Influence, which is the degree to which the user perceives that people whose opinion the user values believe that the user should use the technology.

We tested the influence of this factor in the first Privacy-ABC trial [5] and found no relation to the intention to use Privacy-ABCs. Therefore, we decided to drop this factor. We hypothesize that in the trial environment, this factor may not be applicable, as Privacy-ABCs are only known to the fellow students, and the usage in our scenario did not involve peer pressure (as this would be the case, for example, for social media).

These findings are consistent with the UTAUT and UTAUT2 investigations, where Social Influence was not found to be an important adoption factor, especially for younger users with high experience, as in our sample. We note, however, that for application of Privacy-ABCs in other scenarios and with other (older and less experienced) user populations, Social Influence may be considered.

Additionally, UTAUT considers some factors (age, gender, experience, voluntariness of use) that moderate the relation between the intention to use the systems and the main factors. Considering these moderators does not make sense in our case, however, as our sample is very homogeneous in this respect: The students are of very similar age and experience, all of them use the system voluntarily, and the overwhelming majority is male.

Similar non-applicability considerations apply to the UTAUT2 model that considers additional main acceptance factors: hedonic motivation (the user derives fun or pleasure from using the system), price value (the monetary cost of the system usage), and the habit in using the system.

## B    Measurement Scales for User Acceptance Factors

The constructs considered in this research are presented in Table 2 on page 18.

**Table 2.** Measurement scales for the user acceptance factors; all items were measured on a 5-point scale ranging from 1 = "strongly disagree" to 5 = "strongly agree".

---

**Intention to Use** (adpated from [32,33])

Assuming that the Privacy-ABC system is available for course evaluations, I intend to use it

I would use the Privacy-ABC system for course evaluations in the next semester if it is available

Given that the Privacy-ABC system is available for course evaluations, I would use it

**Perceived Usefulness for Primary Task** (adapted from [32,33])

Using Privacy-ABCs improves the performance of course evaluation

Using Privacy-ABCs enhances the effectiveness of course evaluation

I find Privacy-ABCs to be useful for course evaluation

**Perceived Usefulness for Secondary Task** (adapted from [32,33])

Using Privacy-ABCs improves my privacy protection

Using Privacy-ABCs enhances the effectiveness of my privacy protection

I find Privacy-ABCs to be useful in protecting my privacy

**Perceived Ease of Use** (adapted from [32,33])

Interacting with the Privacy-ABC System does not require a lot of my mental effort

The Privacy-ABC System is easy to use

I find it easy to get the Privacy-ABC System to do what I want to do

**Perceived Risk** (adapted from [24])

I would see the decision to evaluate the course with the Privacy-ABC System as a risky action

**Trust into the Privacy-ABC technology** (adapted from [24])

The Privacy-ABC System is trustworthy

**Situation Awareness** (adapted from [37])

With Privacy-ABCs, I always know which personal information I am disclosing

I find it easy to see which information will be disclosed in order to get a credential

Privacy-ABCs let me know who receives my data

The Privacy-ABC system gives me a good overview of my personal data stored on my Smart Card

I can easily find out when (e.g., at which date) I have received a credential via the University Registration System

I get a good overview of who knows what about my private information from the Privacy-ABC System

I can easily see which and how many Privacy-ABC credentials I have been issued

# References

1. Acquisti, A.: Identity management, privacy, and price discrimination. IEEE Secur. Priv. **6**(2), 46–50 (2008)
2. Acquisti, A.: The economics of personal data and the economics of privacy. Background Paper for OECD Joint WPISP-WPIE Roundtable 1 (2010)
3. Acquisti, A., Grossklags, J.: Privacy and rationality in individual decision making. IEEE Secur. Priv. **2**, 24–30 (2005)
4. Benenson, Z., Girard, A., Krontiris, I.: User acceptance factors for anonymous credentials: an empirical investigation. In: Workshop on the Economics of Information Security (WEIS) (2015)
5. Benenson, Z., Girard, A., Krontiris, I., Liagkou, V., Rannenberg, K., Stamatiou, Y.: User acceptance of privacy-ABCs: an exploratory study. In: Tryfonas, T., Askoxylakis, I. (eds.) HAS 2014. LNCS, vol. 8533, pp. 375–386. Springer, Heidelberg (2014)
6. Bjones, R., Krontiris, I., Paillier, P., Rannenberg, K.: Integrating anonymous credentials with eIDs for privacy-respecting online authentication. In: Preneel, B., Ikonomou, D. (eds.) APF 2012. LNCS, vol. 8319, pp. 111–124. Springer, Heidelberg (2014)
7. Brands, S.: Rethinking Public Key Infrastructures and Digital Certificates: Building in Privacy. MIT Press, Cambridge (2000)
8. Camenisch, J., Van Herreweghen, E.: Design and implementation of the idemix anonymous credential system. In: Proceedings of the 9th ACM Conference on Computer and Communications Security (CCS 2002), pp. 21–30 (2002)
9. Cameron, K., Posch, R., Rannenberg, K.: Proposal for a common identity framework: A User-Centric Identity Metasystem. In: Rannenberg, K., Royer, D., Deuker, A. (eds.) The Future of Identity in the Information Society - Opportunities and Challenges. Springer (2009)
10. Davis, F.D.: Perceived usefulness, perceived ease of use, and user acceptance of information technology. MIS Q. **13**(3), 319–340 (1989)
11. DiMaggio, P.J., Powell, W.W.: The iron cage revisited: institutional isomorphism and collective rationality in organizational fields. Am. Sociol. Rev. **48**(2), 147–160 (1983)
12. Dinev, T., Hart, P.: Internet privacy concerns and social awareness as determinants of intention to transact. Int. J. Electron. Commer. **10**(2), 7–29 (2006)
13. Economics, L.: Study on the Economic Benefits of Privacy-enhancing Technologies (PETs): Final Report to The European Commission, DG Justice, Freedom and Security. London Economics (2010)
14. Field, A.: Discovering Statistics Using IBM SPSS Statistics. Sage, London (2013)
15. Final Report to the European Commission DG Justice, Freedom and Security: Study on the economic benefits of privacy-enhancing technologies (PETs). Technical report, London Economics, July 2010
16. Fischer-Hübner, S., Hoofnagle, C., Krontiris, I., Rannenberg, K., Waidner, M.: Online privacy: towards informational self-determination on the internet (Dagstuhl Perspectives Workshop 11061). Dagstuhl Manifestos **1**(1), 1–20 (2011)
17. Hansen, M., Bieker, F., Deibler, D., Obersteller, H., Schlehahn, E., Zwingelberg, H.: Legal data protection considerations. In: Rannenberg, K., Camenisch, J., Sabouri, A. (eds.) Attribute-based Credentials for Trust, pp. 143–161 (2015)
18. Herath, T., Chen, R., Wang, J., Banjara, K., Wilbur, J., Rao, H.R.: Security services as coping mechanisms: an investigation into user intention to adopt an email authentication service. Inf. Syst. J. **24**(1), 61–84 (2014)

19. Iacovou, C.L., Benbasat, I., Dexter, A.S.: Electronic data interchange and small organizations: adoption and impact of technology. MIS Q. **19**, 465–485 (1995)
20. Laudon, K.C.: Markets and privacy. Commun. ACM **39**(9), 92–104 (1996)
21. McKnight, D.H., Carter, M., Thatcher, J.B., Clay, P.F.: Trust in a specific technology: an investigation of its components and measures. ACM Trans. Manage. Inf. Syst. (TMIS) **2**(2), 12 (2011)
22. Nofer, M., Hinz, O., Muntermann, J., Roßnagel, H.: The economic impact of privacy violations and security breaches. Bus. Inf. Syst. Eng. **6**(6), 339–348 (2014)
23. Patil, S., Patruni, B., Lu, H., Dunkerley, F., Fox, J., Potoglou, D., Robinson, N.: Public perception of security and privacy: results of the comprehensive analysis of PACT's pan-european survey. Technical report, PACT EU Project Public Deliverable D4.2, June 2014
24. Pavlou, P.A.: Consumer acceptance of electronic commerce: integrating trust and risk with the technology acceptance model. Int. J. Electron. Commer. **7**(3), 101–134 (2003)
25. Rogers Everett, M.: Diffusion of Innovations. Free Press, New York (1995)
26. Rubinstein, I.S.: Regulating privacy by design. Berkeley Technol. Law J. **26**, 1409 (2011)
27. Sabouri, A.: Understanding the determinants of privacy-ABC technologies adoption by service providers. In: Proceedings of 14th IFIP WG 6.11 Conference on e-Business, e-Services, and e-Society, I3E 2015 Open and Big Data Management and Innovation, Delft, The Netherlands, 13–15 October 2015, vol. 9373 (2015)
28. Spiekermann, S.: User Control in Ubiquitous Computing: Design Alternatives and User Acceptance. Shaker, Aachen (2008)
29. Stamatiou, Y., Benenson, Z., Girard, A., Krontiris, I., Liagkou, V., Pyrgelis, A., Tesfay, W.: Course evaluation in higher education: the patras pilot of ABC4Trust. In: Rannenberg, K., Camenisch, J., Sabouri, A. (eds.) Attribute-based Credentials for Trust, pp. 197–239. Springer International Publishing (2015)
30. Sun, S.T., Pospisil, E., Muslukhov, I., Dindar, N., Hawkey, K., Beznosov, K.: What makes users refuse web single sign-on?: an empirical investigation of OpenID. In: Proceedings of the Seventh Symposium on Usable Privacy and Security, p. 4. ACM (2011)
31. Tornatzky, L.G., Fleischer, M., Chakrabarti, A.K.: Processes of Technological Innovation. Lexington Books, Lexington (1990)
32. Venkatesh, V., Bala, H.: Technology acceptance model 3 and a research agenda on interventions. Decis. Sci. **39**(2), 273–315 (2008)
33. Venkatesh, V., Davis, F.D.: A theoretical extension of the technology acceptance model: four longitudinal field studies. Manage. Sci. **46**(2), 186–204 (2000)
34. Venkatesh, V., Morris, M.G., Davis, G.B., Davis, F.D.: User acceptance of information technology: toward a unified view. MIS Q. **27**, 425–478 (2003)
35. Venkatesh, V., Thong, J.Y., Xu, X.: Consumer acceptance and use of information technology: extending the unified theory of acceptance and use of technology. MIS Q. **36**(1), 157–178 (2012)
36. Wästlund, E., Angulo, J., Fischer-Hübner, S.: Evoking comprehensive mental models of anonymous credentials. In: Camenisch, J., Kesdogan, D. (eds.) iNetSec 2011. LNCS, vol. 7039, pp. 1–14. Springer, Heidelberg (2012)
37. Wästlund, E., Wolkerstorfer, P., Köffel, C.: PET-USES: Privacy-enhancing technology-users self-estimation scale. In: Privacy and Identity Management for Life, pp. 266–274. Springer (2010)

# Revocable Privacy: Principles, Use Cases, and Technologies

Wouter Lueks[1]([⊠]), Maarten H. Everts[2], and Jaap-Henk Hoepman[1]

[1] Radboud University, Nijmegen, The Netherlands
{lueks,jhh}@cs.ru.nl
[2] TNO, Netherlands Organisation for Applied Scientific Research,
The Hague, The Netherlands
maarten.everts@tno.nl

**Abstract.** Security and privacy often seem to be at odds with one another. In this paper, we revisit the design principle of revocable privacy which guides the creation of systems that offer anonymity for people who do not violate a predefined rule, but can still have consequences for people who do violate the rule. We first improve the definition of revocable privacy by considering different types of sensors for users' actions and different types of consequences of violating the rules (for example blocking). Second, we explore some use cases that can benefit from a revocable privacy approach. For each of these, we derive the underlying abstract rule that users should follow. Finally, we describe existing techniques that can implement some of these abstract rules. These descriptions not only illustrate what can already be accomplished using revocable privacy, they also reveal directions for future research.

## 1 Introduction

Privacy and (homeland) security seem to be at odds with one another: it is a commonly held belief that we cannot strengthen one without weakening the other. And it seems security is winning. The governmental hunger for data—and its ability to actually gather these—seems bigger than ever. And who would argue against collection of these data? Surely we all want to stop terrorists, pedophiles and tax evaders. Yet, security versus privacy does not have to be a zero-sum game [15,17]. Hoepman also argued that this contradiction between security and privacy is a false one, and that we can design systems that have privacy without neglecting security [11].

This paper is based on our earlier technical report on revocable privacy [13]. The work described in this paper has been supported under the ICT theme of the Cooperation Programme of the 7th Framework Programme of the European Commission, GA number 318424 (FutureID) and the research program Sentinels (www.sentinels.nl) as project 'Revocable Privacy' (10532). Sentinels is being financed by Technology Foundation STW, the Netherlands Organization for Scientific Research (NWO), and the Dutch Ministry of Economic Affairs. This research is conducted within the Privacy and Identity Lab (PI.lab) and funded by SIDN.nl (http://www.sidn.nl).

© Springer International Publishing Switzerland 2016
B. Berendt et al. (Eds.): APF 2015, LNCS 9484, pp. 124–143, 2016.
DOI: 10.1007/978-3-319-31456-3_7

Hoepman introduced a design principle to create systems that have both security and privacy: *revocable privacy*. The core idea of revocable privacy arises from the realisation that it is not the data itself that is (or should be) important, but rather the violations of certain rules that manifest themselves in the data. Data related to people who do not violate any rules are irrelevant, and, in fact, these people should remain anonymous, as if no data on their behavior was ever collected. Revocable privacy is a design principle that ensures this property. Informally speaking, a system offers revocable privacy if users of the system are guaranteed to be anonymous except when they violate a predefined rule.

To ensure privacy, the system's anonymity guarantees cannot rely on policy and regulations alone. It is all too easy to ignore policy, to sidestep it, or to change it retroactively. As a result, data that was collected for one specific purpose can easily be reused for another—violating people's privacy. A key aspect of a system implementing revocable privacy is to prevent this type of function creep through technical means: it should not be possible to change the rules retroactively.

It is known that building such systems is possible. One example is the anonymous electronic cash system proposed by Chaum [6], which actually implements revocable privacy (although he did not use this term). Users have electronic coins, which they can spend as if they were physical coins, in effect making an untraceable digital payment system in which the users' privacy is guaranteed. However, to maintain security, this anonymity cannot be unconditional. If it were, it would allow misbehaving users to double-spend the digital coins without consequence. Instead, the revocable privacy aspect of the design guarantees that users are anonymous, as long as they spend the digital coins only once. When they do spend a coin twice, their identity can be recovered from the two transaction records of the two spendings. Any single transaction record, however, gives no information about the identity of the user.

In general, to ensure anonymity for rule-abiding users, data must be collected in a special manner. In Chaum's electronic cash system, the cut-and-choose paradigm is used to ensure that a single transaction record gives no information, whereas two reveal the identity of the culprit. Distributed encryption [12, 14] offers another method for creating threshold based rules. Data is collected for every event, but the user's identity is revealed only if she causes an event to happen at sufficiently many different locations.

While Chaum's electronic cash could be seen as such a scheme with a threshold of two, it differs significantly from distributed encryption. In the first, the user actively partakes in the transaction, whereas in the second, the user deliberately does not take part. As a result, these systems have different privacy guarantees and trust assumptions. These aspects of revocable privacy had not yet been explored.

In all previous work on revocable privacy [11–14], the focus was on identifying users who violate the rules. However, in some situations, such an approach might be too strong. For example, anonymity is the core property of Tor [8], so it should never be possible to deanonimize users. Yet, Tor can also be abused. In order to stop abuse, some approaches, like blacklistable anonymous credentials (BLAC), aim to block misbehaving users, rather than to identify them [18].[1]

Our first contribution, in Sect. 2, is to re-examine revocable privacy in a more general setting, where we consider the implications of different security models, and explore ramifications of users' actions that are less invasive than simply identifying users, for example, blocking users and linking their actions.

Next, we explore and classify some use cases for revocable privacy in Sect. 3. We generalize the underlying rules of the use cases into abstract rules. These use cases illustrate that even if a user has violated a rule, she did not necessarily do something wrong. In fact, we will explore some systems where a violation only means that closer examination is necessary.

The abstract rules for the use cases make it possible to link them to specific techniques. Our final contribution, in Sect. 4, is to give a non-technical overview of existing techniques that can be used to implement revocable privacy. For each technique, we indicate which abstract rules it can implement. This not only shows which use cases we can already solve, but also highlights which abstract rules we cannot yet implement. We analyse the latter in Sect. 5 to reveal interesting new research directions. We also discuss some general limitations of revocable privacy. Finally, we conclude our paper in Sect. 6.

*Revocable Privacy is not a License for Unchecked Surveillance.* The use cases explored in this report come from various sources. Some of them are real, others are purely hypothetical. In many cases the legality and/or morality of the situation described in the use case is debatable. We have included them for the sole purpose of investigating the types of rules a system with revocable privacy might need to implement in the future. Inclusion of a use case in this paper does not mean that we endorse it in any way.

## 2    Revisiting the Concept of Revocable Privacy

In this section we will (re)define revocable privacy. We first explore what it means to be anonymous and what levels of anonymity exist.

### 2.1    Levels of Anonymity

At first sight it may seem that anonymity is an all-or-nothing property: either you have it or you do not. This is false. There are many shades of anonymity, ranging from fully anonymous to fully identified. For example, users might be pseudonymous: their actions are known under a fixed identifier—the pseudonym—but it is not known which pseudonym belongs to which user. In fact, users may have different pseudonyms depending on the situation.

---

[1] Nymble [19] is a related system that can be used to block misbehaving users. However, it relies on a trusted party that can make users linkable if they misbehave, so we do not consider it further in this paper.

Pseudonymity is often even equated with anonymity. However, stronger forms of anonymity are possible. When a user's actions are unlinkable, it is impossible to determine whether two actions were performed by the same user or by different users. (This linking is trivial in a pseudonymous system.) When we say that a system is fully anonymous, we mean that it has this level of unlinkability.

We can traverse the range between fully anonymous to fully identified by adding pieces of information. Some have a small impact on anonymity, like gender, nationality or age. We can also add a pseudonym to make a user's action linkable within a specific domain. The most natural pseudonym is one that does not change. Then all the user's actions will be linkable. However, we can also make pseudonyms that change frequently, and thus make the user's actions linkable within a short time period. Finally, some data, like social security numbers, license plates and bank account numbers, effectively make the user fully identified.

These ranges in anonymity have two consequences when dealing with revocable privacy. First, you can lose anonymity (because you violated a rule) without becoming fully identified. Second, it is better to see losing anonymity in relation to other participants in the system, as some systems may not offer full anonymity in the first place.

## 2.2 Improving the Definition

Hoepman [11] originally defined revocable privacy as follows:

> "A system implements revocable privacy if the architecture of the system guarantees that personal data are revealed only if a predefined rule has been violated."

There are some problems with this specific definition. First, the rule explicitly mentions *personal* data. Companies, however, might have an equally big desire for protecting their corporate data (e.g., their business processes). Moreover, as we explored in the previous section, revealing personal data is not always necessary; there are other ways to lose anonymity.

The definition could also be extended to include cases where revealing a user's personal information could be positive to the user, rather than just negative, as we have discussed so far.[2] One example is privacy-friendly matching on a dating site, where you get each other's contact information only if the profiles match. However, we think that such systems should not be classified as having revocable privacy, as this makes the definition too broad, almost to the point of including all privacy enhancing technologies.

The second problem we have with this definition is that it is very easy to misread it and assume that if a person were to violate the rule then personal data are revealed. However, it does not say that. It states just that personal data *may* be revealed only if the rule is violated.

---

[2] In fact, we suggested this approach in our technical report [13].

We incorporate these suggestions into the following revised definition of revocable privacy. We focus on anonymity rather than personal data and rephrase the rule to clarify that violating a rule does not necessarily imply the release of personal information.

**Definition 1.** *A system implements revocable privacy if the architecture of the system guarantees a predefined level of anonymity for a participant as long as she does not violate a predefined rule.*

As required, this definition does not say anything about the consequences when a participant does violate the rule. In practice there will be a consequence. If the system implements revocable privacy this usually means that the participant loses anonymity, but it can also mean that the participant is blocked from making further actions.

## 2.3 Systems and Rules

In the above definition, we consider the *system* as the environment with which the user interacts, and within which certain rules should be maintained. For example, in Chaum's electronic cash scheme, this system is the payment environment.

Rules are part of the system, and we require them to be predefined, including their parameters. For example, if the abstract rule is "A participant is allowed to cause an event at most $t$ times", then the threshold $t$ should be defined for every instantiation. This requirement prevents function creep and ensures clarity. If, instead, parameters should be configurable afterwards—for example, if certain criteria are not known in advance—the rule should explicitly state this.

We impose no other restrictions on the rules as this allows us to best capture the notion of 'anonymity until violation of the rules' that we see in many systems. In particular, we do not demand the rules to be known to the participants. While it is better that the rules are known, there might be circumstances where they must be kept secret.

We realize that the freedom in choosing rules (and keeping them secret) makes them very powerful. In fact, a rule might simply require all events to be output, or allow parameters to be set to non privacy-friendly values. Thus, careful scrutiny of the rules is of the utmost importance. The designers of the rules must ensure that the reduction in privacy that results from violating a rule is proportional to the detected behavior.

Ensuring proportionality is particularly important when violation of a rule does not necessarily imply that the participant is misbehaving. It may only be an indication of misbehavior (as in the canvas cutters use case, see Sect. 3.1) or even that the participant might be harmed (as in the detecting child abuse case, see Sect. 3.3).

## 2.4 Architecture of a System

What does it mean for the architecture of the system to protect the anonymity of well-behaving users? As we argued before, policies and procedures do not offer sufficient protection against function creep and misuse of the data in the future. We cannot assume that the raw data remain secure forever. Instead, we rely on the architecture of the system (the manner in which it is built, including the cryptography) to guarantee the anonymity of rule-abiding participants.

However, systems implementing revocable privacy cannot always offer unconditional anonymity either. It matters how the user's actions are observed within the system. For example, if the system sees what the user does, but chooses to forget it, we have to trust the system to actually do this. In this section, we explore the trust assumptions in a system implementing revocable privacy.

To determine these assumptions we examine how data is collected—is the identity of the user ever known?—and how it is stored. We consider three conceptually different methods. For reference, we first describe the traditional method where the user is known and the data is stored in the clear. In the second method, the user is still identified, but only processed information is stored. In the third, the user is never identified.

In all of these situations data resulting from the user's actions are stored. A final post-processing procedure, that is based on the rule, takes these data and outputs data such that a negative consequence for the participants can be effected. Usually, these data will reduce the anonymity, but they might also be used just to block further access to the system—as is the case in BLAC. Both how the data is encoded and how it is post-processed depend on the rule. In a system with revocable privacy, it is not possible to change the rule and then reprocess old data (that was collected using a different rule) according to the new rule.

**Plaintext Logging.** For contrast, we first describe the obvious method for implementing a system with rules. Users are never anonymous with respect to the system. Every relevant action by the user—relevant with respect to the rules that are to be enforced—is stored together with the user's identity.

Violations of the rules are detected by checking the rules against the stored data. Since the user's identity is also stored, any consequence to the user's actions can immediately be enforced.

Any anonymity guarantees offered by such a traditional system rely on the policies and regulations that protect access to the stored data and govern the data retention policies. Hence, trust lies in the policies. Because this is not an architectural protection, we say that such a system does not offer revocable privacy.

One way to bolster the protection is to add one or more trusted third parties that decide if the rule is violated and then carry out the desired consequence. Hoepman [11] says such a system, which he calls of the *spread responsibility* type, does have revocable privacy. However, since the system does not enforce the rule we do not consider that to be the case in this paper. Instead, we focus solely on systems that, according to Hoepman, have a *self-enforcing architecture*, where the architecture determines if the anonymity guarantee can be weakened.

**Non-interactive Sensors with Encoding.** The second method is a direct alternative to traditional methods. It drastically improves the anonymity guarantees, without requiring changes to the users of the system. As with plaintext logging, the actions of the participant and its identity are visible to the system, however, in contrast, they are never stored directly. Instead, a sensor (there can be many sensors in a system) observes these actions and identities, and then transforms them, based on the rule, into encrypted data. Only these encrypted data are stored.

The encryption method is special. There is no key that can be used to decrypt the data. Only when the encrypted data corresponds to a violation of the rule, can they be decrypted to produce some useful output.

To guarantee anonymity, we need to trust that the sensors behave as specified. In particular, we trust that sensors do not store their inputs. In addition, many sensors use private keys, in which case we trust them to keep these secret too. These private keys ensure that even if the sensors' outputs are deterministic (i.e., the sensors do not use randomness) an attacker cannot simply confirm a suspected event based on the stored data by simply calculating the same function as the sensor.

Despite these strict trust assumptions on the sensor, these systems can be very useful because they can be used as a drop-in replacement for traditional systems. In particular, they do not require any changes to the user's side. Of course, the sensors and the rest of the system still need to be adapted to work with the encrypted data. In some sense, the sensors act on behalf of the user.

*Mitigating the Trust Needed in the Sensors.* In some cases, like the threshold system that we describe in Sect. 4.1, the sensors are distributed. In this case, it may be possible that some are compromised, while the system as a whole still offers (some) anonymity.

Another approach that is useful in this setting is to make sure that the system is forward secure. Loosely speaking this would imply that if a sensor is compromised, it impacts only future events.

**Interactive Sensors.** In the third and final method, there is no sensor that simply observes the user; the user herself needs to be actively involved and interact with the sensor. The user usually keeps track of some secret information.

The advantage of this approach is that the user's identity is never known to the system, so the user's anonymity does not rely on the trustworthiness of parties within the system. The downside is that the user needs to interact with the sensors.

The sensor cannot rely on its own inputs to verify the correctness of the supplied information. Instead, this burden falls on the participant: she needs to convince the sensor that the supplied information is correct (even if the sensor does not know the content of the information).

# 3   Use Cases

We now present a number of use cases that could benefit from revocable privacy. These use cases are the result of interviews with security experts, internal discussions and privacy enhancing technologies literature. This overview is by no means exhaustive. Instead, it serves as a motivation for revocable privacy and as a source of insight into the abstract rules underlying these cases. We use these abstract rules to determine which cases we can already solve, and for which ones we need to develop new primitives.

We omit some of the use cases from our original analysis [13]. As we discussed in Sect. 2.2, we omit cases where the user would benefit from having its anonymity revealed. Other cases we omit because they are too vague or not interesting. Finally, we omit cases that simply give too much power to a government agency, even if only suspicious behavior would be detected.

We sort and categorise the use cases based on the type of rule that the system should enforce. The rules are roughly ordered by complexity. We start with three simple classes. The first class is that of threshold rules, where an event should not happen too often. The second class, containing predicate rules, consists of rules for logical combinations of simpler events. The third class covers cases where the rule encodes a human decision making element—for example, a judge signing a warrant.

Next, we consider two classes of more complicated rules. The first covers rules that are more complex than any of the aforementioned. For example, rules about flows on graphs (useful in tax situations) and about combining (private) information into the decision making process. The second covers rules that are fuzzy and would normally, even when no anonymity is required, involve machine learning and data mining techniques.

For each of these classes we present several use cases. For every use case, we describe the case, extract an abstract rule and note the consequence of violating that rule. While the use cases focus on specific scenarios, the abstract rules generalize the rule within these scenarios. It ignores the scenario specific details. This makes it easier to determine which use cases have similar rules, and which techniques might be used to solve a use case using revocable privacy. Table 1 records the type of sensor, the source of the use case, and potential solutions.

## 3.1   Threshold Rules

A threshold rule has the form "a certain action should be performed no more than $k$ times within a certain time period". The most common consequence of violating the rule is to reveal the violator's identity, however, it is also possible to block the user. A threshold of one is possible in some of these scenarios. The following use cases work with threshold rules.

**Canvas Cutters.** This case, as well as the following two cases, focusses on detecting bad or suspicious behavior involving cars. As cars are generally not

**Table 1.** An overview of the use cases and their sensor type, source, and applicable techniques. The sensor type is non-interactive (N-I), interactive (I) or both. The techniques are distributed encryption (DE, Sect. 4.1), $n$-times anonymous credentials ($n$-AA, Sect. 4.1), blacklistable anonymous credentials (BLAC, Sect. 4.2), group signatures (GS, Sect. 4.2) and secure multi-party computation (MPC, Sect. 5). A question mark indicates that we are not sure if this technique fully solves the problem. Biskup and Flegel proposed a system [2] to solve the cases marked with an asterisk (*). However, it requires the sensor to store a (partial) record of all events, it thus does not offer the anonymity that our definition of revocable privacy requires. We do not know of a solution for these cases that implements revocable privacy as we defined here.

| Use case | Type | Source | Technique |
|---|---|---|---|
| Canvas cutters | N-I | Dutch National Police (KLPD) | DE |
| Object surveillance | N-I | Dutch National Police (KLPD) | (*) |
| Average speed checking | N-I | Dutch National Police (KLPD) & Lueks et al. [14] | DE |
| Anomalies in logs | N-I | Biskup and Flegel [2] | (*) |
| Sharing anon. resources | I | Camenisch et al. [4] | $n$-AA |
| No-show reservation | I | Internal discussion | Unknown |
| Electronic cash | I | Chaum [6] | $n$-AA |
| Social welfare fraud | Both | Municipality of Groningen | Unknown |
| Terrorist activity | N-I | Internal discussion | Unknown |
| Child abuse | N-I | Internal discussion | DE |
| Anonymous editing | I | Tsang et al. [18] | BLAC |
| Deanonymizing comments | Both | Interview | GS? |
| Wiretapping policy | N-I | Interview | Unknown |
| Riot control | N-I | Dutch National Police (KLPD) | Unknown |
| Money flow anomalies | I | Sharemind application [3] | MPC? |
| Object surveillance 2 | N-I | Internal discussion | Unknown |
| Camera footage | N-I | Internal discussion and Sound Intelligence [16] | Unknown |

able to communicate with roadside equipment, we focus on the scenario where an automatic number plate recognition system reads the license plates of passing cars. This makes using a non-interactive sensor the only option.

Criminals frequently loot trucks parked at rest stops by cutting the canvas that protects the goods. One way to detect these criminals is to look for cars that enter several different rest stops within a couple of hours. These cars are suspicious. While false positives cannot be eliminated—e.g., police cars and roadside assistance vehicles may cause them as well—most hits will correspond to suspicious behavior.

**Abstract Rule.** Given $n$ sensors at different locations, a participant should trigger at most threshold $t$ different sensors within a given time period.

**Consequence.** The system learns the identity of the participant.

**Object Surveillance.** Related to the previous problem is the problem of casing: criminals checking out a location, like a sensitive piece of infrastructure, multiple times. These criminals can be detected by looking for cars that pass by this location rather frequently. This case is not the same as the canvas cutters use case. In particular, here all events contribute to the threshold, whereas for the canvas cutters case the number of different locations of the events matters. Again, false positives cannot be eliminated.

**Abstract Rule.** Given one or more sensors at one locations, a participant should
   trigger at most threshold $t$ sensors (counting repeats) within a given time
   period.
**Consequence.** The system learns the identity of the participant.

**Average Speed Checking.** Besides spot checking with a speed camera, some countries have deployed average speed checking systems which measure a car's speed along a stretch of road [14]. For spot checks it is immediately clear whether an observed car is speeding. However, average speed checking requires some form of storage to determine the time it took a car to traverse a stretch of road. Phrased as a revocable privacy problem: the system should output the license plates of cars that pass two measuring station—one in the beginning and one at the end—within a too short time period.

**Abstract Rule.** Given $n$ sensors at different locations, a participant should
   trigger at most threshold $t$ different sensors in any time period of a given
   length.
**Consequence.** The system learns the identity of the participant.

**Anomalies in Logs.** Servers keep activity logs. These logs can be used to detect attacks. One example of such an attack are repeated log-in attempts from the same remote system. These are easy to spot in the logs as they all originate from the same system. However, it is usually not necessary keep the logs for all the authentic users.

By nature of the system (the remote systems are identified by IP address) we an use non-interactive sensors to detect which remote system makes frequent fraudulent login attempts. These systems can then be blocked.

**Abstract Rule.** Same as for object surveillance.
**Consequence.** The system learns the identity of the participant.

**Sharing Anonymous Resources.** Some systems give people anonymous access to a resource on the basis that they can prove something—e.g., that they have a license to a game, or that they are of a certain age. While this anonymity is good for the user, it also makes it trivial to share the access with any number of people without detection. To limit this sharing, people could be allowed only a limited number of accesses per time period. When this value is exceeded—it should be chosen in such a way that under normal use it is not—the identity of the presumed sharer is revealed or the presumed sharer is blocked from accessing the system.

As the user and the system already interact, we prefer interactive sensors.

**Abstract Rule.** A participant of the system can perform an action at most $n$ times per time period.

**Consequence.** The system learns the identity of the participant.

**No-Shows in Anonymous Reservations.** Consider anonymous reservations of resources like cinema seats, museum access or computing resources based on unlimited access subscriptions. Resources, however, are often scarce, making no-shows undesirable. If the system is fully anonymous, it is not possible to discourage no-shows. Instead, we would like to construct a system that either blocks or deanonymizes a user if she does not use a reservation, or fails to do so too often, but lets honest users be anonymous.

**Abstract Rule.** A participant of the system that reserves a resource may fail to claim this resource only $t$ times.

**Consequence.** The system learns the identity of the participant or the system block the participant from making further reservations.

**Electronic Cash.** As we discussed in the introduction, another common case for revocable privacy is electronic cash [6]. Users are given digital coins that they can spend anonymously. However, they are not allowed to spend the same coin twice. This form of electronic cash is a threshold system with a threshold of two.

As before, using a non-interactive sensor is not desirable as the user already interacts with the receiver of the coin when she is spending it.

**Abstract Rule.** A participant can perform an action (e.g., spend one coin) at most once.

**Consequence.** The system learns the identity of the participant.

## 3.2    Predicate Rules

Not all rules are as simple as limiting the occurrence of an event. In this section we consider a class of rules that combine different indicators, similar to logical formulas.

**Social Welfare Fraud.** In the Netherlands people can receive social welfare when they are unemployed. The amount received depends on the number of people in the household. In particular, they receive less welfare when they share living expenses. Some people defraud the system by incorrectly reporting that they live alone.

To detect possible cases of fraud, the municipality of Groningen looked for people who received social welfare and who indicated living alone but had higher utility consumptions (water, gas, electricity and waste) than would correspond to a one person household.[3] This search required collecting information from different sources. Using revocable privacy, it would be possible to combine these data, and only recover the suspected violations.

Data can be supplied to the system either using non-interactive sensors (for example, the utility companies and the government) or directly by the cooperating welfare recipients (the system verifies that they behave honestly).

**Abstract Rule.** Let every participant have a set of associated data items, and let $P$ be a predicate over these data items. The predicate must be false.
**Consequence.** The system learns the identity of the participant.

**Detecting Terrorist Activity.** Contrary to the canvas cutters use case, a lot of law-enforcement-like cases depend on combining various indicators to find criminals. One rather primitive example works as follows. A person who buys fertilizer, rents a van and scouts a government building in a short period of time may be planning to make and set off a bomb.

Any one of these events might be totally benign. It is only the combination that leads to suspicion. In practice, the rules may be more complicated and involve different data items. Usually, the actual actions and the identity of the person performing them are known, making non-interactive sensors the most obvious choice.

**Abstract Rule.** Same as for social welfare fraud.
**Consequence.** The system learns the identity of the participant.

## 3.3   Decision Rules

All previous rules depend only on the inputs they receive. Given these inputs, the outcome is clear. People do not take part in the decision making process. However, sometimes this decision process is essential. For example, we do not know how to codify the rule "posts should not be offensive." Such a rule is better suited for human decision making. In this section, we discuss a few rules that include human decision making.

---

[3] The original source, http://gemeente.groningen.nl/algemeen-nieuws/2010-1/sociale-dienst-spoort-bijna-driehonderd-gevallen-van-bijstandsfraude-op (Dutch, last accessed January 29, 2012), is currently unavailable. The same technique is mentioned on http://www.nu.nl/politiek/2670044/aanpak-bijstandsfraude-bestand skoppeling.html (Dutch, last accessed May 31, 2015).

**Detecting Child Abuse.** This first rule is actually a threshold rule, but with human decisions as input. Professionals working with children, e.g., doctors and teachers, may suspect abuse. However, for fear of causing undue panic and because reports would become part of the child's record, they may decide not to report this. These concerns would be alleviated if these reports could be made in such a way that a child's identity becomes available only when a predetermined number of professionals agree that a child might be abused. In this situation using an interactive sensor is truly undesirable as it would alert the child or its guardians to the suspicion of abuse.

**Abstract Rule.** Same as for canvas cutters.
**Consequence.** The system learns the identity of the participant.

**Blocking Anonymous Editing.** In the previous case it was essential that there was no interaction with the participant (the child). Here, we consider another case where interaction *is* possible: anonymously editing Wikipedia pages. Given the sensitive nature of some Wikipedia pages, it would be beneficial to allow anonymous edits. Yet, this anonymity can also facilitate abuse, and this abuse is usually not easily detected automatically. Yet, people are good at this task, in fact, Wikipedia is based on this principle.

To protect the system, an anonymous user should be blocked from making further edits if one or several of her edits have been classified as abusive. Even though a moderator can classify an edit as abusive, and thus block a user, she should never be able to recover the identity of the editor.

**Abstract Rule.** Participants are not allowed to perform more than $t$ bad actions.
**Consequence.** The system blocks the participant from performing further actions.

**Deanonymizing Comments.** Like edits on Wikipedia, some posts on an online bulletin board might be made anonymously. Another method of discouraging abusive comments is to actually reveal the identity of the author. However, since this decision is rather invasive, the identity of the author should only be revealed if a sufficient number of moderators agree to do so.

It is possible to build this system with a non-interactive sensor. However, the user already interacts with the system, so an interactive sensor provides better privacy.

**Abstract Rule.** Participants are not allowed to perform actions that are deemed bad by more than $t$ moderators.
**Consequence.** The system learns the identity of the participant.

**Wiretapping Policy.** Typically, law enforcement agencies require permission, for example from a judge or other authority, before they can legally tap phone and internet connections. However, this is enforced only by policy.

To increase privacy, telecom operators could send the requested data to law enforcement agencies in such a way that the agencies can only access this information after the required permission has been obtained. In this case, it is the telecom operator that acts as a non-interactive sensor.

**Abstract Rule.** Participants can perform actions. No trusted party decides that the participant's behavior is suspicious.
**Consequence.** The system learns the future actions of the participant.

## 3.4   Complex Rules

We now discuss rules that are more complex, for example because they operate on graphs and labeled data, or because they use auxiliary information that should be protected as well.

In principle, the rules in this class can be described by any deterministic computer program. However, to illustrate how hard some of these tasks can be, we also discuss fuzzy rules, based on for example machine learning, in the next section.

**Riot Control.** In 2009/2010 there were riots between two ethnic groups in Culemborg (a Dutch city). The police knew that the rioters might receive reinforcements from certain parts of the country. To prevent them from arriving, they wanted to detect these groups en route, and block the exits to Culemborg at the appropriate times.

To detect these groups, they automatically read license plates. If a group of more than four cars originating from the reinforcement area was detected on the highway, they closed the high-way exit.

Two things make this case interesting. First, the goal is not to deanonymise specific cars, but rather to detect a group of cars from a specific area. Second, in order to make this system work auxiliary information is required about where cars are registered.

**Abstract Rule.** A sensor should observe at most $n$ objects (with associated data) satisfying a predicate $\mathcal{P}$ within a time period.
**Consequence.** The system learns that a match has been found.

**Money Flow Anomalies.** Some types of tax fraud manifest themselves in discrepancies in money flows between companies. In particular, whatever company A claims to have sold to B should also be reported as bought from A by B. However, cash flows between companies also reveal strategies and other sensitive economical information that companies would rather not share. Instead of just sharing this information, the tax office and the companies could build a revocable privacy system where a company's name is revealed only if it incorrectly reported its cash flow.

**Abstract Rule.** Given a graph, with the participants represented by nodes and the edges representing money flows between them. Participants should report the flows over their adjacent edges correctly.
**Consequence.** The system learns the identity of the participants.

### 3.5   Fuzzy Rules

Until now we discussed situations where the participants are easy to recognize because they have a unique identifier (e.g., license plate, social security number, name). However, this is not the case, for example, when only video of a person is available. Even if it is possible to recognize people using facial recognition, we may still need to recognize suspicious behavior. This brings us to the realm of fuzzy and probabilistic computation. We consider this class separately because we suspect it is even harder to solve these cases using revocable privacy.

**Object Surveillance Based on People.** This first use case is similar to the object surveillance case earlier, but with the twist we described in the previous paragraph: we have only video of the people in the system. We want to know if someone cases a location, but without the convenience of a fixed identifier.

In a system without revocable privacy, we could (maybe) collect facial features of all recorded people and determine how often they show up. To do this in a privacy friendly manner would require a system that can take faces as input, and keep track of how often a specific face has been seen. Furthermore, even if this works on features that are derived from the image, the original(s) are necessary to make future identification possible. This is why we classify this case as fuzzy.

**Abstract Rule.** As for the object surveillance rule, but now with video as input.
**Consequence.** The system obtains a picture or video of the participant.

**Retrieving Camera Footage After a Crime.** Many cities install cameras to increase safety. One way to use these cameras is as a remote viewing tool, so that it is easier to monitor many locations at once. However, often the camera feeds are also stored in case something untoward happens later on. However, when nothing bad happens, the data can safely be discarded. The data is only stored to obtain more information after a crime has been detected.

If the system automatically detects bad situations (for example based on sounds [16]), the system could encode the data, and only release past records when a bad situation is detected. Hence, the system guarantees that the privacy sensitive recordings are kept and released only when necessary.

Relying on a human operator to make the decision to reveal footage, would put this use case are back in the decision-making class of cases.

**Abstract Rule.** Participants should behave properly on camera (as determined by the system or operator).
**Consequence.** The system obtains footage around the violation.

# 4    Technologies

In this section, we review some technologies from the past twenty years that can be used to implement revocable privacy. Table 1 shows which techniques apply to which use cases.

## 4.1    Threshold Primitives

We begin by discussing primitives that can be used to implement threshold rules.

**Distributed Encryption.** The distributed encryption primitive [12,14] was specifically designed to solve revocable privacy problems with a threshold rule, in particular, the canvas cutters scenario. As such, it describes how non-interactive sensors (ANPR stations at the rest stops) can encrypt messages (license plates) in such a way that only if enough encryptions (by different stations) of the same message are available they can be combined to recover the original message.

Obviously, any corrupted sensor can encrypt any message of an attacker's choosing. So the system guarantees security only as long as not too many sensors are corrupted.

The distributed encryption primitive counts only events, while many of the use cases count events per time period. In most cases, it suffices to restart the system for every new time period. If it is required that no more than a number of events happen in any time interval of a given length, then it is necessary to start overlapping instances of the system. The extensions by Lueks et al. [14] make it efficient to do so and ensures forward secrecy: even if a sensor is corrupted, it cannot be used to obtain information about previous time periods.

Combining the encrypted messages to recover the messages is not very efficient; it is exponential in the threshold. However, if the number of messages is small and they can be enumerated, like for license plates, then another technique by Lueks et al. [14] allows the system to trade space for time, making it reasonably efficient.

**$n$-times Anonymous Credentials.** Whereas the previous primitive uses non-interactive sensors, $n$-times anonymous credentials [4] allow participants to directly interact with the sensors. As a result, the trust assumptions are much weaker. The system gives every user a credential. The user can use this credential to anonymously authenticate $n$ times per time period. If the user authenticates more often, its identity becomes known.

Effectively, the user can create $n$ different (random) numbers per interval. If the user authenticates more often, she is bound to reuse one of the previous ones. This makes it easy and efficient to detect violations of the rule. Extensions make it also possible for a user to exceed the limit a couple of times (possibly in different time periods) before its identity is revealed. These schemes are a generalization of electronic cash schemes [1,5,6] where the limit is to spend every coin only once.

## 4.2  Decision Primitives

We now discuss techniques that can be used to implement decision-based revocable privacy rules.

**Blacklistable Anonymous Credentials.** Blacklistable anonymous credentials [18] make it possible for a service provider to block users from future authentication if the user misbehaved in an earlier session. To enable this, the user uses his (certified) private key to generate a new, random token for every authentication. These tokens are bound to the user (but, without the user's private key it is impossible to determine to which user they belong). In addition, the user proves that it did not generate any of the tokens that the service provider placed on the blacklist.

If the service provider later detects abuse, it can add that session's token to the blacklist. The corresponding user can then no longer prove that its tokens are not on the blacklist and loses access to the service. Alternatively, the user can prove that it has no more than $n$ tokens on the blacklist, thus the system allows a few bad actions.

The complexity of this protocol is linear in the number of items on the revocation list, making it inefficient. Some techniques can be used to reduce the complexity [10].

**Group Signatures with Distributed Management.** A group signature scheme allows members of a group to digitally sign documents on behalf of the group [7]. The signers are anonymous in the sense that it is known only that they belong to the group, not who they are. A special party, the tracing agent, can overcome this anonymity and determine who created a specific signature, thereby revealing the identity of the signer.

Already this scheme can be used to implement the simple rule that you lose your anonymity when the tracing agent decides that this should happen. However, in some sense we are then back to having a single, trusted third party. Instead, we can distribute the powers of the tracing agent. In a group signature scheme with a distributed tracing agent, several agents need to cooperate before the identity of the signer can be recovered [9]. As long as a decent subset of the tracing agents is trusted, the anonymity of the user's identities is guaranteed.

## 5  Analysis

In the preceding section, we reviewed some techniques that can be used for revocable privacy. Unfortunately, we do not know of existing primitives for many of the more complex rules. Only the threshold use cases are covered reasonably well by existing techniques. This suggests that there might be relatively simple techniques that work for the object surveillance and anomalies in logs use cases.

For decision-based rules, there are some existing techniques that help solve some of the use cases. This again suggests that we might be able to develop techniques for the remaining cases (deanonymizing comments and wiretapping policy).

Nevertheless, there are some very generic techniques that could help implement the remaining rules using the revocable privacy paradigm. First, the field of privacy-preserving data mining might help in solving some of the anomalies like social welfare fraud.

Finally, there is multi-party computation. This technique allows multiple parties, each with their own private input, to compute any shared function over the data. All inputs are kept private; only the output is shared. While this technique works, in theory, for any computation, including machine learning algorithms, it is also very computationally intensive. Yet, the Sharemind company successfully used their multi-party computation platform to solve several real-world problems on private data [3], one of which is the money flow problem.

## 5.1 Limitations

We briefly discuss two limitations of revocable privacy. The first is that to obtain better anonymity without losing security, we have to pay in computing power. This is especially the case for the non-interactive sensor techniques that we discussed. However, we think that this cost is often acceptable.

The other limitation stems from the fact that most use cases and all solutions describe positive effects. A participant performs an action, and as a result of doing so, can violate a rule. It seems much harder to handle negative events: what if you follow the rules if you do something, rather than not do it? For example, if you observe someone misbehaving, but fail to report it.

## 6 Conclusions

We have argued why revocable privacy is an important construct that can be used to increase the privacy of a system's participants while maintaining security. We have classified systems with revocable privacy into two classes: those with non-interactive sensors and those with interactive sensors. Furthermore, we have clarified the definition and have generalized it to include different types of consequences for violating the rules.

We have also explored use cases that benefit from a revocable privacy approach. This not only illustrates the usefulness of revocable privacy, but also allows us to compile some abstract rules that revocable privacy techniques should be able to implement. We have described some of these techniques and showed which problems they solve.

The comparison between the abstract rules and existing revocable privacy techniques identifies interesting directions of future work in the area of revocable privacy. Based on the fact that many threshold-based rules and decision-based rules already have corresponding primitives, we expect that the remaining ones may be solvable as well. Furthermore, we identify whole classes of more challenging research direction in finding techniques for the other use cases that lack corresponding techniques, most notably social welfare fraud detection, riot control, and object surveillance based on people.

# References

1. Au, M.H., Chow, S.S.M., Susilo, W.: Short E-cash. In: Maitra, S., Veni Madhavan, C.E., Venkatesan, R. (eds.) INDOCRYPT 2005. LNCS, vol. 3797, pp. 332–346. Springer, Heidelberg (2005)
2. Biskup, J., Flegel, U.: Transaction-based pseudonyms in audit data for privacy respecting intrusion detection. In: Debar, H., Mé, L., Wu, S.F. (eds.) RAID 2000. LNCS, vol. 1907, pp. 24–48. Springer, Heidelberg (2000)
3. Bogdanov, D., Jõemets, M., Siim, S., Vaht, M.: How the Estonian tax and customs board evaluated a tax fraud detection system based on secure multi-party computation. In: Böhme, R., Okamoto, T. (eds.) FC 2015. LNCS, vol. 8975, pp. 227–234. Springer, Heidelberg (2015)
4. Camenisch, J., Hohenberger, S., Kohlweiss, M., Lysyanskaya, A., Meyerovich, M.: How to win the clonewars: efficient periodic n-times anonymous authentication. In: Juels, A., Wright, R.N., di Vimercati, S.D.C. (eds.) CCS 2006, pp. 201–210. ACM (2006)
5. Camenisch, J.L., Hohenberger, S., Lysyanskaya, A.: Compact E-cash. In: Cramer, R. (ed.) EUROCRYPT 2005. LNCS, vol. 3494, pp. 302–321. Springer, Heidelberg (2005)
6. Chaum, D.: Blind signatures for untraceable payments. In: Chaum, D., Rivest, R.L., Sherman, A.T. (eds.) CRYPTO 1982, pp. 199–203. Plenum Press, New York (1982)
7. Chaum, D., van Heyst, E.: Group signatures. In: Davies, D.W. (ed.) EUROCRYPT 1991. LNCS, vol. 547, pp. 257–265. Springer, Heidelberg (1991)
8. Dingledine, R., Mathewson, N., Syverson, P.F.: Tor: the second-generation onion router. In: Blaze, M. (ed.) USENIX 2004, pp. 303–320. USENIX (2004)
9. Ghadafi, E.: Efficient distributed tag-based encryption and its application to group signatures with efficient distributed traceability. In: Aranha, D.F., Menezes, A. (eds.) LATINCRYPT 2014. LNCS, vol. 8895, pp. 327–347. Springer, Heidelberg (2015)
10. Henry, R., Goldberg, I.: Thinking inside the BLAC box: smarter protocols for faster anonymous blacklisting. In: Sadeghi, A., Foresti, S. (eds.) WPES 2013, pp. 71–82. ACM (2013)
11. Hoepman, J.H.: Revocable privacy. ENISA Q. Rev. 5(2), 16–17 (2009)
12. Hoepman, J., Galindo, D.: Non-interactive distributed encryption: a new primitive for revocable privacy. In: Chen, Y., Vaidya, J. (eds.) WPES 2011, pp. 81–92. ACM (2011)
13. Lueks, W., Everts, M.H., Hoepman, J.H.: Revocable Privacy 2012 - use cases. Technical report. 35627, TNO (2012)
14. Lueks, W., Hoepman, J.-H., Kursawe, K.: Forward-secure distributed encryption. In: De Cristofaro, E., Murdoch, S.J. (eds.) PETS 2014. LNCS, vol. 8555, pp. 123–142. Springer, Heidelberg (2014)
15. Schneier, B.: What Our Top Spy Doesn't Get: Security and Privacy Aren't Opposites. Wired, January 2008
16. Sound Intelligence: Sigard, aggression detection. http://www.soundintel.com/uploads/pdf/UK/Sound%20Intelligence%20Brochure%20%28EN%29.pdf. Accessed 31 May 2015
17. Stadler, M.: Cryptographic Protocols for Revocable Privacy. Ph.D. thesis, Swiss Federal Institute of Technology, Zürich (1996)

18. Tsang, P.P., Au, M.H., Kapadia, A., Smith, S.W.: Blacklistable anonymous credentials: blocking misbehaving users without TTPs. In: Ning, P., di Vimercati, S.D.C., Syverson, P.F. (eds.) CCS 2007, pp. 72–81. ACM (2007)
19. Tsang, P.P., Kapadia, A., Cornelius, C., Smith, S.W.: Nymble: blocking misbehaving users in anonymizing networks. IEEE Trans. Dependable Sec. Comput. **8**(2), 256–269 (2011)

# PIP: An Injection Pattern for Inserting Privacy Patterns and Services in Software

Naureen Ali[1], Dawn Jutla[2([⊠])], and Peter Bodorik[1]

[1] Faculty of Computer Science, Dalhousie University, Dalhousie, India
{NaureenAli,Bodorik}@cs.dal.ca
[2] Sobey School of Business, Saint Mary's University, Halifax, NS, Canada
Dawn.jutla@smu.ca

**Abstract.** Increasingly, software engineers in organizations complying with privacy regulations are looking for repeatable ways to embed privacy in their code. We propose the concept of a Privacy Injection Pattern (PIP) for software engineers to use to automate dynamically "injecting" existing privacy patterns in existing or new code. The PIP is composed of a novel tri-abstraction combination of aspect-oriented programming, dependency injection, and mocking. Related work reveals fragmentation in using the software engineering abstractions separately to address privacy, as well as an absence of software injection patterns for privacy. We illustrate our new Privacy Injection Pattern and the simplicity of its implementation with a use case, and downloadable example code, that *injects* well-known de-identification patterns in a banking application. Adoption of our higher-level privacy injection pattern is expected to help software engineers comply more readily with Privacy by Design principles and to enable Privacy by Default. Early evaluation results for the PIP from practising software engineers are yet inconclusive.

## 1  Introduction

According to Alexander [1], a "pattern describes a problem that occurs over and over again in our environment, and then describes the core of the solution to that problem, in such a way that you can use this solution a million times over, without ever doing it the same way twice". Privacy patterns [1–4] in software engineering categorize sets of privacy requirements, and their relationships with system architecture and implementation, into repeatable design groupings that may be applied across software applications. Theoretically, and in practice software engineers' productivity improve with the recognition and use of repeatable patterns.

Numerous privacy patterns exist. For example, Kalloniatis et al. [2] identify authorization, authentication, data protection, anonymization and pseudonymization, unobservability, and unlinkability privacy process patterns. Porekar et al. [3] classify organizational privacy patterns as: Obtaining explicit consent" and "Access control to sensitive data based on purpose", "Time limited personal data keeping", "Maintaining privacy audit trails", "Creating privacy policy, Maintaining (versions of) privacy policies", and Privacy negotiation. Doty and Gupta [7] discuss a privacy policy as a pattern and reference Hoepman's work [19] on privacy strategies and categorization of privacy patterns. Others too

© Springer International Publishing Switzerland 2016
B. Berendt et al. (Eds.): APF 2015, LNCS 9484, pp. 144–157, 2016.
DOI: 10.1007/978-3-319-31456-3_8

(e.g. [17, 39]) discuss collections of privacy patterns. Romanosky et al. [39] specify three privacy patterns (informed consent for web-based transactions, masked online traffic and minimal information asymmetry) for software to support individuals when performing some activity online.

Software patterns are also embedded in updated 2015 standard-track specifications and standards such as the Organization for the Advancement of Structured Information Standards' (OASIS) Security Assertion Markup Language (SAML), the XML Access Control Markup Language (OASIS XACML), the Enterprise Privacy Authorization Language (EPAL), Privacy by Design Documentation for Software Engineers (OASIS PbD-SE), the Privacy Management Reference Model and Methodology (OASIS PMRM) specification of its atomic privacy services, and the PRIPARE project.

Once a privacy pattern is identified as per the above approaches, the pattern or its service implementation still has to be "injected" into existing or new software. This injection issue has not been addressed using patterns in the literature. While it is comparatively simpler to incorporate privacy in new applications, software engineers face challenges to implement even existing privacy patterns and their services' mappings in existing applications without affecting other software modules. In some cases, software engineers would prefer to avoid the recompilation and re-deployment of complex programs, such as found in financial and healthcare systems.

To improve software engineers' productivity, we describe a novel master pattern for privacy pattern injection. To the best of our knowledge, a privacy master-pattern for *automating injection of privacy patterns and their mapped privacy services in software* did not exist before this work. The pattern may be used in distributed SOA, cloud, mobile, as well as in non-web services environments, such as desktop and many existing client-server and legacy applications. With the approach described in this paper, privacy can be incorporated in an existing system without modifying its code, or in some cases modifying the code to a very small extent. In further paper sections, we describe our new privacy injection pattern, demonstrate our privacy injection pattern on a banking use case, present related work that highlights the fragmentation and gaps that exist in the privacy patterns universe, and provide a summary and conclusions.

## 2 Proposal for a Privacy Injection Pattern

A key technical challenge is to *automatically* inject a privacy pattern with its component implementation services in existing software without breaking its functionality and undermining its performance. A complex existing system, for example, should not be altered, or if required, modifications should be minor and minimally affect other existing modules or logic.

To inject privacy in architectures without modifying the existing code, we propose to combine three software engineering abstractions: a mocking framework, dependency injection (DI) pattern, and aspects as defined in aspect-oriented programming [23]. These three concepts exist independently, but have not been composed into a master-pattern before now for use by software engineers to nimbly embed privacy controls in applications.

Table 1 briefly discusses each of the three key techniques in our unifying Privacy Injection Pattern to support software engineers to conduct rapid automated embedding of privacy services in code.

**Table 1.** Combining aspect-oriented programming, dependency injection and mocking for privacy engineering

| Software engineering technique | Terminology and traditional uses |
| --- | --- |
| Aspect-Oriented Programming (AOP) | Aspect-oriented programming (AOP [24]) is a programming technique to separate crosscutting concerns, such as privacy, in a unit of modularization called aspects, instead of fusing them with core modules as is traditionally done in object oriented programming. |
| Mocking | A mock object or isolation framework is implemented as a reusable library. It provides a way to create and configure fake objects at runtime. Isolation frameworks are widely used in test driven development (TTD). The use of dynamic fake object eliminates the need to write classes or provide the implementation of the interfaces. |
| Dependency Injection (DI) | The concept of dependency injection is based on the inversion of control (IoC) design pattern. IoC is a technique that assigns the responsibility of flow of control of an application to a container or a class [30] Dependency injection is mostly used for loosely coupled designs. It is commonly used for unit testing and validation/exception management [13]. |

One of the principles of software engineering is that each element of the program (class, method, procedure etc.) should focus on one task and one task only, aka separation of concerns. According to Sommerville (2011), concerns can be defined as *"something that is of interest or significance to a stakeholder or a group of stakeholders"*. Core concerns are the software system's primary functionalities and purposes, while cross-cutting concerns are those functionalities whose implementation is spread across different modules of the program. The idea of Aspect Oriented Programming was proposed mainly to resolve the issue of cross-cutting concerns [16]. Aspects are the abstractions (such as subroutines, methods and objects) that can be used at several places in the program. For example, transaction logging can be implemented using an *aspect* that can be used wherever logging is required for any type of transaction. Aspects can be included before a method, after a method or when an attribute is accessed [41].

In the PIP superpattern, aspects implement known privacy patterns. Dependency injection may also be considered as a design pattern that is useful to reduce the complexity of the system [21]. Mocking has been successfully used to implement a pattern to introduce fake data to protect users' privacy. The PIP proposal generalizes mocking to allow injection of the universe of privacy patterns and not just fake data.

## 3   PIP: A Privacy Injection Pattern

Combining the three abstractions in Table 1, we develop a new privacy injection pattern to insert known privacy patterns or services in new and existing legacy applications. Figure 1 shows our proposed Privacy Injection Pattern to insert privacy services in a software application using mocking, DI and AOP. It describes our injection pattern's program flow (numbered as 1 to 9) through one pattern instance. The concepts intrinsic to PIP (i.e. combination of AOP, mocking and dependency injection) are extensible to multiple system architectures. However, tightly coupled architectures that lack modularity will require more of a privacy engineer's attention than the more extensible, interoperable, and robust SOA and n-tier architectures.

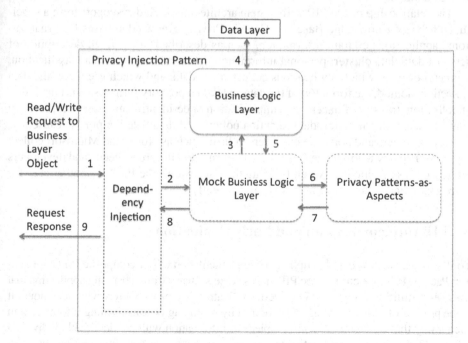

**Fig. 1.**  Privacy injection pattern

Our Privacy Injection Pattern (PIP) implements other privacy-pattern classes in an aspect or privacy service component using AOP. As privacy is a cross-cutting concern across all software collecting or using personal data, software engineers may implement third-party privacy patterns or their components (e.g. masking, encryption) using AOP. Privacy aspects then may be used across software implementation classes.

When using PIP, at the beginning of a software program, software developers load a privacy service DLL (Dynamic Link Library), which consists of privacy pattern services implemented using AOP. An example of such a privacy pattern is obtaining explicit user consent. Dependency injection allows the engineer to load a privacy service DLL without recompiling existing services. A developer simply places the privacy DLL along with other DLLs and the privacy program will automatically load. When the program loads, a mock Business Application Logic (BAL) object of the same type as the original BAL object is created and injected by initializing it. In this way, when a software engineer calls any function of the BAL object (as triggered by (1) in Fig. 1), the mock BAL object function (2) loads. This mock object fetches data from the business layer as normal (3). For de-identification purposes, we use the mock object to apply third-party privacy aspects implementing privacy patterns (6), and to transfer the modified data to the presentation layer (9).

The software engineer may apply privacy patterns or services, implemented as aspects that cater for fine-grain privacy attributes such as role, locations, or any other environmental variables. Thus the PIP enables the software engineer to build rich privacy contexts.

The relationship of the PIP with system architecture includes support from a specialized Privacy Knowledge Base [6]. Generic Privacy Knowledge bases for organizations' applications contain information, such as described in [6, 7, 9]: description of personal data/data cluster, personal information category, personal data classification, source(s) of data, which applications collected the data, and which use them, the data collection method, the format(s) of the data and data repository format(s), the purpose(s) of collection, transfer of data to data minimization or de-identification services, security control during data transfer, data retention policy, and data deletion policy. Currently, privacy engineers and software engineers in firms such as Nokia and Microsoft collect the above Privacy Knowledge Base (PKB) information in spreadsheets, and developers reference these documents when building their software. The PKB is another area for more sophisticated automation that we are currently working on.

## 4    PIP Implementation and Early Evaluation

To illustrate ease of use and simplicity of implementation of our composite Privacy Injection Pattern (PIP), we employ the PIP in a use case scenario from a banking application that uses de-identification patterns. Data de-identification is a privacy-preserving technique. It is the process of de-identifying sensitive data by removing or transforming information in such a way that we cannot associate a piece of information with an identifiable individual [10, 11, 28, 40]. Some identification techniques are substitution, shuffling, nulling out, character masking and cryptographic techniques. We implement the nulling out and character masking privacy patterns for illustration using AOP in our example. We show that the mocking and the dependency injection techniques automatically inject the AOP instance of the de-identification service.

Our technical implementation uses Visual Studio.Net (IDE), PostSharp (AOP), the Unity Container (Dependency Injection) and the Mock library to realize an example injection of our de-identification service into a banking application. We note that the PIP may be implemented with other technologies, e.g. multi-platform heterogeneous technologies. This example's implementation code may be downloaded from https:// web.cs.dal.ca/~naureen/BankExample.

The banking application's use case scenario contains account information that shows individual and account details. We use two roles, manager and operator, to study the behavior of the system before and after applying the proposed pattern. In this case study, we inject the role-based de-identification pattern for access control such that the operator can view only some information while the manager can view all information.

The de-identification service DLL is loaded in the main program. Figure 2 shows the implementation of this added function to load the de-identification service DLL and initialize the de-identification service. This function is required for desktop-based applications. For web-based application, the software developer simply places the privacy DLL with other DLLs.

```
private static void InjectLibraries()
{
    var anonymizationServiceLibName = "SampleBank.AnonymizationService.dll";

    var currentPath = Path.GetDirectoryName(Assembly.GetExecutingAssembly().Location);

    var anonymizationServiceLibCompletePath = Path.Combine(currentPath, anonymizationServiceLibName);

    if (!File.Exists(anonymizationServiceLibCompletePath))
    {
        return;
    }

    Assembly assembly = Assembly.LoadFrom(anonymizationServiceLibCompletePath);
    var anonymizationServiceType = assembly.GetType("SampleBank.AnonymizationService.AnonymizationService");

    var serviceInstance = Activator.CreateInstance(anonymizationServiceType);

    anonymizationServiceType.InvokeMember("Initialize", BindingFlags.Default | BindingFlags.InvokeMethod, null, serviceInstance, null);
}
```

**Fig. 2.** Load de-identification service DLL for desktop applications

When the de-identification service initializes, it creates a mock object of the same type as our business layer object. In our case, our business layer object is CustomerManager, which is an implementation of the ICustomerManager interface. CustomerManager has a method GetCustomer that fetches customer and account details from the database. The software engineer creates a mock object of the ICustomerManager type and then registers it.

The engineer also setups the updated implementation of the GetCustomer method to fetch customer and account details in the same way as the originating object method, and then applies the *de-identification aspect* on this object.

Figure 3 shows the de-identified GetCustomer implementation. Subsequently, when the developer calls CustomerManager.GetCustomer, the updated GetCustomer method is invoked. In the Unity Container, for dependency injection the software engineer first registers the object at the beginning of the program in order to resolve the object to access its methods.

```
public static void Initialize()
{
    SetupCustomerManager();
}

public static void SetupCustomerManager()
{
    if (SampleBank.Common.Ioc.IocContainer.Instance.IsRegistered(typeof(ICustomerManager)))
    {
        return;
    }

    var customerManagerMock = new Mock<ICustomerManager>();

    customerManagerMock.Setup(x => x.GetCustomer()).Returns(() => {

        var customerMgr = new CustomerManager();
        var result = customerMgr.GetCustomer();

        return new CustomerInfoAnonymizedImpl(result);
    });

    SampleBank.Common.Ioc.IocContainer.Instance.Register<ICustomerManager>(customerManagerMock.Object);
}
```

**Fig. 3.** Inject mocking object and invoke IOC

Figure 4 shows how the software developer resolves the ICustomerManager object to fetch customer information. The developer will call the GetCustomer function to fetch the required information. This action calls the mock object's GetCustomer method and applies the de-identification service on the object. After applying de-identification, the system displays the information on the screen.

```
this.customerInfo = SampleBank.Common.Ioc.IocContainer.Instance.Resolve<ICustomerManager>().GetCustomer();

this.lblCustomerName.Text = this.customerInfo.BankUser.FirstName + " " + this.customerInfo.BankUser.MiddleName +" "
    + this.customerInfo.BankUser.LastName;

this.personalInformationUserControl.ShowBankUserInfo(this.customerInfo.BankUser);

if (SampleBank.Common.Ioc.IocContainer.Instance.Resolve<IRoleManager>().UserRole == Role.Operator)
{
    this.personalInformationUserControl.DisableAllControls();
}

this.accountsInfoUserControl.ShowAccounts(this.customerInfo.Accounts);
```

**Fig. 4.** Resolve mocking object at runtime to get customer information

We apply the de-identification service by creating a de-identification aspect with properties or methods. In our case, we apply de-identification on the properties. When we try to access the property, it applies the de-identification aspect on the field and returns a value.

```
[LongStringAnonymization(MaskCharacter = '*', VisibleStringLength = 5)]
public string AccountNumber { get; set; }
```

**Fig. 5.** Apply LongStringAnonymization aspect on AccountNumber

We apply LongStringAnonymization to the AccountNumber property (Fig. 5). In the LongStringAnonymization class, we provide the de-identification logic that will be applied on the field on which we bind as in Fig. 6. We implement the aspect classes for email, date, number, IDs and other fields and then apply these aspects to the properties or methods where required.

```
public override void OnGetValue(LocationInterceptionArgs args)
{
    base.OnGetValue(args);

    if (SampleBank.Common.Ioc.IocContainer.Instance.Resolve<IRoleManager>().UserRole == Role.Manager)
    {
        return;
    }

    string value = (string) args.Value;

    if (String.IsNullOrEmpty(value))
        return;

    if (this.HideFromFront)
    {
        if (value.Length <= this.VisibleStringLength)
            value = this.MaskCharacter.Repeat(this.VisibleStringLength);

        value = string.Format("{0}{1}", this.MaskCharacter.Repeat(value.Length - this.VisibleStringLength),
            value.Substring(value.Length - this.VisibleStringLength));
    }
    else
    {
        if (value.Length <= this.VisibleStringLength)
            value = this.MaskCharacter.Repeat(this.VisibleStringLength);

        value = string.Format("{1}{0}", this.MaskCharacter.Repeat(this.VisibleStringLength),
            value.Substring(0, value.Length - this.VisibleStringLength));
    }

    args.Value = value;
}
```

**Fig. 6.** De-identification implementation in LongStringAnonymization class

Figure 7 shows an operator screen of the sample bank application that results from the use of the PIP for injection of simple de-identification patterns. Recall the operator role does not have permission to view all the private information about the customer.

Different fields' data are de-identified using different de-identification techniques. For example, for the customer id field, we apply character masking; for date of birth, we use date variance; and we null out the street number.

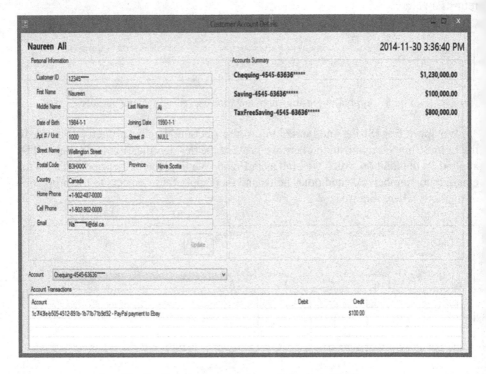

**Fig. 7.** Operator screen of sample bank application

The power of our new PIP pattern lays in its flexibility to inject any privacy pattern in existing code. The PIP pattern can be used repeatedly in many places in a banking application e.g. to also inject a location privacy pattern that disallows the operator from viewing even more of customers' fields from outside of banking hours.

One study that we are currently conducting to evaluate our proposal gives software engineers from large to small participating software organizations a task to embed (1) a simple privacy pattern, and (2) a complex privacy pattern in legacy software. Software engineers are first provided with guidance on using the PIP. They then evaluate the PIP using a validated Technology Acceptance Model (TAM) survey instrument. We sent out electronic surveys to software engineers in software multinationals such as IBM, Intel, Dell, and end user companies with software engineers (e.g. AT&T). We also sent the survey to small software engineering companies, such as Canada's Newpace.

To date, we have received 18 completed and usable responses. These preliminary responses show that the practicing software engineers evaluate the PIP pattern as easy to use. However, responses were mixed with respect to its perceived benefits. While respondents indicated across the board that the pattern would improve their productivity when embedding privacy controls, they were ambivalent about the perceived benefits in general. The respondents did not provide us with outlines or descriptions of any or better alternatives. We are doing a follow-up evaluation exercise to determine whether their response around perceived benefits is due to incompatible technologies (e.g. most engineers in an organization not using the aspect-oriented paradigm), architectural standards and policies that exclude the use of mocking or injected third party code, fear of adding to complexity in the management of their development-operations environments, personal preferences to edit their existing code, lower workplace ranking for adding privacy requirements to code versus product feature requirements, or some other factor or combinations of factors.

## 5  Prior Work

The aspect-oriented programming (AOP) part of our tri-method privacy injection pattern has been used individually in the past to implement security and access control method extensions (e.g. [27, 44]). AOP has been used without automating privacy injection in code via use of mocking and dependency inversion. Sharma et al. [39] propose using AOP for the secure transfer of data over the Internet. They implement privacy patterns for encrypting/decrypting data and key generation using hashing as aspects performed by security agent. Win et al. [42] also use AOP for security and transmission privacy.

Chen and Wang [12] use AOP as a mechanism to implement privacy-aware access control. In their work, application-level access control is extended to enforce privacy policies on personal data using AOP with little impact on the structure of the application. Inter-type declaration (ITD) is used to link privacy preferences of a user with his/her PII, which is then provided to the access control aspect. Inter-type declaration aka member introduction is a mechanism that allows the programmer to modify class members/fields and relationships between classes. Privacy policies are implemented by comparing the purpose of request and the data subject's consent directive. The action manager is used to fetch the purpose of a request while for the data subject's consent or preferences, the preference aspect invokes a preference factory to fetch privacy preferences and link them with the requested data. Lastly, the access control aspect ensures that the requestor is an authorized user, has the authority to perform the requested action, and finally filters user's personally identifiable information (PII) according to privacy preferences attached to the PII.

Many researchers use dependency injection (DI) in their work. Benenson et al. [3] propose a smart card based framework for Secure Multiparty Computation (SMC). Their model consists of multiple processes having a security module that securely interacts with the security modules of other processes. The authors use DI to configure the component that selects the actual algorithm at runtime without recompiling the code. Livne et al. [26] present a health care architecture using dependency injection, AOP, and XML configurations to make the architecture flexible, reusable, loosely coupled and service-oriented. Similarly, Jezek et al. [21] use DI in their work. In their research, they propose a framework that may be used to improve the selection of the injection candidates from multiple candidates based on some extra-functional characteristics such as high performance, low memory consumption etc. In related research, [2] propose a novel service called VAM-aaS (Vulnerability Analysis and Mitigation as-a-service) to mitigate the security vulnerabilities in the cloud environment. It analyzes the online services and in case of vulnerabilities generates a script to block the services or application that can be vulnerable. A list of mitigation actions is maintained by the system. In case of a particular vulnerability, the vulnerability mitigation component injects calls to the security handler classes at runtime based on the required mitigation actions of that vulnerability.

Bender and McWherter [4] use the term "mock" to refer to a family of similar implementations to replace real external resources during unit testing. Indeed, mocking is used primarily during the testing phase of software engineering. It has not been used to automate sophisticated privacy injection patterns in the past, but to provide a simple fake-data pattern to applications to preserve privacy. Beresford et al. [5] propose a modified version of the Android operating system called MockDroid to mock resources accessed by an application. For example, in an application that requests IP connectivity, location data, read-write access to calendar data, the user may provide mock data instead of actual data to the application. Hornyack et al. [20] and Zhou et al. [43], also propose to provide fake or empty data to software applications that require access to users' personal data. A user may view all the permissions that an application requests at the time of installation of the application and then select one of the four modes (trusted, anonymous, bogus, or empty) for each of the permissions.

The OASIS Privacy Management Reference Model and Methodology (PMRM) [8] propose eight atomic privacy services that may be mapped to privacy patterns: Agreement, Validation, Certification, Security, Access, Enforcement, Interaction, and Usage. An Accountability service is recently proposed for addition to the PMRM suite. Doty and Gupta [14] discuss a privacy policy as a pattern with reference to Hoepman's work [19] on privacy strategies and categorization of privacy patterns.

The closest work to this paper's in terms of privacy pattern injection comes from the same research group in Bodorik et al.'s [7] Privacy Architecture for Web Services (PAWS) work that semi-dynamically injects privacy web services for notice and consent in existing web pages built on ROA architectures. Software patterns that *fully automate injecting* privacy patterns are not found in the literature. The literature discussed in this section shows that our abstraction-unifying, higher-level Privacy Injection Pattern helps remove fragmentation from the software engineering landscape for privacy. We expect that patterns for privacy, its constructs, and desirable properties (e.g. unlinkability and unobservability at the data level, and the 7Cs at the user level such as comprehension, choice, consent, consciousness, consistency, confinement, and context [22] - will become increasingly available, as policy levers, such as Privacy by Design in regulations, begin to work.

## 6    Summary and Conclusions

Software engineers can inject other privacy patterns and their service representations in new, existing, and legacy systems without affecting existing systems using the PIP's comprehensive triad-pattern of aspect-oriented programming, dependency injection and mocking. Related work reveals the fragmentation of effort in using the abstractions individually and separately to address privacy. The pattern unification of the three powerful software engineering abstractions to automate the embedding of privacy in applications is expected to increase the productivity of the software engineers tasked with complying with Privacy by Design principles and Fair Information Practices and Principles in code. We illustrate the simplicity of the PIP implementation in a de-identification scenario. This simplicity is at the crux of enhancing its chances of adoption by software engineers.

We will scientifically report on the human performance of our proposed PIP pattern in various use case contexts in future work. We choose to examine the human adoption of our new PIP pattern for two reasons. Not only does the state-of-the art in privacy engineering presently not lend itself readily to automated external verification, engineers' adoption of privacy tools is significant and essential to closing policy-technology gaps. The software engineer is an important stakeholder with respect to the privacy of software applications. Her/his education and the availability of tools in the privacy space remain a major key to progress for Privacy by Design and Default.

**Acknowledgments.**  This material is supported by N. Ali's post-graduate scholarship from the Government of the Province of Nova Scotia, Canada, and D. Jutla's Federal Natural Sciences and Engineering Research Council of Canada (NSERC) grant for privacy and accessibility.

# References

1. Alexander, C., Ishikawa, S., Silverstein, M.: A Pattern Language: Towns, Buildings, Constructions. Oxford University Press, Oxford (1977)
2. Almorsy, M., Grundy, J., Ibrahim, A.S.: VAM-aaS: online cloud services security vulnerability analysis and mitigation-as-a-service. In: Wang, X., Cruz, I., Delis, A., Huang, G. (eds.) WISE 2012. LNCS, vol. 7651, pp. 411–425. Springer, Heidelberg (2012)
3. Fort, M., Freiling, F.C., Penso, L.D., Benenson, Z., Kesdogan, D.: TrustedPals: secure multiparty computation implemented with smart cards. In: Gollmann, D., Meier, J., Sabelfeld, A. (eds.) ESORICS 2006. LNCS, vol. 4189, pp. 34–48. Springer, Heidelberg (2006)
4. Bender, J., McWherter, J.: Professional Test Driven Development with C#: Developing Real World Applications with TDD. Wrox Press Ltd, Birmingham (2011)
5. Beresford, A.R., Rice, A., Skehin, N., Sohan, R.: Mockdroid: trading privacy for application functionality on smartphones. In: Proceedings of the 12th Workshop on Mobile Computing Systems and Applications, HotMobile, pp. 49–54 (2011)
6. Bodorik, P., Jutla, D.N., Dhillon, I.: Privacy compliance with web services. J. Inf. Assur. Secur. **4**(5), 412–421 (2009)
7. Bodorik, P., Jutla, D.N., Bryn, A.: Privacy engineering with PAWS: injecting RESTful privacy web services. Report - 2015–06, Faculty of Computer Science, Dalhousie University (2015)
8. Brown, P.F., Janssen, G., Jutla, D.N., Sabo, J., Willett, M.: Privacy management reference model and methodology (PMRM) version 1.0, OASIS Committee Specification 01, July 2013
9. Cavoukian, A., Carter, F., Jutla, D., Sabo, J., Dawson, F., Fieten, S., Fox, J., Finneran, T.: Annex guide to privacy by design documentation for software engineers version 1.0 OASIS committee note draft 01, 25 June 2014. http://docs.oasis-open.org/pbd-se/pbd-se-annex/v1.0/cnd01/pbd-se-annex-v1.0-cnd01.pdf. Accessed 30 April 2015

10. Cavoukian, A., Emam, K.E.: De-identification protocols: essential for protecting privacy, 25 June 2014. http://www.privacybydesign.ca/content/uploads/2014/09/pbd-de-identifcation-essential.pdf. Accessed 30 November 2014
11. Cavoukian, A., Emam, K.E.: Dispelling the myths surrounding de-identification: anonymization remains a strong tool for protecting privacy, June 2011. https://www.futureofprivacy.org/wp-content/uploads/2011/07/Dispelling. The myth surrounding de-identification anonymization remains strong tool for protectin privacy.pdf. Accessed 15 May 2015
12. Chen, K., Wang, D.-W.: An aspect-oriented approach to privacy-aware access control. In: Proceedings of the Sixth International Conference on Machine Learning and Cybernetics, pp. 3016–3021. IEEE, Hong Kong (2007)
13. Culp, A.: The dependency injection design pattern, 4 May 2011. Retrieved from MSDN: https://msdn.microsoft.com/en-us/library/vstudio/hh323705(v=vs.100).aspx
14. Doty, N., Gupta, M.: Privacy design patterns and anti-patterns. In: Patterns Misapplied and Unintended Consequences. Trustbusters Workshop at the Symposium on Usable Privacy and Security, July 2013
15. Fowler, M.: Inversion of control containers and the dependency injection pattern, 23 de January de 2004. Obtenido de Martin Fowler: http://martinfowler.com/articles/injection.html
16. Groves, M.D.: AOP in.NET Practical Aspect-Oriented Programming. Manning Publications Co., New York (2013)
17. Hafiz, M.: A collection of privacy design patterns. In: Proceedings of the Pattern Languages of Programs Conference (2006)
18. Haque, H.: A curry of Dependency Inversion Principle (DIP), Inversion of Control (IoC), Dependency Injection (DI) and IoC container, 12 de March de 2013. Obtenido de Code Project: http://www.codeproject.com/Articles/538536/A-curry-of-Dependency-Inversion-Principle-DIP-Inversion
19. Hoepman, J.-H.: Privacy design strategies. In: Cuppens-Boulahia, N., Cuppens, F., Jajodia, S., Abou El Kalam, A., Sans, T. (eds.) SEC 2014. IFIP AICT, vol. 428, pp. 446–459. Springer, Heidelberg (2014)
20. Hornyack, P., Han, S., Jung, J., Schechter, S., Wetherall, D.: "These aren't the droids you're looking for": retrofitting android to protect data from imperious applications. In: 18th ACM Conference on Computer and Communications Security. ACM, Chicago (2011)
21. Jezek, K., Holy, L., Brada, P.: Dependency injection refined by extra-functional properties. In: IEEE Symposium on Visual Languages and Human-Centric Computing: Poster and Demos, pp. 255–256 (2012)
22. Jutla, D.N., Bodorik P.: Sociotechnical architecture for online privacy. In: IEEE Security and Privacy, vol. 3, no. 2, pp. 29–39, March–April 2005. doi:10.1109/MSP.2005.50
23. Kalloniatis, C., Kavakli, E., Gritzalis, S.: Using privacy process patterns for incorporating privacy requirements into the system design process. In: The Second International Conference on Availability, Reliability and Security, ARES 2007, pp.1009–1017 (2007)
24. Kiczales, G., Lamping, L., Mendhekar, A., Maeda, C., Lopes, C., Loingtier, J.M.: Aspect Oriented Programming, ECOOP 1997—Object-Oriented Programming, pp. 220–242 (1997)
25. Laddad, R.: AspectJ in Action: Practical Aspect-Oriented Programming. Manning Publications Co., New York (2003)
26. Livne, O.E., Schultz, N.D., Narus, S.P.: Federated Querying Architecture with Clinical and Translational Health IT Application. Springer Science + Business Media, USA (2011)
27. Mourad, A., Laverdière, M.-A., Debbabi, M.: An aspect-oriented approach for the systematic security hardening of code. Comput. Secur. **27**(3–4), 101–114 (2008)

28. Narayanan, A., Shmatikov, V.: Robust de-anonymization of large sparse datasets. In: Proceedings of the 2008 IEEE Symposium on Security and Privacy (2008)
29. Porekar, J., Jerman-Blazic, A., Klobucar, T.: Towards organizational privacy patterns. In: 2008 Second International Conference on Digital Society, pp. 15–19, February 2008
30. Prasanna, D.: Dependency Injection. Manning Publications Co., New York (2009)
31. Raghunathan, B.: Complete Book of Data Anonymization from Planning to Implementation. CRC Press Taylor and Francis Group, Boca Raton (2013)
32. van Rest, J., Boonstra, D., Everts, M., van Rijn, M., van Paassen, R.: Designing privacy-by-design. In: Preneel, B., Ikonomou, D. (eds.) APF 2012. LNCS, vol. 8319, pp. 55–72. Springer, Heidelberg (2014)
33. Romanosky, S., Acquisto, A., Hong, J., Cranor, L., Friedman, B.: Privacy patterns for online interactions. In: Proceedings of the Pattern Languages of Programs Conference (2006)
34. Sadicoff, M., Larrondo-Petrie, M., Fernandez, E.: Privacy-aware network client pattern. In: Proceedings of the Pattern Languages of Programs Conference (2005)
35. Schumacher, M.: Security patterns and security standards - with selected security patterns for anonymity and privacy. In: European Conference on PaBern Languages of Programs (EuroPLoP 2002)
36. Schümmer, T.: The public privacy – patterns for filtering personal information in collaborative systems. In: CHI 2004 (2004)
37. Seemann, M.: Dependency Injection in.NET. Manning, New York (2012)
38. Seemann, M.: Mock Objects to the Rescue! Test Your.NET Code with NMock. MSDN Magazine, October de 2004
39. Sharma, N., Batra, U., Mukherjee, S.: Enhancing security in service oriented architecture driven EAI using aspect oriented programming in healthcare IT. Int. J. Sci. Eng. Res. 5(3), 50–55 (2014)
40. Shapiro, S.: Separating the baby from the bathwater - toward a generic and practical framework for anonymization. IEEE (2011)
41. Somerville, I.: Software Engineering. Pearson Education, UK (2011)
42. Win, B.D., Joosen, W., Piessens, F.: Developing secure applications through aspect-oriented programming. In: Aspect-Oriented Software Development, pp. 633–650. Addison-Wesley (2005)
43. Zhou, Y., Zhang, X., Jiang, X., Freeh, V.W.: Taming information-stealing smartphone applications (on android). In: McCune, J.M., Balacheff, B., Perrig, A., Sadeghi, A.-R., Sasse, A., Beres, Y. (eds.) Trust 2011. LNCS, vol. 6740, pp. 93–107. Springer, Heidelberg (2011)
44. Zhu, Z.J., Zulkernine, M.: A model-based aspect-oriented framework for building intrusion-aware software systems. Inf. Softw. Tech. 51, 865–875 (2009)

# Economic and Legal Implications of Electronic Data Processing

# Surveillance of Electronic Communications in Republic of Serbia

Milana Pisarić[(✉)]

Assistant, Faculty of Law, University of Novi Sad, Novi Sad, Serbia
mpisaric@pf.uns.ac.rs

**Abstract.** The right to privacy, especially the element of communication privacy, as well as right to data protection could be limited only to protect the general interest and this limit should be proportionate and determined by law. In this regard, the question is to what extent and in which cases these rights can be justifiably restricted. In this paperwork the author discusses opportunities given to state authorities by the law to execute surveillance over electronic communications in Republic of Serbia.

**Keywords:** Serbia · Surveillance · Electronic communications · Criminal procedure

## 1 Introduction

The right to privacy is a basic, inalienable and absolute human right of each individual which ensures the integrity and dignity of the human person in order to preserve confidentiality and freedom of his private life. The right to privacy is labeled as "the individual's right to be left alone"[1] more than a hundred years, and several elements of privacy may be recognized: personal privacy, which protects the physical integrity of the individual (i.e. physical privacy); privacy of personal conduct, which refers to the protection of all aspects of individual behavior (especially on the sensitive aspects such as sexual orientation and habits, political activities, religious beliefs, etc.) both in private and in public places (i.e. media privacy); privacy of personal communication, which protects the right of individuals to communicate with one another using a variety of means, without these activities being monitored by unauthorized persons (i.e. communication privacy); privacy of personal data, based on which individuals have a reasonable expectation that the data on them are not automatically available to other individuals and organizations, as well as the ability to exercise control over the processing and use

---

[1] S. Warren, L. Brandeis, 'The Right to Privacy', Harvard Law Review, 5/1890. Cited in: D. Ritchie, "Is it possible to define 'privacies' within the law? Reflections on the 'securitisation' debate and the interception of communications", International Review of Law, Computers & Technology 1–2/2009, 29.

© Springer International Publishing Switzerland 2016
B. Berendt et al. (Eds.): APF 2015, LNCS 9484, pp. 161–177, 2016.
DOI: 10.1007/978-3-319-31456-3_9

of this data (i.e. privacy of information)[2]. This kind of observation could still be considered as the basis for determining the essence of the concept of privacy, as dynamical category that needs to be adjusted to the values in the changed environment. In this regard, it can be considered that there has been a convergence of last two aspects (communication privacy and privacy of information) into so-called informational privacy[3]. Informational privacy can be defined as the right of an individual to voluntarily give up certain elements of privacy rights in the information environment, and in this sense it has become a pressing issue in terms the use of modern information and communication technologies. Due to the convergence of these technologies there has been a change in the process of collecting and processing data, and not just in terms of volume (data are collected and processed in a number of databases, e.g. Google, the user's database of online sales, social networks, etc.), but also by the quality (entirely new kinds of personal data are being collected and processed, for example, information about the location of users of electronic devices, data about user activity on the Internet, etc.), as techniques and methods for data collection and processing have made this process far more intrusive (e.g. automatic recognition, profiling, etc.). On the one hand, individuals are becoming dependent on technologies in everyday activities (which brings a great amount of benefits), but on the other hand, the development of new information technologies has been enabling mass tracking of these activities, especially monitoring and surveillance of electronic communications. Since technology of electronic monitoring and surveillance is dramatically evolving, through creation of unlimited possibilities for concentration of communication data and their use by a wide range of users, question of informational privacy, which may be easily threatened by state's and non-state subjects, is opened. We assume that in order the right to privacy to enable the protection of the right to legal personality and the right to free development of personality in the online environment, it is necessary to ensure that the legislation contain even stricter and more precise rules in relation to the rules that protect these values in offline environment.

The right to privacy, especially the element of communication privacy, could be limited only to protect the general interest and this limit should be proportionate and determined by law. In this regard, the question is to what extent and in which cases these rights can be justifiably restricted. In other words, how to adequately regulate the scope of the authorization of the competent authorities to collect evidence for the purposes of criminal proceedings, by taking certain actions and measures which can greatly interfere with the private sphere of individuals and collect huge amounts of personal data about them. Today in almost all European countries the oversight of electronic communications for the purposes of criminal proceedings is conducted under strict specified assumptions. Surveillance and interception as form of state control are standardized by legal regulations (criminal procedure laws or special laws for combating organized crime) which set boundaries between efficiency in fighting crime and protecting the

---

[2] R. Clarke, "Privacy impact assessment: Its origins and development", Computer Law and Security Review 2/2009, 124.

[3] Y. Poullet, "Data protection legislation: What is at stake for our society and democracy", Computer Law and security review 25/2009, 215.

fundamental rights and freedoms. Each state has different requirements for measures of legal surveillance and interception, but laws in each of them (speaking of ECHR states) require compliance with principle of subdidiarity and proportionality, a relatively short period of time of application of measure and a specific circle of persons to whom the measure may be applied. In all countries, the surveillance of telecommunications for the purposes of criminal proceedings (i.e. the repressive purposes) is regulated by criminal procedure laws or special laws governing the combat against organized crime, and information gained by surveillance may be used as evidence in court in criminal proceedings. In most countries, except for repressive, surveillance may be conducted in preventive purposes as well, and mainly under the provisions of police legislation, where the conditions for application of monitoring are somewhat less stricter comparing to the conditions necessary for the implementation of oversight for repressive purposes. It is understood that the degree of protection of the rights and liberties in the application of surveillance for repressive purposes (which results are to be used as evidence in court) is higher than the level of protection of rights and freedoms that is required for surveillance used in preventive purposes. As almost all European countries have adopted the European Convention for the Protection of Human Rights and fundamental freedoms and have harmonized provisions of their legislation with Convention standards respecting the principles of proportionality and subsidiarity, secret measure of surveillance is today conducted in a very similar way. Serbian legislation has, however, several "suspicious" legal solutions.

## 2    Information Privacy in Serbia

The basic principles of privacy protection of communications can be found in the grounds of legal regulation in the Republic of Serbia. The Serbian Constitution[4] does not recognize the right to privacy as a solid human rights, but does, in the chapter regulating human rights and freedoms, protect several elements of concept of privacy. The article 41 of the Constitution guarantees the secrecy of correspondence and other means of communication, and deviations are permitted only for a limited time and on the basis of a court decision if necessary to conduct criminal proceedings or protect safety of the Republic of Serbia, in the manner provided by law. As for electronic communications in the legal system of Republic of Serbia, they are regulated by special Law on electronic communications[5]. One of the important goals and principles regulating relations in the field of electronic communications is the principle of providing a high level of protection of personal data and privacy, in accordance with the Law on Protection of Personal Data[6] and other laws and the principle of ensuring the security and integrity of public electronic communications networks and services. Although this Law stipulates secrecy of communications, several articles are

---

[4] Constitution of Republic of Serbia ("Official gazette of Republic of Serbia", No. 98/2006).
[5] Law on electronic communications ("Official Gazette of Republic of Serbia", Nos. *44/2010, 60/ 2013 – Decision of Constitutional Court and 62/2014*).
[6] Law on protection of personal data ("Official Gazette of Republic of Serbia", Nos. 97/2008, 104/2009 – other Law, 68/2012 - *Decision of Constitutional Court and* 107/2012).

devoted to regulation of communication surveillance and data retention. These measures are of particular interest if corelated with specific regulations of several other laws. Interception of e-communication that reveals the content of communication is not permitted without consent of user, but it is allowed to record communications for monitoring of commercial transactions or other business relationship, provided that both sides are aware or should have been aware of or are expressly warned that communications are recorded. However, user's consent is not required if the interception done during a certain time and on the basis of a court decision if it is necessary to conduct criminal proceedings or protect national security. The use of e-communications for storage or access information in the terminal equipment of users is allowed on condition that the user is given clear and complete notice of the purpose of the data processing, in accordance with the law governing the protection of personal data, and that he is given the opportunity to refuse such processing. The Law clearly states that the retention of data that reveal the content of communication is prohibited (article 129 paragraph 3), however, the operator is obliged to facilitate interception of electronic communication and also to keep all information about the e-communications for the purposes of conducting the investigation, discovering criminal offenses and criminal proceedings, in accordance with the Criminal procedure Code, as well as the need to protect national security and public safety. Data are to be retained up to 12 months from the date of the communication and in such a manner that data can be accessed immediately, or submitted upon a request to the competent state authorities. State bodies that acquire access to retained data are required to keep records on access to the retained data. Data retention obligation applies on a specific type of withheld data that law states (article 129 paragraph 1) necessary to determine: the source and destination of communication, the beginning, duration and end of communication, the type of communication and location of equipment used. The Law does not define precisely who is authorized to carry out interception of communications and access to retained data, but instead uses the term competent authority, which competence is regulated by other laws.

In addition to guarantees of communication privacy, the Constitution in Article 42 guarantees protection of personal data, and provides that the collection, holding, processing and use of personal data is regulated by law (the principle of legality of the collection and processing of personal data). In addition, it is expressly provided that it is prohibited and punishable to use personal data outside the purpose for which it was collected in accordance with the law, except for the purposes of conducting criminal proceedings or protect safety of the Republic of Serbia, in the manner provided by law (principle of definiteness of purpose and principle of limited use). On the basis of the aforementioned provisions, the Law on Protection of Personal Data was adopted. This Law in Article 8 specifies the cases in which processing of personal data is not allowed (which should be linked with the Criminal Code[7], which in Article 146 stipulates the crime of unauthorized collection of personal data). Article 13 of this Law gives the competences to the authorities to process data without the consent of the person if the processing is necessary for carrying out tasks within the competence specified by law with regard to (among other things) the prevention, detection, investigation and prosecution of crimes, which is in accordance with the aforementioned

---

[7] Criminal Code ("Official gazette of Republic of Serbia", Nos. 85/2005, 88/2005, 107/2005, 72/2009, 111/2009, 121/2012, 104/2013 and 108/2014).

provision Constitution. The Constitution contains one more principle of personal data protection because it guarantees that everyone has the right to be informed about the information collected about his personality, in accordance with the law (Article 42, paragraph 4). In this regard, the Law on Protection of Personal Data stipulates that a person whose data is being processed is entitled to notice of processing (Article 19), access (Article 20) and copy (21 and 22), but that these rights can be limited if the providing of information would seriously undermine the actions of prevention, detection, investigation and prosecution of criminal offenses (Article 23).

The above provisions of the Constitution beside the guarantees, allow restriction of the right to privacy of communication and protection of personal data as human rights, and in order the appropriate legal provisions to have a sense of legitimate restrictions, they must be linked to Article 20 of the Constitution. The human rights guaranteed by the Constitution may be restricted by law if the limit is permitted by the Constitution, for the purposes which the Constitution allows, to the extent necessary to meet the constitutional purpose of restriction in a democratic society and without encroaching upon the substance of the guaranteed rights. At the same time, it should be borne in mind that all state authorities, particularly the courts, in limiting human rights are obliged to consider the substance of the restricted right, pertinence of restriction, nature and extent of restriction, relation of restriction and its purpose and whether there is a way that the purpose of the restriction could be met with less restrictive means.

Therefore, the restriction of the right to privacy of communication and protection of personal data can only be the *ultima ratio* in order to protect certain interests which the Constitution itself recognized, and they are the interest of national security and the needs of the criminal proceedings. However, certain laws in Serbia include provisions allowing restriction of these rights in a much broader, unjustified extent in relation to the limits permitted by the Constitution. At this point we would especially point out the problematic arrangement of special measures of secret data collection, especially of communication data.

## 3   Special Measures of Secret Surveillance in Serbia

At this point it is necessary to define what is considered by special measures of secret data collection. Since these measures are numerous, varied and constantly evolving and changing, it is difficult to give a unique and precise definition[8]. It should be noted, however, that application of these specific measures is mainly justified by two basic purposes: investigation of serious criminal offenses and protection of national security. The Council of Europe as common denominators of "special investigative techniques" used in criminal proceedings accept their secret nature and the fact that their

---

[8] Committee of Experts on Special Investigation Techniques in Relation to Acts of Terrorism (PC-TI). Conclusions of the third meeting, Strasbourg 24.09.2003. PC-TI (2003). http://goo.gl/52RXx0 (coe.int pdf).

application could infringe fundamental rights and freedoms[9]. Special measures may be applied for criminal procedure purpose is usually considered legimit only if the following conditions are fulfilled: that they are expressly provided for in the legal provisions (the principle of legality); that there are not less stringent measures to achieve the same goal (principle of subsidiarity); that they are used regard to very serious offenses (principle of proportionality); that on the basis of the existence of legally prescribed degree of probability (based on suspicion or reasonable suspicion) that a criminal offense is committed or being prepared and if based on the decision of the competent judicial authority, for precise limited period of time; that the control over legality of application exists[10]. Special measures of secret data collection represent sensitive sphere of the state bodies' activities in which full transparency, for obvious reasons, is not possible. However, this does not mean that it is not necessary and possible to achieve a certain level of transparency in this area that would allow external supervision of the implementation of these measures.

So, special measures for secret collection of communication data mean that national authorities apply secretly actions which temporarily impinge on the privacy of citizens and limit certain rights guaranteed in the Constitution of Serbia. Supervision of electronic communications restricts two civil rights (in our case, the inviolability of letters and other means of communication and the protection of personal data) and involves two types of activity: interception of communications and access to retained electronic data. The Constitution allows these restrictions only for two important reasons.

When it comes to the application of specific measures to collect data, they are differently defined, depending on the reasons for their application and the actors who apply them. These measures are "hidden" in different laws under a variety of names: the special evidentiary actions, measures of targeted search, special procedures and measures for covert data collection, secret surveillance of communications and information systems. Depending on the purpose of collecting data - whether it is the protection of national security or interest of criminal proceedings - there are two legal regimes governing the use of special measures. The interception of electronic communications and access to stored data without the user's consent are permitted only for a limited time and on the basis of the court's decision. The actors who carry out lawful interception of communications and access stored data should not threaten civil rights and in addition to the prescribed reasons, it is necessary to comply with the legal procedure. The procedure differs depending on which reason is concerned, the prosecution of criminal offenses or the protection of national security.

As for protection of national security secret monitoring by specific measures are regulated by the Law on Military Security Agency and Military Intelligence Agency[11]

---

[9] Council of Europe Committee of Ministers. Recommendation of the Committee of Ministers to member states on "special investigation techniques" in relation to serious crimes including acts of terrorism. Adopted by the Committee of Ministers on 20 April 2005 at the 924th meeting of the Ministers' Deputies. Rec(2005)10 http://goo.gl/X3QiRb.

[10] T. Bugarski, Dokazne radnje u krivicnom postupku, Novi Sad 2014, 25.

[11] Law on Military Security Agency and Military Intelligence Agency ("Official Gazette of Republic of Serbia", Nos. 55/2012 - *Decision of Constitutional Court* and 17/2013).

(Law on VBA and VOA) and the Law on Security Information Agency (Law on BIA)[12]. The first-mentioned Law provides that Military Security Agency and Military Intelligence Agency can apply secret data collection (Article 10) to counter threats to the Ministry of Defence and the Serbian Army, and only against the employees of these bodies, and to other entities only in cooperation with the police or the BIA. Among special procedures and measures, agencies may apply covert surveillance and the contents of letters and other means of communication, and in addition there is also possibility of covert electronic surveillance of telecommunications and information systems in order to collect the retained data on telecommunications traffic, without insight into their content (Article 12). The latter Law in Article 9 provides that the Agency may apply special measures against a person, group or organization for which there are reasonable grounds to undertake or preparing acts directed against the security of the Republic of Serbia, more precisely appropriate operational methods, measures and actions, as well as the appropriate operational and technical means which enable the collection of data and information in order to eliminate and prevent activities aimed to undermining or destruction of the constitutional order of the Republic of Serbia and jeopardizing security in the country. Also among special measures derogating the inviolability of letters and other means of communication, the Law provides for surveillance and recording of conversations, as well as statistical electronic surveillance of communications and information systems in order to collect communication data or location used mobile terminal equipment (Article 13). When it comes to protecting national security, authorities propose to court to approve enforcement. It can not be done, however, by any of the employees in agencies or the police. The law provides who is authorized proposer and which court has jurisdiction for each of these actors. So, on behalf of the BIA proposal for the application of special measures may be only director of the Agency and the authorization is made by the President or his authorized judge of the Special department (for organized crime) of the Higher Court in Belgrade. On the basis of a proposal by the VBA Director for making decision on the application of special measures authorizing interception of communications is in jurisdiction of judges of the Supreme Court of Cassation, and when it comes to accessing the retained data decisions-maker are judges of competent Higher court. The application of special measures by the police is proposed by a director of police, and is approved by the President or authorized judge of the Supreme Court of Cassation.

As for purpose of criminal procedure, relevant articles are found in Criminal Procedure Code[13] (CPC) that among special evidentiary actions regulates secret surveillance of communications. These measures may be applied only if certain material and formal conditions are fulfilled. When it comes to the criminal proceedings, the object of secret surveillance of communications can be a person for whom there are grounds for suspicion of committing or preparing any of the serious crimes listed in the Criminal Procedure Code. Material requirement (defined in Article 161) for the implementation of

---

[12] Law on Security Information Agency ("Official Gazette of Republic of Serbia", Nos. 42/2002 and 111/2009).
[13] Criminal procedure code ("Official Gazette of Republic of Serbia", Nos. 72/2011, 101/2011, 121/2012, 32/2013, 45/2013 and 55/2014).

specific evidentiary action consists in the cumulative fulfillment of two conditions, namely: (1) the necessity of the existence of grounds for suspicion that any of the offenses referred to in Article 162 is committed, and (2) a requirement that applies to evidentiary problems from which it follows that the special investigative actions is to be imposed as a kind of evidence ultima ratio, meaning that otherwise evidence for prosecution can not be collected or it would otherwise be significantly more difficult. This special evidentiary action may be exceptionally determined if there are grounds of suspect of the preparation of a separate criminal offense, and the circumstances of the case indicate that such it would not be able to detect an offense otherwise, prevent it or prove it, or that would cause disproportionate difficulties or a great danger. Secret surveillance of communication may be ordered against person, against whom there are predefined grounds for suspicion, but only upon court decision. An action can be determined only by reasoned order of the judge for preliminary proceedings on a reasoned request of the public prosecutor. When deciding on the application and the duration of this action, competent authority is required to take into account the proportionality, and especially to evaluate whether the same result could be achieved in a way that is less restrictive to the rights of citizens.

This court order must contain explanation. This is especially important as it encroaches on the area of privacy and the judge is obliged to explain what are the reasons that justify the use of these special investigative actions. The Code provided for mandatory elements of order on the secret surveillance of communications: available data on the person against whom the secret surveillance of communication is determined (this means that the secret surveillance of communications can be determined against known as well as against and unknown suspect), the legal name of the crime (the legal qualification), indication of the famous telephone number or address of the suspect or the phone number or address for which there are reasonable grounds to believe that the suspect uses them, the reasons on which the suspicion is based, manner of implementation, the scope and duration. All those are mentioned in the operative part of the order, except for reasons, which underlie the suspicion and are placed in the explanation.

This special evidentiary action includes monitoring and recording of communication by telephone or other technical means as well as surveillance of electronic or other address of the suspect and the seizure of letters and other consignments (but neither of e-mails nor other messages transmitted using electronic communications services). Implementation of surveillance is interrupted as soon as the reasons for its application cease, can last up to three months, and for the reason of necessity of further evidence gathering it can be extended up to three months (and for criminal offenses in jurisdiction of special Public Prosecutor, secret surveillance may be exceptionally extended for a maximum of two times for a period of three months). Action is executed by the police, Security Information Agency or Military Security Agency. The authority determined to conduct secret surveillance of communications shall constitute the daily reports that along with the collected material is submitted to the judge for preliminary proceedings and the public prosecutor, at their request. In order to facilitate application of the surveillance, the postal, telegraphic and other enterprises, companies and persons registered for transmission of information are obliged to assist the authorities who execute the action by enabling the implementation of surveillance and recording of communications and to, with acknowledgment of receipt, submit letters and other items. The Code provides for the possibility of expansion of secret surveillance of communications, and if in the course of conducting secret surveillance of communications the authority that executes the command concludes that the suspect uses another phone number or address, it may expand the secret surveillance to that another communication and phone number or address. In that case they shall immediately notify the public prosecutor, who submits to the court a proposal for subsequently approval of the expansion of secret surveillance of communications (the court decides within 48 h of receipt of the proposal). If the proposal is adopted, the judge for preliminary proceedings will subsequently approve the expansion of secret surveillance of communications, and if the proposal is rejected, the material collected by extended surveillance is destroyed.

When secret surveillance of communication is complete (the expiry of the period for which a specific measure was idetermined or earlier before the expiration of the deadline if reasons for the application of control ceased), the authority which implemented action will submit to the judge for preliminary proceedings recordings of communications, letters and other items and the special report. This special report must include: time and date of start and end of surveillance, details of the official who conducted monitoring, a description of the technical means used, the number and available information on persons covered by the supervision and the assessment of the purpose and results of the implementation of surveillance. The judge for preliminary proceedings will prepare a report on the opening of letters and other parcels and must take care when opening them not to violate seals, as well as bags and store address. Complete material obtained by secret surveillance of communication judge will deliver to a public prosecutor, and he will order the material obtained using technical means to be prescribed and described in whole or in part.

As regards the treatment of the collected material, it is anticipated that the judge for preliminary proceedings issue a decision on the destruction of the material collected, if the public prosecutor does not initiate criminal proceedings within six months from the day when introduced with the material collected using a special evidentiary action, or if he declares that it will not be used in the process, or that he will not require proceedings against the suspect. About this decision the judge for preliminary proceedings may inform the person against who evidentiary action of secret surveillance of communication was conducted, provided that during the implementation of these actions the identity of the person is established and if informing this person would not jeopardize the possibility of conducting criminal proceedings. It is noteworthy also that the data collected can not be a base for a judicial decision if when conducting this special evidentiary actions authorities acted contrary to the provisions of this Code or court order.

## 4   Concerns About Some Solutions in Serbian Legislation

In Serbia exists data retention and anyone who uses an electronic communication service can count with the data retained about him, but he can not find out if someone asked or gained access to these data. Article 128 of the Law on Electronic Communications provided that the operator is obliged to keep data on electronic communications for the purpose of investigating, detecting offenses and criminal proceedings (in accordance with the law governing criminal procedure) and for the protection of national and public security of the Republic of Serbia (in accordance with the laws governing the work of the security services of the Republic of Serbia and the work of the internal affairs) as well as to submit the retained data without delay at the request of those bodies. The provisions of Article 128 of the part that read: "in accordance with the law governing criminal procedure", "in accordance with the laws governing the work of the security services of the Republic of Serbia and the work of the internal affairs" and "at the request of the competent state organs" ceased to apply on the basis of decisions of the Constitutional Court[14]. Also the provision of Article 129, paragraph 4, by which it was anticipated that the ministry responsible for telecommunications and information society, after obtaining the opinion of the ministry responsible for judicial affairs, the ministry responsible for internal affairs, the ministry responsible for defense affairs, the Security information Agency and the body responsible for the protection of personal data, shall prescribe the requirements regarding data retention was terminated. The Constitutional Court declared unconstitutional the provisions of Article 128 which established the obligation of operators to make retained data (regardless of the fact they do not reveal the content of communications) available to the competent authority without a prior court decision, because this regulation infringes the inviolability of the right to confidentiality of communication of the users of electronic communications. Law on Amendments to the Law on Electronic Communications, amended Article 128 in general[15], so the operator is required to retain certain data on electronic communications, as well as to keep them for 12 months from the date of the communication.

Access to such retained data is not permitted without the consent of the user, except for a limited time and on the basis of a court decision if it is necessary to conduct criminal proceedings or protect national security of the Republic of Serbia, in the manner provided by law. An important still opened issue related to the above is the way the competent authorities gain access to retained data, given the inviolability of the secrecy of communications. Given the fact that the Constitution permits derogation from the secrecy of letters and other means of communication only for a specific time on the basis of a court decision if it is necessary for the conduct of criminal proceedings in the manner provided by law (Article 41, paragraph 2), it means that for the purposes of criminal procedure the simple retention and storing of communication data could be ordered only by a court decision and in accordance with the law governing criminal procedure. Therefore, we think that regulation of the matter should be fully withdrawn from the retention of data in the manner stipulated by the Law on Electronic Communications, but prescribed by corresponding provisions in the Criminal Procedure Code. In order the competent authorities to obtain access to information necessary to identify the suspect, it is necessary to adequately commit service providers, who have in possession or control over necessary information, to keep them, but only regarding certain data for

---

[14] Decision of the Constitutional Court ("Official Gazette of Republic of Serbia", No. 60/2013).

[15] Law on Amendments to the Law on Electronic Communications ("Official Gazette of Republic of Serbia", No. 62/2014).

the purpose of concrete criminal proceedings. So, the only proper solution, is to foresee in the Code provisions which would regulate measures of expedited preservation of communication data (for instance, like measures provided by COE Cybercrime Convention) in order ensure that data relevant for criminal proceedings are secured in expeditious manner from loss/modifications till the completion of formal procedures in which the competent authorities entitled to access such data (by issuing appropriate orders by the court). Since preservation of data, by using this measure, only applies to issuing orders to secure and maintain data and does not involve the realization of access to the content of these data, the measure could be also ordered by public prosecutor, in order to achieve expediency. However, access may be achieved only upon court decision.

There are several concerns regarding the lawful interception of communications and access to stored electronic data and they are in correlation with the absence of a bylaw that would describe in detail the procedures and define the technical requirements for the implementation of these actions. The proposal of such an act is drawn up in 2013, but has not yet been adopted. The main problem is the way that authorized person of the operator, who is responsible to deal with the request of the police, BIA and VBA to intercept or access stored data, is determined. The operator has no legal obligation to designate such persons and to secure that they receive a security certificate. However, they would have to have special training and permission, given that they come into contact with classified information. Concrete demands to operator may submit only the authorized person of the competent authority, and only if present an adequate legal basis or judicial decision. This means that upon receipt of the request, the operator is obliged to assess whether all the conditions for access are fulfilled. If it comes to an unauthorized person or incompetent authority, or if there is no court authorization, access should not be enabled. It is therefore very important that the person receiving the demands before the operator have appropriate training. Another problem is that the interested public is not presented clearly whether VBA, BIA or the police can directly intercept communications and access stored data, i.e. without prior submission of the application, even without the knowledge of the operator. This is important because the operators are obliged to record only received requests for interception or access to data, why such direct approaches remain out records. However, it seems that the wording of the Law on electronic communications leaves the possibility of the direct approach as competent authority addresses the operator only if it can not implement the measure without access to the premises, network, associated facilities or equipment operators (and not always, but only in special circumstances).

Illegally obtained and unused data is destroyed. All material collected by applying these measures in a manner that is not in line with law or is not in the short time subsequently approved by the court is destroyed, whether it was collected for a criminal procedure or protection the national security (Article 84, 163i 169 CPC, Article 15b Law on BIA, Article 15 Law on VBA and VOA). Also lawfully collected material is destroyed if it has not been used for the purpose for which it was collected. When it comes to the prosecution of crimes, destroying the material that is not used six months to institute criminal proceedings, or for which the public prosecutor declares that he will not use it. The same applies to data collected by the police after lawful application of special measures for the capture and detention of persons and which may not be evidence in criminal procedure (Article 163 CPC, Article 83 ZP). The way VBA and BIA maintain and destroy data collected by lawful specific measures in order to protect national security is governed by the by-laws and internal rules (Article 32 Law on VBA and VOA). So in the Instruction on the regulation of BIA, issued by the Director of the Agency, the destruction of data is provided in a few cases: (1) if activity according to which the Agency is competent to act is not confirmed; (2) to relieving the burden of documentation funds, unnecessary data is successively being destroyed; (3) when deleting of certain persons from the registers, as provided in the Ordinance on internal reporting, documentation and records of BIA. Also, the provider of electronic communication is required to destroy all electronic data kept if they have not been accessed within period 12 months starting from moment of data retention (Article 130(4) Law on electronic communications).

In terms of notification of persons that information about him were collected for the purpose of criminal proceedings, it should be provided the right of individuals to be aware that the personal data were collected and processed for the purposes of criminal proceedings, but that such a right of access may be restricted, if necessary and proportionate to the protection of certain interests, among other things, in order not to interfere with the criminal proceedings. In order to protect the interests of the criminal proceedings, the exercise of the right to information can be limited or time-deferred until the expiry of a certain period. In doing so, any refusal or restriction of access shall be granted in writing to the person whose data is processed. A written decision should contain an explanation (which may be absent in cases where there is reason to limit the right of access to information). We believe that it is necessary to foresee in the Code a provision by which the public prosecutor's office or the court would be obliged upon individual's application to deliver notification of whether personal data have been the subject of gathering and processing for the purposes of criminal proceedings. Obligation of noticing persons whose personal data is being collected and stored is of particular importance in connection with special evidentiary actions that are secret and intrusive by their nature. The Criminal Procedure Code provides for the possibility of informing person just in one single article. In Article 163, which regulates the handling of the material collected by applying a special evidentiary action of secret surveillance of communications, and which will certainly not be used in criminal proceedings. Namely, if the public prosecutor does not initiate criminal proceedings within six months from the day when material collected using a special evidentiary action was presented to him or if he declares that it will not be used in the proceedings, the judge for preliminary proceedings decides on the destruction of the collected material, about which he may inform the person against who a special evidentiary action was carried out, if during the implementation of the action his identity was established and if this would not jeopardize the possibility of criminal proceedings. We believe that such a solution is not in accordance with the principles and standards of protection of personal data for several reasons. Notification is provided only as a possibility, and not as an obligation, so it can be completely avoided. The Code should foresee adequate duty for state authorities, which can be time-delayed until there is danger to criminal proceedings, but that kind of disposal should also bind to a specific deadline. Furthermore, the possibility of notification applies only to the use of secret surveillance of communications, but not to other special evidentiary actions, which we believe is unjustified. In addition, the person may be notified only on the adoption of the resolution on the destruction of the material, which means that he has neither legal nor factual means available to gain insight into collected data, so of such notification has no meaning in terms of the legal protection of personal data.

Moreover, Article 165 provides that the information on the proposal, decision-making and implementation of special evidentiary actions represent secret information in terms of Law of confidentiality of data. Given the fact that the implementation of special evidentiary actions is secret information to which the access is possible only in the manner and under conditions established by Law, it follows that a person against whom a special evidentiary action was applied can in no way be informed about the personal data collected by applying the actions of secret surveillance of communications as long as the material is not destroyed in accordance with Article 163 of the Criminal Procedure Code. Two years after obtaining the status of classified information, the information on the proposals, decision-making and implementation of special evidentiary actions cease to be secret, so the person could hypothetically request these information, which does not make any sense because material generated by using secret surveillance actions could have already been destroyed in accordance with the aforementioned provision of the Code.

Prementioned articles are in the line with standardized conditions regarding special investigative actions found in national legislation of European countries. However, some of the solutions are to be reconsidered. The Code determines authorities who can implement this special investigative action: the police, the Security-Information Agency and Military Security Agency, but we believe that it is justified to authorize by the Code of Criminal Procedure only the police for taking such action, and not national security agencies and that the results of actions taken by these authorities should not be used as evidence in criminal procedure (especially as this agencies are not "proceedings authority" within the meaning of Article 1, paragraph 15). Although the Constitution provides that state authorities, when limiting human rights, are obliged to consider the substance of the restricted right, pertinence of restriction, nature and extent of restriction, relation of restriction and its purpose and whether there is a way to achieve the purpose of the restriction with less restrictive rights, we consider that such a duty may be problematic in relation to solutions that give relevant state authorities broad powers and do not provide adequate system of control. In addition, the Code, as a regulation which should more precisely address possibility of restriction of civil rights to protect the interests of the criminal proceedings, however, does not contain any provision which aims to protect personal data that may be infringed by secret collection of communication data. Therefore, we believe that, for the sake of greater legal certainty, the Code should foresee explicit provisions that would be related to the collection, use and protection of personal data for the purposes of criminal proceedings. As for the restrictions on the right to privacy of communications, we think that a legal solution is to some extent satisfactory, but due to not taking into account the need to protect personal data, such a solution is not adequate enough.

There are three types of actors who carry out external supervision of the application of special measures in Serbia. The judiciary is primarily responsible for prior or ex ante control of the authorization for enforcement, and only if these measures are executed within criminal procedure. Independent state bodies, relevant for the monitoring of the implementation of special measures, are Ombudsman and the Commissioner for Information of Public Importance and Personal Data Protection. They control those aspects of security institutions falling within the scope of their competencies. The third actor responsible for oversight of the implementation of specific measures is the National Assembly of the Republic of Serbia. Since the retained electronic data belong to the personal data which enjoy special constitutional and legal protection, the Commissioner supervises handling of them. Moreover, such monitoring was conducted twice, over the mobile phone operators in 2012, and over the Internet providers in 2014[16]. Also, the competent authorities and the operators keep additionally records on requests for access to retained data on an annual basis and submit them to the Commissioner. These logs are quite general, do not contain any details, and relate only to requests for access to the data, not the interception of communications. They contain information about the total number of submitted and fulfilled requirements, as well as the period between the date of data retention and the date they are requested. Commissioner revealed in 2012 not only that access to stored data without sending a request to the operator occurs, but also that their number is far greater than the number of claims filed. However, only one of the monitored mobile operators had information about such accesses[17].

Uncontrolled use of these measures may lead to human rights violations, abuse of authority and causing needless significant financial costs to taxpayers. These risks are not only "theoretically". In the last few years in Serbia there were several scandals related to the use of special measures. The public, during 2012 and 2013, shook the media reports about telephone tapping of high government officials. In early 2014, the former deputy head of the special investigative methods of the Criminal Police was arrested for tipping organized criminal group on measures that were applied against its members. In addition to these scandals, there are indications that the institutions of special measures are applied in a very wide scale. For example, an operator of mobile and fixed telephony reported that the authorities in one year 270,000 times accessed the electronically retained data of its customers. All this indicates that the need to strengthen external oversight, because he is fundamentally important to increase the accountability of state actors for special measures. However, it is of great importance to reassess laws allowing state authorities to exercise wide competences.

## 5    Concluding Remarks

The decision of Constitutional Court of Republic of Serbia is commendable, but the mere retention of data in the manner prescribed by the Law on Electronic Communications could be a subject of examination by the Court, bearing in mind that the constitutional courts in several European countries found laws implementing the EU Directive

---

[16] http://www.poverenik.rs/images/stories/dokumentacija-nova/izvestajiPoverenika/2012/izvest aj2012final.pdf.
[17] Ibidem.

on data retention unconstitutional (which solutions are used as inspiration for prescribing provisions in the Law on Electronic Communications), and the Court of European Union annulled the Directive. Although the retention of data might be justified by the need of the competent authorities to, if necessary, require from service providers some specific data, we believe that regulation of the obligation to retain data of a large indefinite number of people, for unspecified purpose and in one an act that does not regulate criminal procedure is not justified with the aspect of the guaranteed human rights and legal security in general.

Although the surveillance of electronic communication in CPC related to collection of communication data specified in the Law of electronic communication (retention and access to retained data) could be seen as an appropriate measure for achieving the goal, which is to combat serious crimes, the way the Law due to the lack of clear and precise requirements in its provisions interfere with basic human rights is not adequate to justify this interference as absolutely necessary. First, it refers to data on all persons who are users of electronic communications services, without any closer determination or refinement. In addition, the Law does not provide any criteria that would ensure that the authorities gain access to data and to use them solely for the purposes of preventing and revealing a serious criminal offense and prosecution of the perpetrators of those acts, or on the basis of which the proportionality and justification of such a serious interference in basic human rights could be assessed. In addition, the Law does not provide neither material nor the formal conditions under which the competent authorities may require service providers from obtaining access to retained data, moreover, such an approach is not in any way preconditioned by judicial decision or decision another independent body. Also the period of data retention is problematic, because there is no difference between the various categories of data which does not ensure that the measure of data retention to be limited to the necessary duration. Similar arguments were used in the decision of the Court of European Union on 8 April 2014 by which the Data retention Directive[18] was proclaimed invalid[19]. The retention of traffic data may represent even more intrusive measure comparing to intercepting the contents of communications or collecting traffic data in real time, for it is clear that traffic data are personal data (since they can identify individual) in respect of which it is also necessary to comply with the prescribed principles of data protection. If we apply the standards set in the ECHR case law, we conclude that the application of these measures is neither required nor appropriate regulated and neither proportionate and justified in a democratic society. This measure is extremely intrusive in terms of the rights guaranteed by Article 8 of the ECHR, given that the right to respect for private life and communication can be restricted only to the extent necessary in a democratic society and in accordance with the principle of proportionality. The Law does not even contain the limitation in terms of serious

---

[18] Directive 2006/24/EC of the EEuropean Parliament and of the Council of 15 March 2006 on the retention of data generated or processed in connection with the provision of publicly available electronic communications services or of public communications networks and amending Directive 2002/58/EC, http://eur-lex.europa.eu/LexUriServ/LexUriServ.do?uri=OJ:L:2006:105:0054:0063:EN:PDF.

[19] C-293/12 и C-594/12, http://curia.europa.eu/juris/documents.jsf?num=C-293/12.

crimes, so the principle of proportionality is almost nullified. Data retention has much wider coverage compared to the action of collecting traffic data in real time or communication interception - competent authority collects and records data by using technical means or requires providers of electronic communications in accordance with their technical capabilities to collect or record or to help and cooperate with the competent authorities in the collection of data relating to a specific particular communication which is realized by means of a computer system - while retention refer to indefinite amount of communication. Since the ECHR found that simple storing of personal data represents a threat to freedom of the citizens, requirements for the retention of data by service providers represents an even greater threat to the rights guaranteed by Article 8 of the Convention. Bearing in mind that in European Union regulation as well as in case-law of the ECHR a violation of privacy (and Personal Data Protection) exists when disabling person to be informed whether the data is collected about him, as well as storing data for longer period of time than necessary for achieving the purpose for which the data were collected, we believe that it is absolutely necessary to proscribe the appropriate provisions in the Criminal Procedure Code relating protection of personal data in connection with criminal procedure (especially regarding communications interception as a special investigative measure) which would be in accordance with the basic principles of protection of personal data.

Since Serbia is country candidate for membership in European Union, in order Serbian legislation, that regulates the surveillance of electronic communications and related collection of personal data for the purposes of criminal proceedings, to be in accordance with the relevant legal standards, we believe that it would be necessary to review and reconsider the constitutionality of some provisions of the Law on Electronic Communications (referring to the obligation to retain data) as well as articles of other laws regulating collection of communication data, especially Code's regulation of surveillance of electronic communications.

# References

1. Bugarski, T.: Dokazne radnje u krivicnom postupku, Novi Sad (2014)
2. Clarke, R.: Privacy impact assessment: its origins and development. Comput. Law Secur. Rev. **2**, 123–135 (2009)
3. Committee of Experts on Special Investigation Techniques in Relation to Acts of Terrorism (PC-TI). Conclusions of the third meeting, Strasbourg 24.09.2003. PC-TI (2003). http://goo.gl/52RXx0 (coe.int pdf)
4. Constitution of Republic of Serbia ("Official gazette of Republic of Serbia", No. 98/2006)
5. Council of Europe Committee of Ministers. Recommendation of the Committee of Ministers to member states on "special investigation techniques" in relation to serious crimes including acts of terrorism. Adopted by the Committee of Ministers on 20 April 2005 at the 924th meeting of the Ministers' Deputies. Rec(2005)10. http://goo.gl/X3QiRb
6. Criminal procedure code ("Official Gazette of Republic of Serbia", Nos. 72/2011, 101/2011, 121/2012, 32/2013, 45/2013 and 55/2014)
7. Decision of the Constitutional Court ("Official Gazette of Republic of Serbia", No. 60/2013)

8. Directive 2006/24/EC of the European Parliament and of the Council of 15 March 2006 on the retention of data generated or processed in connection with the provision of publicly available electronic communications services or of public communications networks and amending Directive 2002/58/EC. http://eur-lex.europa.eu/LexUriServ/LexUriServ.do?uri=OJ:L:2006:105:0054:0063:EN:PDF
9. EU Court Decision, C-293/12 и C-594/12. http://curia.europa.eu/juris/documents.jsf?num=C-293/12
10. http://www.poverenik.rs/images/stories/dokumentacija-nova/izvestajiPoverenika/2012/izvestaj2012final.pdf
11. Law on Amendments to the Law on Electronic Communications ("Official Gazette of Republic of Serbia", No. 62/2014)
12. Law on electronic communications ("Official Gazette of Republic of Serbia", Nos. 44/2010, 60/2013 – Decision of Constitutional Court and 62/2014)
13. Law on Military Security Agency and Military Intelligence Agency ("Official Gazette of Republic of Serbia", Nos. 55/2012 - Decision of Constitutional Court and 17/2013)
14. Law on protection of personal data ("Official Gazette of Republic of Serbia", Nos. 97/2008, 104/2009 – other Law, 68/2012 - Decision of Constitutional Court and 107/2012)
15. Law on Security Information Agency ("Official Gazette of Republic of Serbia", Nos. 42/2002 and 111/2009)
16. Poullet, Y.: Data protection legislation: what is at stake for our society and democracy. Comput. Law Secur. Rev. 25, 211–226 (2009)

# Legal and Technical Perspectives in Data Sharing Agreements Definition

Claudio Caimi[1], Carmela Gambardella[1], Mirko Manea[1],
Marinella Petrocchi[2(✉)], and Debora Stella[3]

[1] Hewlett-Packard Italiana, Milan, Italy
{claudio.caimi,carmela.gambardella,mirko.manea}@hpe.com
[2] IIT-CNR, Pisa, Italy
marinella.petrocchi@iit.cnr.it
[3] Bird and Bird, Milan, Italy
Debora.Stella@twobirds.com

**Abstract.** An electronic Data Sharing Agreement (DSA) is a human-readable, yet machine-processable contract, regulating how organizations and/or individuals share data. In this paper, we shed light on DSA engineering, i.e., the process of studying how data sharing is ruled in traditional legal human-readable contracts and mapping their fields (and rules) into formats that are machine-processable, leading to the transposition of the traditional contract into the electronic DSA. Tangible creation of the electronic DSA is possible through the design and implementation of a three-step DSA definition phase, with an associated authoring tool. The tool is specifically tailored for encoding not only the terms of law but also the rules that an organization may have put in place (e.g., corporate internal policies, or privacy policies, or data processing agreements) to manage the data, as well as end users' privacy preferences.

## 1 Introduction

Sharing data among groups of organizations and/or individuals is essential in a modern web-based society, being at the very core of scientific and business transactions. Data sharing, however, poses several problems including trust, privacy, data misuse and/or abuse, and uncontrolled propagation of data. In this paper, we focus on preserving privacy whilst sharing data based on electronic Data Sharing Agreements (DSA).

An electronic DSA is a human-readable, yet machine-processable contract, regulating how organizations and/or individuals share data. Figure 1 sketched the basic components of a DSA lifecycle.

The *template definition* stage is a preliminary phase in which a pool of available DSA templates is created, according to the purpose of the data sharing and

The research leading to these results has received funding from the EU Seventh Framework Programme (FP7/2007–2013) under grant no 610853 (Coco Cloud).

© Springer International Publishing Switzerland 2016
B. Berendt et al. (Eds.): APF 2015, LNCS 9484, pp. 178–192, 2016.
DOI: 10.1007/978-3-319-31456-3_10

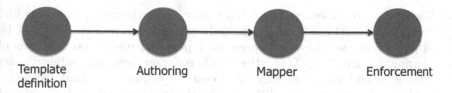

**Fig. 1.** Basic DSA lifecycle

the classification of data whose sharing is regulated by the DSA. The *authoring* stage is an editing tool-assisted phase, during which the stakeholders prepare the DSA itself. The result of the authoring stage is an electronic, still human readable, DSA document. The data sharing rules in the DSA are then translated to a set of enforceable security policies during the *mapper* stage. The *enforcement* stage is the phase in which the DSA is enacted on the specific data being shared.

DSA are the digital transposition of traditional legal contracts to regulate the terms and conditions under which organisations and individuals agree to share data. A first key problem in the digital world is that the constraints expressed in such (not digital) contracts remain inaccessible from the software infrastructure supporting the data sharing and management processes and, consequently, they cannot be automatically enforced. This is mainly because fields in the contract, such as its validity, the involved parties, the kind of data to be shared, and the data sharing rules themselves, still need to be interpreted and translated (primarily by humans) into meaningful technical policies, to ensure degrees of enforcement and auditing.

Overall, DSA definition, i.e., the process of creating the machine-processable document by starting from the traditional paper contract regulating data sharing, is a complex task. The main obstacles that currently prevent its successful achievement are that the process is prone to error and quite reductive (e.g., from the end users' point of view).

On the one hand, transposition of paper contracts into digital DSA involves a deep understanding of jurisdictional and intra/inter-organisations matters: as an example, legal constraints may vary from country to country, and the enactment of data sharing rules defined, e.g., at organisational level, could be subject to contextual conditions that must be considered and evaluated case by case. Traditional legal contracts may summarise in few words a series of exceptions that, if fulfilled, may change the effect of the data sharing (either allowing or denying the data access, for example). If such shades are not adequately expressed and represented in the DSA, the software infrastructure responsible for the DSA enforcement will uselessly operate.

On the other hand, standard online forms highly reduce the capabilities of end users to control how their data can be shared, by whom, and for which purposes. Usually, when end users' data is going to be processed by organisations, end users are asked to accept online the terms that will govern the data processing, by simply clicking on buttons like "Review and Accept the Terms and Conditions" or "I accept the privacy policy". Furthermore, end users find it difficult to understand these terms and conditions, how their data will be shared practically, and how to express their potential preferences in terms of data sharing and handling. This introduces burdens on users and usability issues of solutions for end-to-end automation of contract definition and enforcement.

In this paper, we study traditional data sharing contracts with the aim of creating the corresponding enforceable data sharing agreements. In particular, we contribute by (i) evaluating which fields in a traditional data sharing contract are representable in an electronic data sharing agreement, and under which format; and (ii) showing the design and implementation of an authoring tool satisfying the representation of such fields in such formats. The authoring tool supports the creation of the contract, by leveraging on a vocabulary of reference, which defines the terms and the reference context (ontology). The tool supports a process defined on three levels of interaction and it assists an even a non-technical author (e.g., a legal expert) in the definition of the data sharing rules. Finally, the tool provides the possibility to get the user preferences and tune some rules in a final step of editing.

*Roadmap.* This paper is structured as follows. Section 2 expands the concept of DSA and gives a panoramic view on tools for editing privacy policies. Section 3 gives an example of legal terms contained in a traditional contract and defines fields and formats of the corresponding electronic DSA. In Sect. 4, we present architecture and functionalities of the authoring tool, through which formation of a DSA is enacted within a three-step editing phase. Finally, we conclude the paper in Sect. 5.

## 2    Background and Related Work

As highlighted in [5], "sharing data among groups of organizations and/or individuals is a key necessity in modern web-based society and at the very core of business transactions". A DSA is an agreement between two or more parties who wish to exchange data in several specific domains and contexts: it regulates which data to use, for which purposes and how to use it. Basically the aim of DSA is (i) to capture the data sharing policies that restrict both the party(-ies) that provide(s) the data and the party(-ies) that receive(s) the data, and (ii) to govern the data flow between them, see, e.g., [16]. Furthermore, a DSA also defines the legal obligations and the organisation policies according to, e.g., the data classification. The data classification allows to distinguish between personal data - both common data, e.g., contact details, and data belonging to special categories, like medical data - and non personal data, as, e.g., administrative and business data. In recent years, DSA have become common both in the scientific community, see, e.g., [17], and between enterprises that want to share data. In the scientific world, the importance of sharing information and making it available within the community also clashes with the assurance need that data privacy and confidentiality must be maintained. Likewise, organizations (both in the private and in the public sector) share data, on the base of agreements: nowadays, any ecipient of services must sign a contract with the provider. The goal is not only to protect the latter from improper or unauthorized usage of those services, but also to protect the recipient with respect to the misuse the provider could do over the data the recipient has provided when signing the agreement (or s/he provides and produces, using the services over the duration of the agreement). Thus, beyond defining relationships among the involved parties, an agreement also is a tool for managing risk and liability.

Initially, DSA was the electronic implementation of the common contracts stipulated in any relationship of sharing data. Currently, we assist to an evolution of electronic DSA towards not only the description of policies that govern the data sharing, the parties involved in the contract, the period of validity and other legal and business information, but also towards the DSA automatic enforcement and the verification of the effective compliance of the parties to the agreement. Thus, the rich framework for the management and the enforcement of the DSA includes authoring tools, to guide the users in the creation of comprehensive and consistent DSA; repositories to facilitate the authoring of DSA, even starting from a catalogue of DSA templates, and to manage the life-cycle management of DSA; agents to monitor and enforce the terms of the DSAs, when the checks are programmable and automatically verifiable, see, e.g. [16,17]. Contributing to move to that direction is main goal of this paper, that concentrates on the evolution of electronic DSA supported by a devoted authoring tool.

*Policy Authoring Tools.* Series of work in [3,4,8,9,15] connect policy authoring tools with the capability of common users to use them. In [9], the authors carry out a laboratory evaluation of a variety of user-centered methods for privacy policies authoring, to identify which design decisions should be taken for flexible and usable privacy enabling techniques. Work in [3] continues this line of research, by providing a parser which identifies the privacy policy elements in rules entered in natural languages: identification of such elements is a key step for subsequent translation of natural sentences in enforceable constructs (such as the XACML language [14]). Authors of [15] recall security and privacy policy-authoring tasks in general, and discover further usability challenges that policy authoring presents. In [4] the authors present the Coalition Policy Management Portal for policy authoring, verification, and deployment, with the goal of providing "easy to use mechanisms for refining high-level user-specified goals into low-level controls". Recently, work in [8] advances the notion of template-based authoring tools, for users with different roles and different skill sets, such as, e.g., patients, doctors, and IT administrators could be in a e-health scenario. The authors propose different templates to edit privacy policies, each of them needing different user skills to compose high-quality policies.

The FP7-EU project *Consequence* (Context Aware Data Centric Information Sharing) designed and developed an integrated framework for the authoring, analysis, and enforcement of DSA. The authoring tool developed within the project was intended for users with some knowledge on policy specification, see, e.g., [6,13]. The insertion of a help-on-line facility partly mitigates usability issues, whose complete solution needs however further investigation.

From a business perspective, Axiomatics [2] offers an authorization framework based on the XACML standard [14], that covers all the phases of the policy life-cycle, including policy creation, exploiting a graphical user interface for policy authoring, validation, deployment and enforcement.

From a social networking perspective, we may cite work in [18], which presents a *collaborative* authoring tool, allowing several individuals to specify policies over data published on social networks, and whose disclosure may affect their privacy. The authors acknowledge some usability issues in their prototype implementation, and future work are foreseen towards a user-friendly authoring interface.

## 3   DSA: From Legal Contracts to Machine-Processable Agreements

An electronic Data Sharing Agreement (DSA) regulates how organizations and/or individuals share data. It can be between two organisations and/or individuals (bilateral agreement), or more (multilateral agreement). DSA can also be adopted to share information inside an organisation, e.g., between its different business units.

A DSA consists of:

– Predefined legal background information (which can be derived following, e.g., the text of traditional legal contracts). A legal expert (e.g., in-house legal counsel) provides such description most of the times. This kind of data is unstructured by nature, that is data that are not organized in a predefined manner.
– Structured user-defined information, including the definition of the validity period, the parties participating in the agreement, the data covered and, most importantly, the statements that constrain how data can be shared among the parties (such statements usually include policy rules). Business policy experts and end users can be those who usually fill up this information and implement these fields.

For the aim of this paper, we define a DSA specification to be encapsulated (or wrapped) as an XML (eXtensible Markup Language) file. The XML format facilitates the task of programmatically accessing and working on the different DSA sections; furthermore, the XML fosters the interoperability with different tools and parties. The XML structure is described by an XSD (XML Schema Definition). An example will be given in the following.

From the analysis of many types of traditional legal data sharing contracts – and of some guidance issued by data protection authorities [7] – we identify the following sections to appear in an electronic DSA.

These are the examples of the *minimum essential* DSA sections:

– the *DSA title*, a label to identify the DSA into a repository of DSA.
– the *parties* involved into the DSA. For each party, we need to specify

- its role in the DSA: borrowing the language from the privacy and data protection context, the DSA usually involves the Data Controller, the Data Processor and the Data Subject, terminology adopted in the European Parliament Directive 95/46/EC to indicate the parties involved in an agreement governing the sharing of personal data[1], and
- its responsibility, i.e., the organisations duties which cannot be expressed in terms of authorisations and obligations by a data sharing rule, and for which the compliance checks cannot be enforced automatically (e.g., the role that each party will play in terms of gathering, sharing and storing the relevant data).

– the *validity* of the DSA: its start and end date, the duration of the any surviving obligations (especially, in relation to the use of data) after the expiration of the DSA and the duration of *off-line licences* for data access. The latter information allows the DSA actors to manage so called "off-line cases", as an example, when data are accessed by a mobile without Internet connection. This means that, in certain circumstances, data may be kept by the recipient also after the contract expires, for a predefined time.

– the *vocabulary* used for the DSA, which provides the terminology for authoring DSA statements. In our implementation, the vocabulary is defined by an ontology, written in OWL (Ontology Web Language) [1], that is a formal explicit description of a domain of interest. It provides the terminology for authoring DSA rules representing the semantics of terms in the context in which they are used and the relationships between them. Also, an ontology allows the reasoning and deductions in the scope of use. Such vocabularies are domain specific (e.g., medical context, legal context, etc.), but vocabularies describing cross-domain abstract aspects can be common for different context. The W3C (World Wide Web Consortium)[2] recommends some ontologies to describe objects and relationships across a number of domains. For instance, Org (The Organization Ontology)[3] is about organizational structures and the rules within them. FOAF (Friend of a Friend)[4] is one of the many available specifications about people and the relations between people and objects. The Platform for Privacy Preferences Project (P3P)[5] can be useful to express legal rules in different domains. The user can use a basic or proprietary vocabulary to describe rules about the parties or people involved in the agreement. However, in order to be more precise and specific in the DSA referring context, a domain specific ontology is more flexible. For example, the just mentioned Org may be suitable to the context of sharing data to and from mobile applications, moreover Core Person[6] can be very appropriated for the context of

---

[1] With a little abuse of notation, in this paper we use these terms also referring to other kind of data, to identify the actors involved in a general data sharing agreement.

[2] www.w3.org.

[3] www.w3.org/TR/vocab-org/.

[4] http://xmlns.com/foaf/spec/.

[5] http://www.w3.org/P3P/2004/040920_p3p-sw.html.

[6] https://joinup.ec.europa.eu/asset/core_person/description.

E-government and Public Administration, because it describes the fundamental characteristics of a person and it has already been used in public administrations contexts. Furthermore, the ontology SNOMED CT[7] is the most standardized terminology for health and it involves all radiological terms and procedures, thus it is very suitable to describe medical domains.

- the *data classification*, describing the nature of the data covered by the DSA. We consider two main data categories: personal data and non personal data. Additionally, we can propose a deeper data taxonomy for each of these classes, in order to identify better the object of the DSA. A (non-exhaustive) example follows:
  - Non personal data
    * Business data
      · Highly Confidential (e.g., strategic business plans, etc.)
      · Confidential (e.g., price lists, etc.)
      · Public (e.g., a list of products)
    * Administrative data (e.g., customers invoices, etc.)
  - Personal data
    * Common personal data
      · Identification details (e.g., name and surname)
      · Contact details (e.g., address, phone number)
      · . . .
    * Special categories
      · Sensitive data (e.g., medical data)
      · Judicial data (e.g., data relating to offences or criminal convictions)
      · . . .
- the *purpose* of the DSA, which is linked to the data classification; we assume that there is only one purpose for a DSA. If more than one purpose is needed, another agreement must be made. According to the data classification, the purpose can be:
  1. Administrative and Accounting (e.g., for booking, for payment);
  2. Healthcare services (e.g., for diagnoses);
  3. Scientific Research;
  4. Statistical (e.g., public costs control, epidemiological);
  5. Marketing (e.g., for commercial proposal of services/needs);
  6. Profiling (e.g., aggregation/grouping of users depending of certain user characteristics to propose specific products/services tailored to those characteristics);
  7. Fulfil law obligations (e.g., to access or share data in case of legitimate requests of public authorities).

It is worth noting that the Platform for Privacy Preferences Project (P3P) defines a long list of further purposes that could be considered.

We define also additional *technical* fields to support the DSA metadata:

- the *template id*; since a DSA can derive from another DSA in the three phases definition process (see the following Sect. 4), a template identifier can be useful to trace the original DSA.

---

[7] www.ihtsdo.org/snomed-ct/snomed-ct0.

- the *status*, that identifies the DSA into the three-steps process explained in Sect. 4 – possible values are: TEMPLATE, CUSTOMISED, and COMPLETED.

The following *optional* sections contain examples of the data sharing *rules* for a DSA:

- the *authorizations* section contains rules about permitted operations for each party (e.g., the possibility of sharing data with an identified third party);
- the *obligations* section contains rules about the duties of each of the parties in relation to the data sharing (e.g., the duty of not to transfer the data outside the country).

The Authorisation section contains a subsection specific for data subject rights, for example rights of viewing the data collected by the Data Controller, the source of data (where data has been obtained from, like from a public registry, etc.), cancellation, update, and their rights in front of third parties with whom the data have been shared (e.g., data can be stored, but cannot be accessed), grants/revokes, etc. Moreover, we distinguish among different types of obligations:

- Privacy: about personal data;
- Confidential: (usually) about business data;
- Audit: including obligations in relation to inspection of supervisory authorities (this may comprehend to specify logging actions related to data access);
- Warranties: concerning features, quality, and characteristics of the data: these obligations guarantee that the data are up to date, right, and complete (i.e., parties must share all the agreed data);
- Termination or expiration conditions for disposal of the DSA either for breach of contractual obligations, natural contract conclusion or convenience; they can include also what will happen to the data after the DSA disposal (i.e., delete or destroy data);
- Transfer of data: about only geographical movement of data (e.g., "not outside European Union");
- Other obligations (IPR, etc.).

It is worth noting that, even if we have defined Authorizations and Obligations to be optional sections, to have a significant DSA at least one authorisation – or one obligation – must be specified. Indeed, if both sections are empty, then the DSA does not explicitly impose any constraints.

While the required sections are not formal fields, but supporting metadata for the DSA, Authorizations and Obligations are authored using (semi)formal languages such as CNL4DSA [12] to define the data sharing rules, possibly using placeholders (strings), in case user preferences are needed for a statement (see next section for illustrative details of the use of placeholders).

Additional information can be provided by users:

1. Economics: the parties can specify fee for use of data, indemnities in case of breach in the use of data or penalties in case of improper sharing of data.

2. Governing Law: which law(s) the parties choose to apply to the business arrangements in the contract (i.e., commercial and jurisdiction clauses). In many countries, however, this field does not apply to the basic rules about processing personal data, because, according to many privacy and data protection laws, the identification of the applicable privacy and data protection law is based on mandatory criteria defined by the law.

An example of the XSD definition for DSAs defined according to the above sections is available online at www.iit.cnr.it/staff/marinella.petrocchi/dsa_schema.xsd.

## 4   DSA Authoring

The DSA Authoring Tool (hereafter also referred to as DSAAT) is a Web application for authoring DSAs. DSAAT allows organizations to define DSA, including the referring laws/regulations and acquiring end users' privacy preferences.

The actors involved in the DSAAT are:

**A Legal Expert.** S/He is very familiar with legal and contractual perspective content of agreement but s/he is not able to translate them in a high-level formal language which facilitates automatic processing of the policies. S/he is responsible for the creation of a DSA template, containing legal rules and optionally pending policies, that need to be completed by an end user. The use of a placeholder in a rule defines a pending policy.

**A Policy Expert.** S/He is responsible for defining business policies and other DSA metadata (as the ones listed in Sect. 3), specific to the context of a use case, starting from a DSA template. A business policy may require user preferences, so also a policy expert might include pending policies to be completed by the end user of a business application.

**The End User.** S/He may be involved when the DSA contains pending policies that require a user input to be finalized.

The process of authoring a DSA consists of three phases, each of them is managed by one of the above-cited actors though the DSAAT. The DSA can have the following status:

1. TEMPLATE: the legal expert creates the DSA template, i.e., a draft version of the DSA, containing the legal policies. It can be reused between different business use cases.
2. CUSTOMISED: the policy expert populates the DSA template with business policies, specific for the context of a use case. The DSA moves from template status to customised status. A customised DSA might still contain policy placeholders, used to gather a end user preference. Pending policies take the form of check-boxes (e.g., "allow consent to use data for marketing purposes. (Yes, No)") or free text fields (e.g., "delegate access to (XYZ) person").
3. COMPLETED: if there are no rules that require specific choices of the end user, or after the user preferences gathering, the DSA can be considered completed.

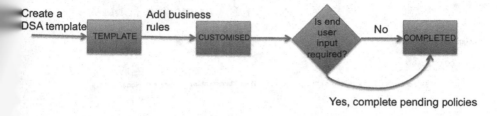

**Fig. 2.** The DSA state-chart diagram

Figure 2 shows a state diagram of DSA authoring in the DSAAT context.

*DSA Authoring Tool Storyboard.* The DSAAT home page shows the content of a DSA repository (see Fig. 3). For each entry in the repository the interface shows the UUID (Universal Unique Identifier), which is the name of the DSA file (in XML format), the size of the file, the title of the DSA and its status. The figure shows that user is logged as legal expert, meaning that s/he can either create a new DSA template, or edit and view an existing one.

# DSA Authoring Tool

**Logged as: Legal Expert**

| UUID* | Size | Title | Status |
|---|---|---|---|
| DSA-5c5f0223-b85e-45cf-92bf-00b434b952aa.xml | 599 | Business Data Template | TEMPLATE |
| DSA-6d05l9f5-c647-49fc-9f0e-aef6f5ab7b56.xml | 593 | new untitled DSA | TEMPLATE |
| DSA-8aef961a-c374-46e1-b423-70c7ff53726b.xml | 601 | Medical Data Template | TEMPLATE |

View DSA Template | Create DSA Template | Edit DSA Template | Logout

**Fig. 3.** DSAAT home page interface

The following gives details on the actions which the DSA actor can perform via the DSAAT interface:

1. create a new DSA template - Typically a legal expert creates a new DSA template. First of all, a reference to the vocabulary, for the definition of terms and actions used by the policies, is required. In DSAAT, different ways of loading a vocabulary (technically, a file written in OWL - Ontology Web Language) can be supported: a user can provide a URL, so that the DSAAT can access it through HTTP or a path from his/her file system, if the vocabulary is stored locally. The DSAAT takes care of fetching and processing the ontology defining a vocabulary, and of using it when the user edits a DSA.

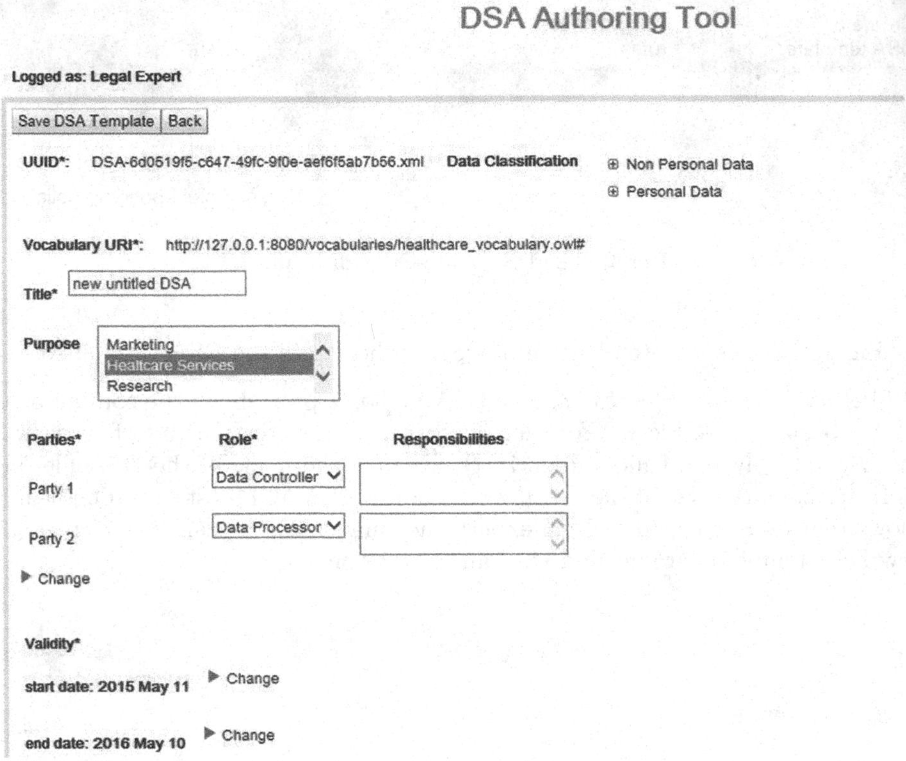

**Fig. 4.** DSA (template) creation

Once a vocabulary has been selected, the web page shows to the user an input form with information to be filled, describing the DSA.

Thus, the user must specify for a DSA according to the structure described in Sect. 3 (XML container) and through the interface illustrated in Fig. 4:

- a DSA *title*;
- the *parties* involved into the DSA. S/he can select the parties from a drop-down list menu. For each party, the user must specify a role in the DSA, selecting one item from another menu and, optionally, specifying the party's responsibility in the agreement. The responsibilities are hosted in a free-text field because no enforcement will be provided for this information. It is worth noting that the figure shows only the role of the parties defined. Indeed, being the form at DSA template level, the specific name of the parties remains generic. The policy expert at organization level will be responsible for fill them in.
- the *validity* of the DSA; its start and end date, and the duration, in days, of off-line licences for the data access. This field may be refined by the policy expert at the organization level.

- the *data classification*; note that to support the taxonomy of the data classification, once the legal expert selects the kind of data, the user interface allows to go in depth with a drop down menu, as shown in Fig. 5, where business data, which in their turn belong to the "non personal data" category, are expanded into "highly confidential", "confidential", and "public";
- the *purpose* of the DSA, which is strictly connected with the data classification. The legal expert can select items in the menu containing the possible value, according to the XML schema (see details in Sect. 3);
- at least one statement in either *Authorization* or *Obligation* sections of the DSA, as defined into the schema. We remind the reader that legal experts are supposed to encode at DSA template level terms of law that apply for the purpose of sharing data belonging to a certain class. In the advanced phase of authoring, the policy expert and - optionally - the end user will append organisation-specific data sharing rules and end user privacy preferences.

Data sharing rules include both authorisations and obligations. In the following, we will focus on authorisations, even if the same reasoning hold for obligations. Thus, when the generic user is going to add a new authorisation, a pop-up will be displayed to ask if s/he is going to define a data subject authorisation, so that the tool can put the rule in a new separated section, as Fig. 6 shows.

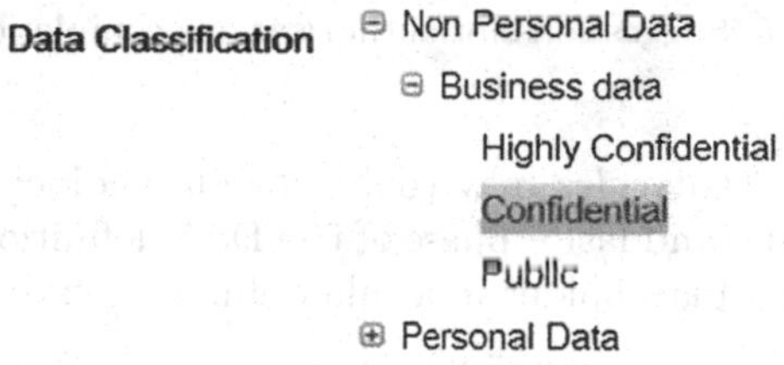

**Data Classification**    ⊖ Non Personal Data
  ⊖ Business data
     Highly Confidential
     Confidential
     Public
  ⊕ Personal Data

**Fig. 5.** DSA data classification (excerpt)

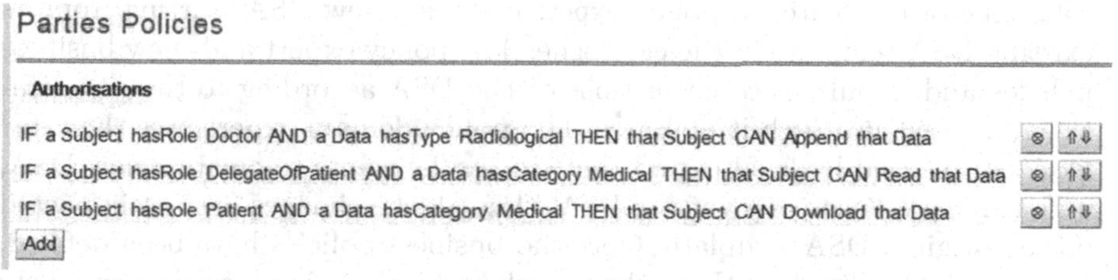

**Parties Policies**

**Authorisations**

IF a Subject hasRole Doctor AND a Data hasType Radiological THEN that Subject CAN Append that Data    ⊗ ⇅

IF a Subject hasRole DelegateOfPatient AND a Data hasCategory Medical THEN that Subject CAN Read that Data    ⊗ ⇅

IF a Subject hasRole Patient AND a Data hasCategory Medical THEN that Subject CAN Download that Data    ⊗ ⇅

Add

**Fig. 6.** A detail of the authorisations section

A dedicated section about sharing the data with other organisations exists in the DSA: it contains the definition of policies where third-parties are involved.

It describes if and how the receiving party of the DSA is permitted (or not) to share the data with any third party and any relevant restriction.

Each definable rule is expressed in terms of authorisations and obligations. The user is continuously supported in the editing of the various sections of a DSA, especially in the definition of the rules, in an intuitive and assisted way. The DSAAT provides suggestions in the definition of the rules according to the initially chosen vocabulary. For instance, if the user is writing a rule about a certain entity in the vocabulary, the user interface provides a pop-up containing only the predicates and then the objects for which a reference in the ontology defining the vocabulary exists. The definition of the rules is error free (from a semantic point of view): this approach allows the user to insert only well-formed rules according to the reference ontology. Figure 7 shows an example of the kind of suggestions shown to the user when editing the Authorisations section.

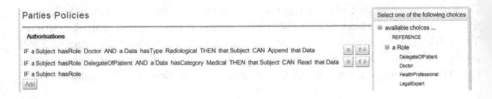

**Fig. 7.** Suggestions for authorisations completion

It is worth noting that rules may contain a placeholder to acquire the end user input in the third – and last – phase of the DSA definition process described in Sect. 1. The use of a placeholder in a rule defines a pending policy.

2. Create a new DSA starting from a template. Once the legal expert provides the first round of authoring, the DSA is in TEMPLATE status. It means that this DSA can be loaded and used as a starting point by a policy expert to create a custom copy of the DSA, according to the use case.

    Organisations may establish specific DSA with other parties starting from a catalogue of templates: a policy expert creates a new DSA starting from an existing DSA template in the catalogue. The policy expert adds new business policies and populates some sections of the DSA according to the organizational context in which it operates. The policy domain expert uses the same DSA editor used by legal expert, but since s/he wants to create a new DSA, s/he can save a new copy of the DSA, thus all the changes are not impacted on the original DSA template. Once the business policies have been defined, DSA can be finalized (with all the metadata): if there is no need to complete pending policies by end users, the DSA moves directly to the COMPLETED status. Otherwise, a business application loads the DSA and presents it to the end user to get his/her privacy preferences.

3. Edit an existing DSA. All kinds of DSA editing actors can modify a DSA or a DSA template stored into the DSA repository during any of the phases of

the authoring process. The DSA can remain in the same status it was stored or pass to the following phase according to the user actions.
1. View an existing DSA. As mentioned before, the home page of the DSAAT shows the content of the DSA repository. From this view, a user can select an existing DSA and view its content in a XML format.

## 5   Concluding Remarks

In this paper, we have proposed fields (and format) of an electronic data sharing agreement following guidelines for traditional paper contracts. The creation of the agreement is supported by an authoring tool for the definition of the contractual clauses as well as appropriate metadata rendering the original paper document.

The authoring phase depicted above is a three-step process, where first legal experts define terms of Law and regulations applicable according to the data classification and the purpose of data sharing; then, policy experts at organization level define specific business policies. Finally, end users may insert preferences for sharing data referring to them. A well formed DSA implies that the rules defined at the three levels of authoring do not conflict one with each other. A conflict may arise when two applicable rules deny and allow, at the same time, the access to the same data, by the same subject, under the same contextual conditions. Thus, a sound management of DSA should involve the support of a policy conflict analyser, detecting conflicts between rules edited at DSA template level and organisation level, and between rules edited at organisation level and end users' preferences. An example of conflict analyser is in [13], which we are currently adapting to be usable in our framework. Once a conflict is detected, we also envisage to have an automatic conflict resolution procedure that chooses, among conflicting policies the "right" one, to be enforced. Our research effort turns around technical compliance with terms of Law. Thus, an appropriate strategy for conflict resolution could be, e.g., the "Lex superior derogat legi inferiori" Roman law principle, meaning that the higher ranking legal source overrides the lower ranking one. Furthermore, other strategies could be exploited as well (like the principle "Lex specialis derogat legi generali", a complementary principle meaning that exceptions may override a more general regulation). In past work, we developed a prototypal conflict solver that can be easily adapted to prioritise data sharing rules according to the authoring level at which they have been edited [10,11]. Evolution of the conflict analyser and adaption of conflict solving strategies are left for future work. Finally, the direct involvement of end users in the specification of policies expressing privacy constraints paves the way for usability studies on the proposed three-step authoring phase. We are currently investigating how individuals can be actively and easily involved in specifying their preferences. As a running scenario, we consider the constrained access to patients' radiological examinations being stored at a Cloud provider.

# References

1. Antoniou, G., Harmelen, F.V.: Web ontology language: OWL. In: Staab, S., Studer, R. (eds.) Handbook on Ontologies in Information Systems, pp. 67–92. Springer, Heidelberg (2003)
2. Axiomatics. www.axiomatics.com. Accessed 22 December 2015
3. Brodie, C., et al.: An empirical study of natural language parsing of privacy policy rules using the SPARCLE policy workbench. In: SOUPS. ACM (2006)
4. Brodie, C., et al.: The coalition policy management portal for policy authoring, verification, and deployment. In: POLICY, pp. 247–249 (2008)
5. Casassa Mont, M., Matteucci, I., Petrocchi, M., Sbodio, M.: Towards safer information sharing in the cloud. Int. J. Inf. Secur. **14**, 319–334 (2015)
6. Consequence Project. Infrastructure for data sharing agreements, December 2010. http://goo.gl/is7cpR
7. Information Commissioner's Office (ICO). Data sharing code of practice, pp. 26, 41–45 (2011). https://goo.gl/11vXHb. Accessed 22 December 2015
8. Johnson, M., Karat, J., Karat, C.-M., Grueneberg, K.: Optimizing a policy authoring framework for security and privacy policies. In: SOUPS, pp. 8:1–8:9. ACM (2010)
9. Karat, J., et al.: Designing natural language and structured entry methods for privacy policy authoring. In: Costabile, M.F., Paternó, F. (eds.) INTERACT 2005. LNCS, vol. 3585, pp. 671–684. Springer, Heidelberg (2005)
10. Lunardelli, A., Matteucci, I., Mori, P., Petrocchi, M.: A prototype for solving conflicts in XACML-based e-Health policies. In: Computer-Based Medical Systems, pp. 449–452. IEEE (2013)
11. Matteucci, I., Mori, P., Petrocchi, M.: Prioritized execution of privacy policies. In: Di Pietro, R., Herranz, J., Damiani, E., State, R. (eds.) DPM 2012 and SETOP 2012. LNCS, vol. 7731, pp. 133–145. Springer, Heidelberg (2013)
12. Matteucci, I., Petrocchi, M., Sbodio, M.L.: CNL4DSA: a controlled natural language for data sharing agreements. In: SAC: Privacy on the Web Track, pp. 616–620. ACM (2010)
13. Matteucci, I., Petrocchi, M., Sbodio, M.L., Wiegand, L.: A design phase for data sharing agreements. In: Garcia-Alfaro, J., Navarro-Arribas, G., Cuppens-Boulahia, N., de Capitani di Vimercati, S. (eds.) DPM 2011 and SETOP 2011. LNCS, vol. 7122, pp. 25–41. Springer, Heidelberg (2012)
14. OASIS. eXtensible Access Control Markup Language (XACML) version 3.0, January 2013
15. Reeder, R.W., Karat, C.-M., Karat, J., Brodie, C.: Usability challenges in security and privacy policy-authoring interfaces. In: Baranauskas, C., Abascal, J., Barbosa, S.D.J. (eds.) INTERACT 2007. LNCS, vol. 4663, pp. 141–155. Springer, Heidelberg (2007)
16. Rosenthal, S.S.: Specifying data sharing agreements. In: Seventh IEEE International Workshop on Policies for Distributed Systems and Networks, pp. 157–162 (2006)
17. Swede, S.: Enforcing scientific data sharing agreements. In: IEEE 9th International Conference on e-Science, pp. 271–278 (2011)
18. Wishart, R., Corapi, D., Marinovic, S., Sloman, M.: Collaborative privacy policy authoring in a social networking context. In: POLICY, pp. 1–8. IEEE (2010)

# Towards Reinventing Online Privacy

Gabriela Gheorghe[(✉)] and Thomas Engel

SnT, Université du Luxembourg, 4 rue Alphonse Weicker,
2721 Luxembourg City, Luxembourg
{gabriela.gheorghe,thomas.engel}@uni.lu

**Abstract.** In this opinion paper, we examine several challenges to privacy online, for both enterprises and individual users. We argue that we have come to a turning point and we need to regain control over how our data is handled even when outside our reach. We give an overview of a set of measures at the intersection of legal and technical domains, to underline that only a combined approach can really put online privacy back in the hands of the users.

## 1 Challenges in Online Privacy

We live in an age when raw data is power. Data is the blood of advertising, and the prices of harvesting and storing it will continue to go down, as investments in data science are on the rise [1]. On the other hand, enterprises have to rely more and more on managed services [5]. Managed services are cheap, but using them comes at the expense of losing control over what data is gathered, how it is processed and what third-parties it reaches. These two trends have a privacy footprint that we are just beginning to fathom.

The flurry of cloud services at very low prices makes outsourcing an unavoidable practice for enterprises, and turns security and privacy into 'somebody else's problem'. Service-Level Agreements focus on availability and reliability measured in a number of *nines*, but that is as far as they reach. There is little to no choice whatsoever in qualitative aspects such as: who has access to our data? how is that access handled? is our data protected? what are any system configurations used that impact data (e.g., backups)? Indeed, no cloud provider is transparent about cloud data access controls, data flow restrictions, or security settings at service provision. Such aspects are at best hinted to in the terms of contract but with no transparency, enterprises can only 'take it or leave'.

It is hard to estimate how data is protected in the cloud anyway. The blurring of responsibilities that comes from different jurisdictions makes reporting complicated. Legal jurisdictions are delimited by regions or countries but service usage is not. With enterprises losing control over what happens to their customers' data in the cloud, the users at the end of the chain will be even further from ever finding out what happened. This is already happening: for example, only 15 out of approximately 50 US states have mandatory data breach notification laws [2]; also, for many economic reasons companies are reluctant to report on occurred data breaches and leave a lag between the date of the breach and the

© Springer International Publishing Switzerland 2016
B. Berendt et al. (Eds.): APF 2015, LNCS 9484, pp. 193–196, 2016.
DOI: 10.1007/978-3-319-31456-3_11

day of the announcement [3]. Worse happens in healthcare scenarios: patients are unsure about how to react to medical data breaches, therefore hospitals are not making security efforts since these are not really visible to patients [8].

On this background, security and privacy are about to become expensive for companies. Since 2012 the European Parliament has been elaborating a new and ambitious privacy directive to be applied homogeneously across all EU countries [4]. This directive is raising the bar in data protection by massive fines to data processors of up to 5 % of the annual turnover, in case of non-compliance. In response, enterprises have started to consider data protection and data protection officer roles more seriously than before[1]. Fear of fines might work as an argument supporting privacy compliance.

The presence of privacy legislation is beneficial, but there is a long way to go in actual compliance. Directives give us some definitions of what is sensitive data. They also suggest that "appropriate measures" should be in place. Yet, little is known about these measures in practice, and how to objectively measure their "appropriateness". One reason for this difficulty is that privacy is an abstract *must-have*, related with the meaning of the service, the threat model, the infrastructure, and to the risks for the organisation itself (e.g., data collection and storage practices). No regulation or standard tells us how to actually become compliant, nor how to measure levels of compliance in protecting customer data.

## 2   The Road Ahead

One of the biggest issues to affect online privacy and safety is that service clients do not have any visibility or control over how their data should flow. Enterprises cannot oppose market trends to outsource, nor competition from the big players offering attractive cloud services. On this background, we believe that the corrosion of good privacy and data protection practices could be stopped by fusing two main areas: legal and technical. Legal measures cannot survive without an accurate understanding of the standpoint of technology. Technology-only measures cannot be sustained without legal support, as long as they are not as much about *what* technology does but rather about *how*.

From the law and regulatory standpoint, it is imperative that regulations call for more specific data protection controls for cloud services to adhere to. A form of standardisation of constraints about data flow and management should be in place; for example, currently the Terms and Conditions whenever using new software are very heterogeneous across providers, and are binary in terms of sending data to third parties. Data protection bodies need to make efforts to standardise requirements of sharing and managing data, that could be present in the Terms and Conditions so that clients could have a clearer idea *how safely* data is handled, before agreeing to the contract. A more uniform specification of *how* can greatly benefit users when choosing among application/service providers,

---

[1] Google Trends reports a massive increase in searching for 'data privacy compliance' in the UK since 2005 [7].

s long as these terms are user-understandable[2], and to some extent checkable. However, clearer regulations are only part of the solution; the other part is to have mechanisms to either impose adherence to them, or to economically incentivise them. Right now the online market favours reliability for service provision, and reliability is typically self-assessed by the provider. A privacy or security logo – especially when assessed externally – could potentially be turned into a commercial advantage with support from the state and data protection authorities. This is a more constructive approach from that of applying fines.

From a technological point of view, privacy online can greatly benefit from investing more efforts into researching topics such as:

**Metrics to measure how safely an online service handles data.** Improving comes hand in hand with measuring. Instead of taking the service provider's word for the safe management of data, metrics are needed to quantify the management of data when given away. For example, there are Mozilla Firefox plugins to graphically show the spread of user data to third-party trackers. Hopefully, similar approaches can be taken for cloud service provisions. More than examining how far off into the chain data propagate, other possible metrics for safety can be local to the provider and focus on anonymisation quantification, basic encryption details other than key strength, and the practiced transparency levels (such as privacy reports and mandatory breach notifications).

**Allowing for user privacy preferences.** Whenever installing new applications or signing in to new services, users should be allowed to choose among different privacy profiles permitted by the service. Such profiles should differ in the way the collect and share data about users, and by their existence users would be allowed to choose between more features and less privacy, or more privacy and less functionality. This could make sense if privacy would be stimulated by economic incentives for companies. It will become challenging to understand how to monetize data from users of different privacy preferences, and what proofs to offer to controllers and users that those preferences are met.

**Privacy-friendly data processing strategies.** User privacy preferences could be translated into data handling policies for the enterprises providing online services. Such policies could look at data storage restrictions, data aggregation, data splitting, and security and privacy configurations. Such policies will need to be enforced into the application and infrastructure. The strategy of how much to store and how much to distribute or centralise user information must (1) satisfy the basic requirements of privacy/anonymity of the users, (2) consider the minimum performance levels of the provider, and (3) consider the current constraints, context and threat model of the service provider.

Privacy is a basic right in a normal society, and we must invest efforts in building data protection controls for the online life to protect privacy and help

---

[2] Indeed, we still have a long way towards readable terms of licence and similar usage agreements.

users feel safe online. This process will not be easy, but will have to rely on transparency, choice, and verification. This opinion paper has briefly suggested a few steps in that direction.

# References

1. Accenture: Accenture big success with big data survey (2014). https:// www.accenture.com/lu-en/_acnmedia/Accenture/Conversion-Assets/DotCom/ Documents/Global/PDF/Industries_14/Accenture-Big-Data-POV.pdf
2. Bisogni, F.: Data breaches and the dilemmas in notifying customers. In: WEIS (2015)
3. Edwards, B., Hofmeyr, S., Forrest, S.: Hype and heavy tails: a closer look at data breaches. In: WEIS (2015)
4. European Commission: Proposal for a general data protection regulation (2012). http://ec.europa.eu/justice/data-protection/document/review2012/com_ 2012_11_en.pdf
5. Gartner: gartner survey reveals that SaaS deployments are now mission critical (2014). http://www.gartner.com/newsroom/id/2923217
6. Gembasu, R., Levy, A.: Vanish: self-distructing digital data (2009). http://vanish. cs.washington.edu/
7. Google: google trends statistics on the keyphrase "data protection compliance" since 2005 in the UK (2015) http://www.google.com/trends/explore# q=data%20protection%20compliance&cmpt=q&tz=
8. Kwon, J., Hofmeyr, S., Johnson, B.: The market effect of healthcare security: dopatients care about data breaches? In: WEIS (2015)
9. Perlman, R.: The ephemerizer: making data disappear. J. Inf. Syst. Secur. 1, 51–68 (2005)
10. Reardon, J., Basin, D., Capkun, S.: SoK: secure data deletion. In: Proceedings of the 2013 IEEE Symposium on Security and Privacy, SP 2013, pp. 301–315. IEEEComputer Society, Washington (2013)

# Multidisciplinary Aspects of Privacy by Design

# Privacy by Design: From Research and Policy to Practice – the Challenge of Multi-disciplinarity

Pagona Tsormpatzoudi[1(✉)], Bettina Berendt[2], and Fanny Coudert[1]

[1] Center for IT and IP Law, Leuven, Belgium
{pagona.tsormpatzoudi,fanny.coudert}@kuleuven.be
[2] Department of Computer Science, KU Leuven, Leuven, Belgium
bettina.berendt@kuleuven.be

**Abstract.** The concept of Privacy by Design (PbD) is a vision for creating data-processing environments in a way that respects privacy and data protection in the design of products and processes from the start. PbD has been inspired by and elaborated in different disciplines (especially law and computer science). Developments have taken place in research and policy, with the General Data Protection Regulation to be adopted by the European Parliament in 2016 and to enter into force in 2018. It is now time to use the results for practical guidance on how to achieve the goals defined by the legislation. In this paper, we summarise lessons learned from the special session on Multidisciplinary Aspects of PbD organised at the Annual Privacy Forum 2015. In particular, we identify important current and future implementation challenges of PbD. These are: terminology, legal compliance, different disciplines' understandings, the role of the data protection officer, the involvement of all stakeholders, and education. We conclude by emphasising the importance of approaching PbD in an interdisciplinary way.

**Keywords:** Privacy by design · Multi- and interdisciplinary approaches · General data protection regulation · Education

## 1   Introduction

The concept of Privacy by Design (PbD) is a vision for creating data-processing environments in a way that respects privacy and data protection in the design of products and processes from the start, rather than treating these as desiderata that may be treated as additional, ex-post, and lower-priority requirements. PbD has, from the start, been inspired by, and elaborated in, different disciplines (especially law and computer science). Also from the start, PbD was meant to be deployed as a practice in organisations, as something to be codified into actual laws and as a way to enforce law. At the moment it has been codified in the EU, with the new General Data Protection Regulation expected to be adopted by the European Parliament in early 2016 and to come into force in 2018. However, the concept is still not known to large parts of the public and industry.

While developments have taken place in the fields of research and policy, practical guidance on how to achieve the goals defined by the legislation is still lacking. In this context, PbD is becoming a huge multidisciplinary opportunity for "bringing research

B. Berendt et al. (Eds.): APF 2015, LNCS 9484, pp. 199–212, 2016.
DOI: 10.1007/978-3-319-31456-3_12

and policy together", the core theme of the Annual Privacy Forum 2015. At the same time, however, PbD faces many challenges. These include common terms that evoke vastly or subtly different concepts, absence of or uncertainties concerning implementation methods, and disagreement about evaluation criteria.

These observations motivated us to organise a session on the multidisciplinary aspects of PbD at APF 2015. In the present article, we first give an overview of the concept and development of PbD and then summarise lessons learned from the panelists' contributions and the discussions surrounding the panel. This paper does not intend to attribute views and statements to any individual participant but rather identify important challenges for implementing PbD and other take-home messages from the overall debate. The goal is to illustrate current and future implementation challenges of PbD. Amongst them we highlight the importance of teaching PbD concepts and skills, reporting on experiences with students and practitioners. We conclude by emphasising the importance of approaching PbD in an interdisciplinary way.

## 2 Context: Privacy by Design (PbD)

Privacy by Design (PbD) has in recent years developed as a legal and technological concept that helps enforce data protection obligations and make privacy a priority in an organisation. PbD has developed within experts communities both from the technological side that produced privacy-respecting methods and tools, and from the legal and policy side that reflected on the usefulness and limits of the concept as a new way to enforce the privacy and data protection frameworks.

The idea first emerged in the 1990s with the concept of Privacy Enhancing technologies (PETs), as alternative to the traditional focus on legal and administrative instruments that are exhausted with policy development and monitoring (van Rossem et al. 1995; Koorn et al. 2004). PETs, first, developed in relation to two data protection principles, data quality and data security[1], thus contribute to the protection of the confidentiality of personal data. However, technologists also started proposing PETs as a solution for the implementation of other data protection principles such as transparency or accountability (Phillips 2004; Gürses and Berendt 2010; Diaz and Gürses 2012). PETs grew as a solution for personal data management in general (Danish Ministry of Science Technology and Innovation 2005). This wider scope is reflected in the terms under which the concept has been popularised since the 1990s, including "data protection by technology" (ULD 1996) and "privacy by design" (Cavoukian 2011). From the start, PETs/PbD have been developed by computer scientists and lawyers, sometimes jointly, sometimes in parallel. Thus, bringing the different perspectives on PbD together remains an ongoing challenge. Technical, legal and other stakeholders should work together and have a role to play in delivering products and services that take privacy into account from the start. In the remainder of this section, we will

---

[1] The principle of data quality (Article 6 Directive 95/46/EC) includes the principles of fairness (data must be processed fairly), lawfulness (data must be processed according to a legitimate legal ground), purpose limitation, data minimisation, and accuracy. PETs are able to ensure confidentiality of personal data as an attribute of information security.

riefly sketch important elements of today's views from these two disciplines, and identify
mplementation as a key challenge.

## 2.1  PbD as a Computer-Science Concept

The increasing use of the term PbD in computer science reflects the concept's increasingly generalised scope: from the focus on *tools* or *instruments* in PETs to a focus on
more comprehensive *design* guidelines, processes and practices (see also Gürses et al.
2011; Hansen 2015). Computer scientists now consider PbD from a variety of perspectives (many of these are described in the overview in Danezis et al. 2014). These
perspectives range in granularity from desirable properties of data (e.g. degrees of
anonymity or type of encryption) and constraints on algorithms (Monreale et al. 2014)
to methodologies for requirements engineering and the whole process of software development (Gürses 2010; Wuyts 2015). The perspectives range in formalisation from
mathematical proofs of datasets and algorithms having certain properties to investigations of human privacy-related behaviour and recommendations for the design of
human-computer interfaces (Jameson et al. 2014).

This multitude of approaches also implies that the notion of privacy itself as the goal
of PbD is not uniform: it ranges from IT Security's data confidentiality to psychologi-
cally and sociologically informed notions of privacy. A matching to legal notions of
privacy and data protection is also not always straightforward. A computer-science
method that promises to deliver, protect, enhance, etc. "privacy" or "data" therefore has
to be investigated closely for the degree to which it can implement legal notions and
possibly also the degree to which it does something else.

## 2.2  PbD: The Emergence of a Legal Obligation

From a legal perspective, PbD is an approach to privacy that places technology at the
service of the law, i.e. it seeks for technical solutions to address privacy and data protection requirements posed by the legal framework (Tsormpatzoudi and Coudert 2014).

The emergence of PbD as a legal obligation followed up on a lively policy debate.
During the 2000s, the ideas of PETs and PbD gained recognition at EU level, and in
2007 the European Commission published a Communication promoting the use of PETs
as complementary mechanism for the enforcement of the data protection framework
(European Commission 2007, p. 6). In this Communication, the EC defines PETs as "a
coherent system of ICT measures that protects privacy by eliminating or reducing
personal data or by preventing unnecessary and/or undesired processing of personal data,
all without losing functionality of the information systems". In 2009, under the prepar-
atory works for the reform of the European Data Protection framework, the Article 29
Data Protection Working Party (2009) advocated the introduction of a *principle of
privacy by design* that would emphasize the need to implement PETs, "privacy by
default" settings and the necessary tools to enable users to better protect their personal
data (e.g., access control, encryption). This was seen as a way to move data protection
"from theory to practice" and make technology developers responsible for the systems
they produce. Like the other data protection principles, this principle would have to be

defined "in a technologically neutral way" to keep pace with the fast-changing techno-logical and social environment. Similarly, the wording should be flexible enough to allow stakeholders to translate the principle into concrete measures adapted to each specific case.

After long negotiations, the compromise text for the draft General Data Protection Regulation (GDPR) includes the concepts of data protection by design and by default (Council of the European Union 2015, Article 23 and Recital 61). The two concepts represent the more comprehensive concept of PbD, which was tailored into these two derivatives for consistency with the scope of the particular legal instrument (GDPR). Data protection by design requires that "the controller shall, both at the time of the determination of the means for processing and at the time of the processing itself, implement appropriate technical and organisational measures, such as pseudonymisa-tion, which are designed to implement data protection principles, such as data minimi-sation, in an effective way and to integrate the necessary safeguards into the processing in order to meet the requirements of the Regulation and protect the rights of data subjects". Data protection by default requires that "the controller shall implement appro-priate technical and organisational measures for ensuring that, by default, only personal data which are necessary for each specific purpose of the processing are processed".

### 2.3  Implementation Challenges Facing PbD

PbD refers to the design process, but it cannot be understood separately from the whole organisational context in which it develops. This is acknowledged in Recital 61 of the Draft GDPR, which points out that the controller should adopt internal policies and measures to comply with the principles to data protection by design and by default (Council of the European Union 2015). Being related to the general context, PbD is naturally affected by different disciplines. Technical, legal and business stakeholders should work together and have a role to play to deliver products and services that take privacy into account from the start.

The concept of PbD has developed within experts communities both from the tech-nological side that produced privacy-respecting methods and tools, and from the legal and policy side that reflected on the usefulness and limits of the concept as a new way to enforce the privacy and data protection frameworks. However, PbD has so far not reached companies. One rationale for turning the principle into a legal obligation was to drive companies to implement it in practice. Yet, companies lack practical guidance on how to achieve the goals defined by the legislation. Conceptual and terminological challenges are exacerbated when legal provisions get translated into descriptions and instructions for stakeholders from other disciplines, such as engineers or business actors.

## 3  Overview of the APF 2015 Session on Multidisciplinary Aspects of Privacy by Design

The Computer Science Department and the Center for IT and IP Law of KU Leuven co-organised a session on 7th October 2015 at the Annual Privacy Forum in order to discuss he challenges faced by companies when deciding to integrate Privacy by Design into he development of products and services. The objective of the Annual Privacy Forum, upported by DG Connect and ENISA, is to provide a forum to academia, industry and olicy makers, and among other things discuss the uptake of PbD in industry. Although orivacy technologies are widely discussed in various research communities, their mere existence is often unknown to the general public. Hence PETs need the support of policy o find their way into IT products. The session received funding by the EU FP7 project PARIS, which aims at defining and demonstrating a methodological approach for PbD in the development of surveillance systems.

The session consisted of a keynote given by Marit Hansen, Privacy & Information Commissioner of the State of Schleswig-Holstein, Germany, who introduced the need of a motivated interdisciplinary approach to privacy and data protection by design. This was followed by a panel that included three more participants who brought different viewpoints to the table. Dan Bogdanov, Product manager for Sharemind at Cybernetica (Estonia), focused on the challenges raised for product development. David Stevens, Data Protection Officer at Telenet (Belgium), related his experience in interacting with other departments from a same organisation (such as marketing or engineering) in order to look for a solution that takes into account all requirements. Matthias Pocs, representing the European Association for the Co-ordination of Consumer Representation in Standardisation (ANEC) (Germany), stressed the importance of involving consumers in the PbD process. The session was moderated by Antonio Kung, CTO, Trialog, France and coordinator of the PARIS and PRIPARE EU projects.

## 4    Current Challenges for PbD

In this section, we describe four main areas in which clarification and guidance are needed. The first challenge is related to the way the concept is described in the GDPR. The second is the challenge of the interpretation of the concept: we argue how even from a legal standpoint, focussing only on legal compliance can threaten the success of PbD. From an engineering standpoint, viewing privacy only in terms of *risks* (to be guarded against by trying to comply with a law) is even more restrictive; a positive view as a *goal* is more likely to help PbD succeed. The third challenge is the different understandings of PbD across disciplinary boundaries. The fourth challenge is the role of the data protection officer in an organisation– a person who needs to integrate multiple interests and who needs to be loyal to the law as much as to his or her organisation and its (e.g. business) goals. Throughout all challenges, we can see how applying a certain disciplinary lens can enable PbD practitioners to zoom in on and pan around new questions, which in turn require the lens of yet other disciplines.

### 4.1    Challenges Arising from the Wording in the GDPR

A factor contributing to the lack of understanding of the principle of PbD and how to implement it in practice, is the way it has been worded in the Draft GDPR. The Communication of the Commission that launched the discussion for the data protection reform initially referred to 'Privacy by Design', as the discussion at the beginning of the reform permitted a general and broad view on the matter (European Commission 2010). In the first draft of the GDPR the choice was made to introduce the concepts of data protection by design and by default due to the scope of such instrument, which intends to protect the fundamental rights and freedom of individuals, and in particular the right to the protection of personal data, in relation to the processing of such data (Article 1) (Tsormpatzoudi and Coudert 2015a).

In the compromise text of the GDPR, the principle of *data protection by design* mandates data controllers both at the time of determination of the means for processing and during the processing itself, to take technical and organisational measures, such as pseudonymisation, which are designed to implement data protection principles, such as data minimisation, in an effective way and to integrate the necessary safeguards into the processing (Article 23). *Data protection by default*, which is introduced in addition to data protection by design in Article 23 (2) and Recital 61, requires privacy settings on services and products that by default comply with the general principles of data protection, such as data minimisation and purpose limitation (Council of the European Union 2015).

Furthermore, Recital 61 provides a non-exhaustive list of examples of data protection by design measures such as minimising the processing of personal data, pseudonymising personal data as soon as possible, enhancing transparency with regard to the functions and processing of personal data, enabling the data subject to monitor the data processing, and enabling the controller to create and improve security features. These concrete examples enhance the clarity of the provision. However, Article 23 then provides an extensive list of factors related to data processing to be taken into account when deciding about the implementation of data protection by design measures, and these factors blur the picture. Besides the available technology and the cost of implementation, the factors also include the nature, scope, context and purposes of the processing as well as the likelihood and severity of the risk for rights and freedoms of individuals posed by the processing. Balancing these factors is expected to be a challenging task, given that there is no further explanation on how to interpret and prioritise them in relation to one another. This may eventually be a difficulty for implementing data protection by design in practice (Tsormpatzoudi and Coudert 2015b).

## 4.2 Legal Compliance for Implementing PbD

When developing technologies, system requirements come to fulfil different considerations. This is a challenge to be addressed in complex ecosystems of private organisations, where different departments function with different assumptions of privacy deriving from political, economic, business, legal, or technical interests.

For instance, in a given system, a privacy expert may argue for data minimisation, which will imply that the minimum amount of information should be stored in the system. This may also be a legal requirement. At the same time, a security expert may propose data integrity from a security point of view, which may require a considerable amount of data that is accurate, consistent and reliable. This would be in principle contradictory to data minimisation but also very essential for the system.

Gathering such interests, including compliance with the law, often represents risks to be taken into account in product development. Legal compliance as a risk often results n legal workarounds which may take place for the sake of compliance only. In the above example, an organisation may take a series of data minimisation measures and this may seem to comply with the law, but may not be the case if storage is not really needed at all (see also Schaar 2010).

The inclusion of the principle of data protection by design in Recital 61 and Article 23 of the draft GDPR creates a legal obligation for data controllers. However, this obligation should be detached from the goal of addressing it only because it may create a compliance risk. Preserving privacy should rather become a goal in itself in product development. Rather than just taking measures to demonstrate that the PbD has been taken into account, data protection by design and by default should penetrate the actual working culture and the decisions taken in an organisation.

## 4.3 Difficulties of Understanding Between Disciplines

PbD does not provide fixed solutions. It rather suggests that IT solutions alone cannot ensure sufficient respect of privacy in an organisation. In several cases PbD requires a running system with clear responsibilities and tasks that may be process-oriented, taking into account the full lifecycle of system evolution. PbD is therefore a means of involving all relevant stakeholders active in engineering, law, organisational processes, business models, user interaction, or organisational culture. The purpose of the system is the common starting point that allows all stakeholders to discuss about the requirements the system should comply from the perspective of each discipline and further justifies the necessary data processing, the appropriate protection levels and measures to implement privacy.

Involving the relevant stakeholders in this process is not an easy task given that each comes with different systems of beliefs and values even with different vocabulary. This leads to lack of cross-disciplinary understanding. For example, when talking about "erasure" as a good PbD practice, one needs to clarify what exactly is necessary to erase. For instance, a stakeholder who operates on the assumption of storage by default, may exclude logfiles and temporary files from a privacy assessment, even though such files may contain significant amounts of personal data. Thus for a developer of a particular component this may be an acceptable – or even altogether harmless – practice, however, a privacy manager or a compliance officer who may look into the system more holistically will identify the pitfall. The added value of the joint interdisciplinary work would help bring these views together and define solutions that satisfy all involved experts.

## 4.4 The Data Protection Officer (DPO): A Key Actor to Communicate About Privacy Internally and to Coordinate the Different Needs

The introduction of the function of a DPO may be a cornerstone in the implementation of PbD as an interdisciplinary concept (Article 34 GDPR). DPOs will have to monitor compliance with data protection law and engage in several activities to promote data protection in their organisation. DPOs may link between different functions of an organszation and as such promote the interdisciplinary aspects of the principle Privacy/Data Protection by Design. DPOs as employees of the data controller have a quite sensitive but pivotal role. They will be the ones to promote the dialogue between different depart-ments and eventually strike the balance between different interests under the common goal of implementing privacy/data protection by design. Their skillset should include the ability to compromise –but without losing sight of the obligation to comply with the law-, be part of a negotiation process, and be ready to accept other views reflecting different system of beliefs and values coming from different stakeholders.

The sensitivity of the role of the DPO has been recognised in the discussions of the draft GDPR, which takes steps to promote their independence. It thus states in its report that Data Protection Officers should be protected from being penalised or dismissed for reasons other than not performing well their data protection compliance tasks (Article 36 para 3, Article 35 para 7). Nevertheless, even though the Regulation obviously tries to avoid situations of conflict of interest (Article 36 para 4), it should be noted that DPOs will always have as agenda to defend the best interests of the company. Yet, their freedom within the organisation to talk equal-to-equal with other departments will contribute to a higher level of privacy protection.

## 5   Challenges Ahead: Involvement of Stakeholders Outside the Data Controllers' Organisation, and Education

Implementation of PbD has so far been understood mainly in relation to obligations of an organisation as the data controller. This section elaborates on challenges ahead in the implementation of PbD. First, organisations will have to re-assess their focus on the data processing lifecycle. New technologies will illustrate that PbD is a responsibility not only of data controllers but also of data subjects and technology providers. The next steps will be to broaden the scope of application of PbD and find ways of involving end users and technology providers. Second, limited understanding or experience with the concept as illustrated in the sections above will create a significant need to invest in awareness, knowledge and skills. Education will thus be an important future imple-mentation challenge.

### 5.1   End Users

PbD as a negotiation process amongst all stakeholders should not only focus on data controllers but also involve end users, who are meant to ultimately profit from PbD. This idea has been reflected in the GDPR Article 33 para 4, which introduces the obligation of the data controller to perform a Privacy/Data Protection Impact Assessment. Specif-ically, "the controller shall seek the views of data subjects or their representatives on the intended processing, without prejudice to the protection of commercial or public interests or the security of the processing operations". However, the involvement of end users in privacy negotiation is far from trivial. It presupposes awareness and under-standing of the core issues that happen in the value chain.

Being the last part in the value chain, end users are often less aware or interested in PbD implementation. This may explain why despite the policy efforts to foster imple-mentation of PbD, the take-up of PETs remains low. As a result, privacy as competitive advantage is still not a mature idea on the market. Some users perceive usability and privacy as a trade-off. Others will only accept any change (e.g. an increase in privacy-friendliness) if it is also accompanied by a usability improvement. Yet others find it hard to accept any change "because they have always worked in this way" – even if, for example, the change consists of storing or processing data that these users never used in the first place. These examples illustrate why also a challenge that sounds relatively specific ("involve end users") calls for contributions from several disciplines, such as usability design and process change.

Education and additional ways to involve end users in PbD implementation will help overcome such challenges. Recently, standardisation initiatives have been emphasised as a means to furthering PbD implementation. In January 2015, the European Commission issued an Implementing Decision including a standardisation request to the European standardisation organisations as regards European standards and European standardisation deliverables for privacy and personal data protection management in the field of security industrial policy (European Commission 2015). Standardisation may function as an enabling method for involving end users in PbD. However, as consumers (end users) represent only one voice and are in a minority, it may be difficult to be heard in a community established to defend the interests of industry.

## 5.2 Technology Providers

In the compromise text adopted on December 15, 2015, the Regulation introduces the obligation for data controllers to adopt technical and organisational measures appropriate to comply with the requirements of the Regulation and protect the rights of data subjects ("data protection by design") (Article 23) (Council of the European Union 2015). Yet in several cases, the data controller only operates at the very end of the supply chain and this may be too late for the obligation to be effective.

Because of the scope of data protection law, the obligation to data protection by design is only applicable for the data controller from the moment that personal data are collected and processed. In a case of a drone or remotely piloted aircraft, this would be once the drone is ready to use by the drone operator. However, the drone operator (data controller) comes very late and has no influence in the choice of the components or of the apps chosen to operate the drone. Such decisions that take place during the development phase of the drone, such as whether to integrate automated deletion or to insert a visible sign that its camera is "on" are taken by providers of drones or of its components (sensors, cameras etc.) who act earlier in the supply chain and are excluded from the scope of the data protection framework. "Even though their technologies can (and will) be used to process personal data and even if they can reasonably expect that their technology may severely impact individuals' rights to privacy and data protection, they are not bound to respect the principles of data protection" (Tsormpatzoudi and Coudert 2015b).

This issue has been identified has been extensively discussed in the GDPR. Eventually the compromise text (Recital 61) requires that technology providers, when developing, designing, selecting and using applications, services and products, shall "be encouraged to take into account the right to data protection when developing and designing such products, services and applications and, with due regard to the state of the art, to make sure that controllers and processors are able to fulfil their data protection obligations". Even though it is not worded as a clear obligation, these actors, in addition to the data controllers, should be responsible for PbD implementation.

Standardisation may be a way to clarify and implement PbD in the supply chain. The standardisation request in the Commission's Implementing Decision M530/2015 explicitly refers to a standard for privacy management in the design, development, production, and service provision processes of security technologies (European Commission 2012). Standardisation, followed by relevant certification, is expected to become increasingly important, as the compromise text of the GDPR specifically refers to an approved certification mechanism as an element to demonstrate compliance with data protection by design and by default (Article 23 (2a) Council of the European Union 2015).

### 5.3   Education: PbD Teaching and Training

As the previous sections have shown, the implementation of PbD by all relevant stakeholders (companies, technology or component providers, the public at large) requires an *awareness* of the relevance of the issue and of the challenges posed by a multi-discipline, multi-stakeholder concept. It also requires *knowledge* of concepts and methods: for example, which legal rights and values are to be protected (and what counts as protection), which methods and technologies are currently available to process data while ensuring these protections, how available, usable and economical these are, how to deal with the tradeoffs necessitated by conflicting interests, etc. Last but not least, PbD requires *skills* for transforming this knowledge into action.

Books and other materials alone are ill-suited to creating complex meshes of awareness, knowledge and skills, the more so for concept under continuous development such as PbD. We therefore argue that the development, testing and improvement of teaching and training methods is vital for transporting lessons learned about PbD – such as those described above – into practice. As an outlook, we therefore want to illustrate what we consider key elements of such teaching/training, using two case studies from our own work.

The first case study was a lesson series given to computer science Masters students (Berendt and Coudert 2015). It involved a collaboration between two courses at KU Leuven during the last third of the semester. In the first course, student teams had developed and begun to carry out a project in which they started from a research question, gathered data from the Web, and analysed it with statistical and data-mining methods. In the second course, students had been instructed on privacy from various disciplinary perspectives, including an introduction to the legal view of privacy and data protection. The students grouped themselves into "developer teams" and "consultancy teams", respectively. For the assignment, each consultancy team specified a possible app that could be built based on one developer team's data-analysis project. The consultants then worked out an "initial privacy impact assessment (PIA) and design advice" based on guidelines that (a) helped them draw on their computational and legal knowledge and (b) were inspired by existing PIA guidelines (Coudert and Berendt 2014).

This resulted in good presentations and discussions and some excellent written reports. Of course, the analysis was not perfect, but we were surprised to find that the description of data flows by the consultants was often incomplete or faulty, although this should be a basic skill of computer-science students. We also discovered that even though all developer teams reflected the PIA/design advice input in their final projects, early (privacy-unfriendly) modelling choices could be sticky. Both challenges indicated that learning could profit from either more time or a simpler assignment. After the successful first run, the second route was chosen: In the current (2015) run of the course, the privacy course students' semester project is to develop a PIA/design advice for an existing online/mobile application in the outside world (rather than a fictitious one that is being developed by their peers).

The second case study was a two-day workshop for IT practitioners, organised in the context of the EU FP7 PRIPARE project. The day started with a Welcome and Introduction, followed by two lectures on Privacy Motivation and Introduction (given by Claudia Roda and Susan Perry) and Data Protection and Privacy Principles (given by Pagona Tsormpatzoudi) and ended with a practical session. The exercise was an assignment covering aspects that were discussed mainly during the session 'Data Protection and Privacy Principles'. Its design was based on the assignment of the first case study.

The exercise was designed in a way that allowed follow-up of the use case presented during the Welcome and Introduction of the Participants. The intention was to use the same case in order to perform the exercises of the workshop. The use case was based on the facts of the Patras pilot on anonymous course evaluation from the EU FP7 Project ABC4Trust (Bcheri et al. 2012). It presented a roughly specified flawed IT solution adjusted as follows: "A university hired an IT professional to provide an online course evaluation solution in order to allow professors receive feedback for their classes. The professional provided a typical IT solution, as presented during the introductory session." The assignment was: "Could you help him specify the solution in a privacy preserving manner? The questions below represent the basic steps of a privacy impact assessment. Please use them to complete the task."

A feedback questionnaire that participants filled out at the end of the workshop illustrated that IT practitioners recognised the topic of the lecture (privacy and data protection law) as very important. On specific aspects, participants considered it useful to learn about data protection principles in a logical order determined by the time of the processing they become relevant. In contrast to the Master students of the first case study, the practitioners were able to identify technical aspects (data flows, who has access to what data). However, they tended to have a narrow perspective when they called upon to identify expectations of the different actors regarding the goals of the system.

Furthermore, the discussions and comments showed that the practitioners had difficulties in working on the basis of a use case that was presented to them with no technical details. The reason for this was that in the PRIPARE methodology the legal assessment takes place only before the technical design and assessment of the solution. As an illustration of the methodology, the 2-days workshop started with the legal training; the technical part followed. Therefore, even though we managed to make legal reasoning more explicit and to improve the way we teach PIA, we think that in order to make this use case more successful, we need interdisciplinary assignments, where law and technology are merged together throughout the design process. These assignments will go beyond the principle that was already applied in this workshop: presenting the data protection principles in a logical order determined by the time of the processing. By this extension, we will be able to guide participants to think of legal aspects at the different stages of the actual design (when they become relevant) and not only on the basis of fictitious examples. Whereas education and training should be adapted to the needs of each stakeholder group, such an approach may be useful to bring law and technology together.

## 6   Conclusions

The challenges that we identified in the sections above illustrate that implementation of PbD will play a significant role in organisations' efforts to respect privacy. In the years to come we will come across initiatives to specify and apply the concept of PbD during the design process. PbD specification and implementation will go much beyond systems design and will have an impact at different levels. First, it will affect the whole organisational context including stakeholders with diverse interests from different disciplines; and second, the whole supply chain, starting from the component/technology provider and ending at end users. This is the reason why interdisciplinary work may be useful.

Interdisciplinary work is sometimes difficult and time-consuming. But it is reasonable for research (even if not valued in the respective disciplines' metrics) and to some extent necessary for workable solutions. As "the whole is more than the sum of its parts", interdisciplinary approaches will be useful in order to bring to the market products/services that fulfil the common good and serve end users' needs. Yet, it remains a challenge to inform and educate all stakeholders and engage them in a dialogue that will clarify what their goals behind their stated interests are in each case. Openness to understand the underlying incentives of other disciplines will be the first step to move away from (biased) discipline-specific beliefs and values and embrace truly interdisciplinary methods for research and implementation of PbD in practice.

**Acknowledgements.**   This paper was made possible by the funding of the PARIS project (PrivAcy pReserving Infrastructure for Surveillance), EU FP7, under Grant Agreement No: 312504, andof ENISA. We thank Marit Hansen, Dan Bogdanov, Matthias Pocs, David Stevens and Antonio Kung for their inspiring keynote, panel contributions, and discussions during the planning of the session, and the APF 2015 participants for their valuable arguments during the session.

## References

Article 29 Data Protection Working Party: The future of privacy. Joint contribution to the consultation of the European commission on the legal framework for the fundamental right to protection of personal data (WP168, 2009) (2009) http://ec.europa.eu/justice/policies/privacy/docs/wpdocs/2009/wp168_en.pdf

Scheri, S., Goetze, N., Liagkou, V., Pyrgelis, A., Raptopoulos, C., Stamatiou, G., Storf, K., Waengmark, P., Zwingelberg, H.: D5.1 scenario definition for both pilots. ABC4Trust Deliverable (2012)

Berendt, B., Coudert, F.: Privatsphäre und Datenschutz lehren - Ein interdisziplinärer Ansatz. Konzept, Umsetzung, Schlussfolgerungen und Perspektiven. [Teaching privacy and data protection - an interdisciplinary approach. Concept, implementation, conclusions and perspectives.] In: Neues Handbuch Hochschullehre. [New Handbook of Teaching in Higher Education] (EG 71, 2015, E1.9), pp. 7–40. Raabe Verlag, Berlin (2015)

Cavoukian, A.: Privacy by design: the 7 foundational principles. Information and Privacy Commissioner of Ontario, Toronto, Ontario, Canada (2011). Revised version, originally published 2009. https://www.ipc.on.ca/images/resources/7foundationalprinciples.pdf

Coudert, F., Berendt, B.: Guidelines for initial privacy impact assessment and related design advice (2014). http://people.cs.kuleuven.be/~bettina.berendt/teaching/kaw/guidelines.pdf

Council of the European Union: Proposal for a regulation of the European parliament and the council on the protection of individuals with regard to the processing of personal data and on the free movement of such data - Analysis of the final compromise text with a view to agreement. Presidency to Permanent Representatives Committee, 15 December 2015. http://www.statewatch.org/news/2015/dec/eu-council-dp-reg-draft-final-compromise-15039-15.pdf

Danezis, G., Domingo-Ferrer, J., Hansen, M., Hoepman, J.-H., Le Métayer, D., Tirtea, R., Schiffner, S.: Privacy and data protection by design – from policy to engineering. ENISA report (2014). https://www.enisa.europa.eu/activities/identity-and-trust/library/deliverables/privacy-and-data-protection-by-design

Danish Ministry of Science Technology and Innovation: Privacy enhancing technologies, META group report v1.1 (2005). https://danskprivacynet.files.wordpress.com/2008/07/rapportvedrprivacyenhancingtechlologies.pdf

Diaz, C., Gürses, S.: Understanding the landscape of privacy technologies. Extended abstract of invited talk in Proceedings of the Information Security Summit, pp. 58–63 (2012). https://www.cosic.esat.kuleuven.be/publications/article-2215.pdf

European Commission: Communication from the commission to the European parliament and the council on promoting data protection by privacy enhancing technologies (PETs) COM/2007/0228 final (2007). http://eur-lex.europa.eu/legal-content/EN/TXT/?uri=CELEX:52007DC0228

European Commission: Communication from the commission to the European parliament, the council, the economic and social committee and the committee of the regions: a comprehensive approach on personal data protection in the European union COM(2010) 609 final (2010). http://ec.europa.eu/justice/news/consulting_public/0006/com_2010_609_en.pdf

European Commission: Communication from the commission to the European parliament, the council and the european economic and social committee: security industrial policy action plan for an innovative and competitive security industry brussels. COM(2012) 417 final (2012). http://eur-lex.europa.eu/legal-content/EN/TXT/?uri=uriserv:OJ.C_.2013.076.01.0037.01.ENG

European Commission: Implementing decision of 20.1.2015 on a standardisation request to the European standardisation organisations as regards European standards and European standardisation deliverables for privacy and personal data protection management pursuant to article 10(1) of regulation (EU) No 1025/2012 of the European parliament and of the council in support of directive 95/46/EC of the European parliament and of the council and in support of union's security industrial policy, M530 102 final (2015). http://ec.europa.eu/growth/tools-databases/mandates/index.cfm?fuseaction=search.detail&id=548

Gürses, F.S.: Multilateral privacy requirements analysis in online social network services. KU Leuven, Department of Computer Science: Ph.D. Dissertation (2010). https://www.cosic.esat.kuleuven.be/publications/thesis-177.pdf

Gürses, S., Berendt, B.: PETs in the surveillance society: a critical review of the potentials and limitations of the privacy as confidentiality paradigm. In: Gutwirth, S., Poullet, De Hert, P. (eds.) Data Protection in a Profiled World. Dordrecht etc., S. 301–321 (2010)

Gürses, S., Troncoso, C., Diaz, C.: Engineering privacy by design. In: Conference on Computers, Privacy and Data Protection (CPDP 2011) (2011)

Hansen, M.: Verabschiedung von Dr. Thilo Weichert und Amtsantritt von Marit Hansen als Landesbeauftragte für Datenschutz Schleswig-Holstein. [Presentation on the occasion of Dr. Thilo Weichert taking leave and Marit Hansen taking office as the Data Protection Commissioner of the German Land Schleswig-Holstein] (2015). https://www.datenschutzzentrum.de/uploads/uld/verabschiedung-weichert/20150903_Hansen_Uebergang-LD_Langtag-Kiel.pdf

Jameson, A., Berendt, B., Gabrielli, S., Cena, F., Gena, C., Vernero, F., Reinecke, K.: Choice architecture for human-computer interaction. Found. Trends Hum.-Comput. Interact. **7**(1–2), 1–235 (2014)

Koorn, R., van Gils, H., ter Hart, J., Overbook, P., Tellegen, R., Borking, J.: Privacy enhancing technologies: white paper for decision-makers. Ministry of Interior and Kingdom Relations, Directorate of Public Sector Innovation and Information Policy (2004). https://is.muni.cz/el/1433/podzim2005/PV080/um/PrivacyEnhancingTechnologies_KPMGstudy.pdf

Monreale, A., Rinzivillo, S., Pratesi, F., Giannotti, F., Pedreschi, D.: Privacy-by-design in big data analytics and social mining. EPJ Data Sci. **3**, 10 (2014)

Phillips, D.J.: Privacy policy and PETs. New Media Soc. **6**(6), 691–706 (2004)

Schaar, P.: Privacy by design. Identity Inf. Soc. **3**(2), 267–274 (2010)

Tsormpatzoudi P., Coudert, F.: Chapter 3: legal perspective on privacy by design. In: Troncoso, C. (ed.) Pripare Deliverable D.5.1 State-of-Play: Current Practices and Solutions, pp. 22–27 (2014). http://pripareproject.eu/wp-content/uploads/2013/11/D5.1.pdf

Tsormpatzoudi, P., Coudert, F.: Chapter 3: gaps in the legal frameworks and lack of awareness. In: Le Métayer, D. (ed.) Pripare Deliverable D.5.2 Multilateral Gap Analysis: Identification of Research Gaps, pp. 23–36 (2015a)

Tsormpatzoudi, P., Coudert, F.: Technology providers'responsibility in protection privacy… dropped from the sky? Paper presented at the Amsterdam Privacy Conference, Amsterdam, October 2015b

ULD: Sommerakademie Datenschutz durch Technik – Technik im Dienste der Grundrechte. [Summer Academy Data Protection by Technology – Technology at the Service of Fundamental Rights.] (1996). https://www.datenschutzzentrum.de/sommerakademie/1996/sa96prog.htm. Summarised in a report https://www.bfdi.bund.de/SharedDocs/Publikationen/Entschliessungssammlung/DSB undLaender/52DSK-KurzberichtZum_DatenschutzDurchTechnik_.pdf?__blob=publicationFile

van Rossem, H., Gardeniers, H., Borking, J., Cavoukian, A., Brans, J., Muttupulle, N., Magistrale, N.: Privacy-enhancing technologies, the path to anonymity. Volumes I and II. Registratiekamer, The Netherlands and Information and Privacy Commissioner, Ontario, Canada (1995). https://www.ipc.on.ca/english/Resources/Discussion-Papers/Discussion-Papers-Summary/?id=329 and https://www.ipc.on.ca/images/Resources/anoni-v2.pdf

Wuyts, K.: Privacy threats in software architectures. KU Leuven, Department of Computer Science: Ph.D. Dissertation (2015). https://lirias.kuleuven.be/bitstream/123456789/472921/1/wuyts2014_thesis_online.pdf

# Author Index

Printed in the United States
By Bookmasters